'No aspect goes unexamined, from the charities which encourage donation of unwanted clothing, to 'upcycling' – using old clothes as the basis for new fashions: style with one eye on the environment … It's impossible to deny the force of the arguments on show.'
Geographical

'*Clothing Poverty* should be of immense intellectual stimulation to individuals wanting to be a better (and more depressed) consumer, or those searching for inspiring examples of writing about a capitalist system as a whole rather than isolated capitalist actors.'
LSE Review of Books

'Thought-provoking and insightful. A fascinating, must-read text for those interested in the ethics surrounding sustainability in fashion and design.'
**Alison Gwilt, author of *Fashion Design for Living* and
*A Practical Guide to Sustainable Fashion***

'A book that sparks with intelligence, mapping a world that connects inequalities, Vivienne Westwood, post-consumption and second-hand garments.'
Kate Fletcher, London College of Fashion

'By bringing global systems of clothing provision into clearer view, the book offers valuable resources for vigorous debate over what an alternative world might look like.'
Gillian Hart, University of California, Berkeley

'A lively exploration of the hidden world of fast fashion and second-hand clothing that invites us to think of where our clothes come from.'
Karen Tranberg Hansen, Northwestern University

'This engaging and well-written book focuses on some of the least explored outcomes of the fast-fashion system we all live in – that is, what we increasingly and quickly cast off.'
Alessandra Mezzadri, SOAS, University of London

T0286503

Clothing Poverty

ABOUT THE AUTHOR

Andrew Brooks is a Senior Lecturer in Development and Environment, in the Department of Geography, King's College London. His research examines connections between production, consumption and waste, and particularly the geographies of economic and social change in Africa. Following the publication of the first edition of *Clothing Poverty*, Andrew was interviewed by international media including Al Jazeera, BBC News, CNN, *The Economist*, *The Guardian*, *Le Monde*, *The New York Times* and *Newsweek*. Fieldwork has taken him across sub-Saharan Africa as well as to Portugal, Papua New Guinea, the United States and Hong Kong where he also leads an undergraduate fieldtrip. Research in Africa has included extensive investigations of local markets, national politics and international investments in Malawi, Mozambique and Zambia. He was an editor of the *Journal of Southern African Studies* (2015–19). Andrew is also the author of *The End of Development: A Global History of Politics and Prosperity* (Zed Books, 2017) and more than 25 journal articles and chapters in edited books.

Clothing
Poverty

THE HIDDEN WORLD OF
FAST FASHION AND
SECOND-HAND CLOTHES

Second Edition

ANDREW BROOKS

LONDON · NEW YORK · OXFORD · NEW DELHI · SYDNEY

Zed Books
Bloomsbury Publishing Plc
50 Bedford Square, London, WC1B 3DP, UK
1385 Broadway, New York, NY 10018, USA
29 Earlsfort Terrace, Dublin 2, Ireland

BLOOMSBURY and Zed Books are trademarks of Bloomsbury
Publishing Plc

First published in Great Britain 2015
This edition was published in 2019
Reprinted 2021

Copyright © Andrew Brooks 2015, 2019

Andrew Brooks asserted his right under the Copyright, Designs and
Patents Act, 1988, to be identified as Author of this work.

Typeset in Book Antiqua by Swales and Willis Ltd, Exeter, Devon
Index by John Barker
Cover design by Caro Gates
Font: Napo Family by Zetafonts

All rights reserved. No part of this publication may be reproduced or
transmitted in any form or by any means, electronic or mechanical,
including photocopying, recording, or any information storage or retrieval
system, without prior permission in writing from the publishers.

Bloomsbury Publishing Plc does not have any control over, or
responsibility for, any third-party websites referred to or in this book. All
internet addresses given in this book were correct at the time of going
to press. The author and publisher regret any inconvenience caused if
addresses have changed or sites have ceased to exist, but can accept no
responsibility for any such changes.

A catalogue record for this book is available from the British Library.

A catalog record for this book is available from the Library of Congress.

ISBN: PB: 978-1-78699-737-1
ePDF: 978-1-78699-739-5
ePub: 978-1-78699-738-8
Mobi: 978-1-78699-740-1

Printed and bound by CPI Group (UK) Ltd, Croydon, CR0 4YY, UK

To find out more about our authors and books visit www.bloomsbury.com
and sign up for our newsletters.

CONTENTS

ACKNOWLEDGEMENTS

Global poverty, inequality and environmental crises are among the most pressing issues of our time, yet it is frustrating how often work on these topics falls short of offering answers, a compelling argument or an engaging narrative. We have to work rigorously to understand how the world has changed and developed, yet in doing so it can be hard to make the analysis interesting and clear, as well as authoritative. My hope is that this book goes some way to bridging between the real experiences of the poor and vulnerable and the privileged and often out of touch academic community. *Clothing Poverty* tells a story of uneven development that is interesting for a broad audience and discusses the hidden world of fashion through diverse and colourful examples, while drawing upon rigorous evidence and maintaining a critical perspective. Thank you to all those who helped me with this book. I could not have written it without the research assistants, factory workers, managers, business people, charity staff, government officials, market traders and others, most of whom are unnamed, who gave their time to be interviewed or in other ways facilitated the writing. I am also indebted to family and friends, especially Barra and colleagues at King's and elsewhere who have offered encouragement, support and guidance, for which I am very grateful. A special mention goes to Kate Fletcher, Robert A. Francis, Emma Dulcie Rigby and Thomas Roberts with whom I worked on the research of micro-fibre pollution and closed loop recycling. Kim Walker and others at Zed Books have also always been very helpful. Any errors are of course my sole responsibility. Finally, special thanks must go to David Simon and Alex Loftus who inspired me to develop *Clothing Poverty* in the first place.

PREFACE TO THE SECOND EDITION

What is fast fashion? In simple terms fast fashion is the rapid production of stylish, yet ever-changing and inexpensive new clothing designs for mass market retail. In the last few years, since the publications of the first edition of *Clothing Poverty*, the speed of fashion has accelerated. Like 5G mobile phones and fibre optic broadband, it's gone superfast. Evolving technologies have facilitated the rise of popular online-only retailers, such as Boohoo and Nova Fashion. Simultaneously Instagram, WeChat and other social media have become ever more effective in rapidly communicating new trends. Manufacturing lead times are shrinking. Brand new media-inspired styles, primarily targeted towards female Gen Z and younger millennial consumers, can be reproduced from initial designs as fresh, affordable fashion products in as little as five weeks. Material and garment construction standards have declined as budget fashion items are only destined to lead short lives. As the speed of new production cycles and the rates of disposal have increased the broader consequences of clothing over-consumption have expanded and touched lives around the world. Impoverished factory workers, vulnerable ecological systems and transnational recycling industries all experience the hidden impacts of globalized fashion.

Consuming masses of cheap clothes has social and environmental impacts that are garnering greater attention. Stories from emerging economies such as China, Bangladesh and India about poverty wages, gender-based violence against female workers, and the relentless pace of workloads driven by targets imposed by fast-fashion retailers have proliferated in the mainstream media. Environmental campaigns have also focused attention on the oversized ecological footprint of fashion, such as the impact on stressed agricultural lands and huge volume of water use associated with clothing production. In response advocacy organizations like the Clean Clothes Campaign and Fashion Revolution have drawn attention to widespread labour abuses and environmental scandals. British members of parliament have asked how retailers can justify selling T-shirts for £2 ($3) and law-makers have begun to scrutinize the greenhouse gas emissions of fast fashion, yet many aspects of the industry remain hidden from view and escape media and political attention. This new edition casts further light on the clothing scene's dirty secrets.

Fast fashion promotes a throwaway culture. A huge amount of emissions, pollution and waste are generated by one of the world's largest industrial sectors, with far-reaching ecological consequences. New research is demonstrating how the widespread use of synthetic fibres, including acrylic, nylon and polyester, is having a devastating impact on the environment. These effects are linked to the problem of ocean plastics pollution, but occur on a different scale. News reporting has highlighted the huge problem of plastic debris – bags, bottles, wrappers – that wash up on beaches, but pollution from microscopic textile fibres is also causing irreversible damage as they end up in the guts of fish and other marine creatures. Strands of synthetic materials smaller than a human hair are shed as clothes are worn and laundered, then enter waterways and can be ingested by marine organisms as they feed. The effects are fearsome for fragile ecological systems and food chains that ultimately lead to humans eating contaminated seafood. Micro-fibre pollution is part of a suite of irreversible global environmental changes, alongside ocean acidification and climate change that has trigged debate among scientists and led to the emergence of the Anthropocene concept. This new idea is a way of understanding how humans have caused permanent geological-scale changes to the planet. In the new concluding chapter, the problems of microfibre pollution are explored within the framework of the Anthropocene alongside proposed solutions to fast fashion's waste problems. The ill-thought-out and deeply problematic circular fashion initiative that envisages a virtuous cycle of clothing manufacturing, use and recycling is dissected.

At the heart of this book is an exposé of the flipside of fast fashion, which puts two means through which international inequalities are reproduced at the front and centre of the debate. First, although the awful employment conditions of workers who make clothes for Europeans and North Americans are well documented, more attention is needed on the livelihoods of poor people on the other side of the world. Factory workers get low wages and work hard to make low-cost garments. The story behind the made in Bangladesh or China label in fast-fashion clothes is fleshed out through detailed discussion of industrial practices and in the conclusion new examples and evidence of changing, yet still unjust labour relations are reviewed. Second, this book highlights that production of new clothing is only half of the story, as when fast-fashion items are thrown away they do not just go away, they go somewhere. Many items return to be sold again in Africa, Asia or South America. The under-belly of the global fashion industry is the enormous, although obscure, trade in used clothing from the world's richest to the most underdeveloped countries: worth over $4 billion and amounting to tens of billions of garments. Here it is argued that this trading relationship stifles economic progress and is a fundamental issue of global inequality and human dignity. Billions of people are locked in relationships of dependency that leave them with little choice but to wear unwanted fast fashion. In particular original fieldwork and colourful examples from Africa are used to support and animate many of the arguments through this book because the world's poorest continent is normally forgotten in studies of the fashion and textile industries. The first edition of *Clothing Poverty* led to publicity and debate on this topic, but the new conclusion offers further insight into what should be done to address the poverty that is reproduced through global patterns of second-hand trade. Political momentum has built around the issues. In 2015 the East African Community (EAC) voted to ban the import of used clothes by 2019 and this has begun to come in to force. Controls on second-hand clothing imports are contentious and the United States has opposed this restriction on free trade. The context behind this dispute and why the EAC actions are commendable is explained in the conclusion alongside what should be done with unwanted clothing. Bringing together the changing environmental and developmental contexts of the global new and second-hand trades in fashion necessitated a new edition of *Clothing Poverty*.

INTRODUCTION

Everyone knows that most Africans are poor. Life
expectancy is low, education is basic, food is simple,
and clothes are few. Curving around the south-east
coast of the continent, Mozambique has a typically
African economy. Many Mozambicans are dependent on subsistence agriculture or low-value exports
such as cashew nuts, cotton and Indian Ocean
shrimps. Beneath the shrimps and the warm waters
are rich natural gas reserves, which could fuel development, but these resources are more likely to be
stolen or squandered overseas, as recent economic
growth has contributed to rising inequality rather
than a reduction in poverty. Like much of Africa,
Mozambique's national budget is dependent on support from overseas aid, and the liberalized economy
is wide open to both exports and imports. The capital, Maputo, is an important regional port 30 miles

from South Africa. Tree-lined avenues, a legacy of Portuguese colonialism, stretch out from the city centre towards poorer neighbourhoods. At the end of one of these avenues on the edge of downtown is the sprawling and bustling Mercado do Xipamanine – Xipamanine market.

On any weekday morning the entrance to Xipamanine market is crowded; minivans clog the narrow approach road and hawkers circle, touting cheap Chinese manufactured goods such as plastic clothes pegs, polyester socks and pressed steel cutlery. Entering the market one passes through narrow alleys, between market stalls selling a mix of local food and international products: coconuts, mangoes, pineapples, fresh fish, suitcases, school stationary and stereos – pumping out the latest R&B beats from New York and Los Angeles. It is lively and vibrant, rich in all sorts of smells and muddy under foot. Moving further into the market you begin to encounter noisy traders negotiating the sale of cheap, low-quality, imported new clothing. There are soccer shirts with English Premier League logos or Mozambican flags, brightly coloured floral ladies' tops, and Bob Marley branded belt buckles. Beyond these new clothing vendors is the heart of the market, and here we find Mario's used-clothing stall.

Mario is in his early thirties; he migrated to Maputo from rural Inhambane province in search of work. He makes a living selling second-hand jeans imported from North America and Europe. Six days a week he comes to his simple wooden market stall and sets out his stock. The jeans are carefully arranged according to quality. Pristine pairs of Calvin Kleins and Levi's hang on display on improvised coat-hangers, while low-value torn and soiled denim is heaped on the ground on polythene sacks. Mario buys mixed consignments of used jeans shipped to Mozambique from rich countries. All of the jeans have their own unique and unknown stories; maybe they were outgrown by an American teenager, discarded by a fashion-conscious Canadian student, or worn out by a British construction worker. At one time the jeans have all been bought, owned and worn by someone in North America or Europe, and then recycled and ended up far away in an African marketplace. Some jeans show the marks of their previous lives; there are rips, scuffs and stains, and scraps of paper in the pockets. The dirtiest and most torn jeans won't be sold, and if Mario ends up with too many low-quality pairs he will lose money.

Traders in Xipamanine market are familiar with Western popular culture and work hard to identify clothes which will appeal to customers who are poor but nevertheless caught up in the currents of global fashion. Mario enjoys American hip hop and English football. He knows all the results and soccer gossip, and what tracks are in vogue with Mozambican teens. Although Mario recognizes Beyoncé songs, Manchester United players and what styles of denim sell well, he does not know where the jeans come from or how they get to Maputo. Globally the used-clothing trade is a large and growing sector, but here in this cramped market business is usually slow during the long, stiflingly hot afternoons. Between sales Mario is preoccupied with more pressing matters than thinking about how second-hand jeans from the West end up on his stall. He faces the persistent dilemma of deciding whether to take a risk and spend more money on another package of used denim, save funds to pay for further education so he can try to find a formal job, or use the cash to provide for his young family. Like the other thousand or so second-hand traders in Xipamanine market, Mario has a precarious small business; while he is able to provide for his household, he still faces the constant demand for basic necessities at home. Ultimately he cannot escape poverty through selling second-hand clothes. For him this is his only means of making a living, and he does not dwell on the origins and impacts of the second-hand clothing trade.

Thousands of miles away in rich countries like the United States and Britain, few people ever think about what happens to their clothes after they have finished wearing them and given them away to a recycling company or charity. In many instances they will end up somewhere like Mario's stall in Mozambique. People often express disbelief when they hear that their unwanted clothes are sold in Africa, rather than freely distributed, and that companies profit through this business (as well as cheat, steal and smuggle). Billions of second-hand garments are traded globally ever year.[1] This book explores how second-hand clothing supply chains cut across continents, linking Americans, Canadians, Britons and other Europeans to Mozambique; spanning North and South America, connecting Europe with East and West Africa and stretching across Asia and around the Pacific. Used-clothing networks are different to other trade patterns as they reverse the flow of commodities; while new clothes are mainly manufactured in low-income countries and emerging economies like Bangladesh and China, used clothing goes from the rich to the poor. Moreover they are intimate connections as they physically link consumers who wear new clothes in the global North (Australia, Europe, Japan and North America) to some of the poorest people in the global

South (Africa, most of Asia, the Middle East and South America), who are dependent on buying and re-wearing the same garments.

The story of second-hand clothing is just one of the many sides to the hidden world of clothes that is exposed through this book. Using research from across the globe, colourful stories and hard data demonstrate how the clothing and textile sectors have played a major part in making different regions of the world affluent and impoverished. Starting with a biography of jeans, this investigation of the global economy first uncovers how one of the world's most common garments has grown to be so popular. It considers the origin and spread of jeans, and then maps out the production process from design to cotton growing, denim milling, manufacturing, advertising and retail. The lifespan of jeans offers an insight into the complex international journeys new clothing goods follow around the globe. A narrow biography of jeans provides one slice through the world economy, like cutting through a layered cake; some of the patterns of globalization are exposed, but it is equally important to understand the broader clothing sector as a whole. Therefore the following chapter provides more historical breadth and examines how today's global trade in clothing has been linked to the international spread of a free-market economy. Cotton, cloth and clothing production played an important role in driving forward global trade. Textile factories underpinned the Industrial Revolution and the development of capitalism. The expansion of this mode of production and economic globalization is explored. Recent trends, and the reasons behind the global shift in clothing production away from Europe and North America, are then introduced. Next, light is cast on the shadowy world of second-hand clothing, which has been less documented, despite used clothing being an important source of garments for hundreds of years. One example that is put to work here is an in-depth analysis of the collection, recycling and export of used clothing in the UK. Britain is one of the major exporters of second-hand clothing and the trade is long-standing and well established; yet it involves an uneasy cast of actors, including charities, immigrant traders, companies and even criminals.

Tracing the evolving roles of different countries in garment manufacturing and markets explains some of the divergent economic trajectories of various regions of the world; in particular some of the poorest and least-known places are discussed here. Field research from Mozambique, Zambia and elsewhere in Africa makes up the body of many of the core arguments.

Africa has largely been neglected in writing on the clothing sector, yet the world's most impoverished continent has played an important role in the global history of garment production, especially in cotton growing. In the colonial period cotton was one of the major export crops, and through patterns of uneven exchange relationships of dependency between Africa and Europe emerged. After political independence, terms of trade hardly improved; here the long-term structural exploitation of African farm workers is investigated using evidence from Mali, Mozambique and Senegal. Africans are not just involved in the clothing trade as cotton growers, but like everyone are also consumers of clothes. Over a billion Africans are deeply impoverished, and clothing availability is an important livelihood issue as the poor lack access to affordable, good-quality, basic garments. Few clothes are made in Africa for local markets; understanding why there is so little manufacturing helps to explain how this part of the world remains so poor.

Today, China plays the dominant role in global clothing manufacture, while North America and Europe still generate the demand that structures the geographies of production and consumption, although the balance of market power is swinging east. Predominantly female workers in garment factories make clothes for export, generating profits that are driving Chinese gross domestic product (GDP) growth; the reasons behind large-scale labour exploitation are considered. As China rises it is leading the reconfiguration of the global economy, and part of this new shift is a growing embrace of Africa by China. In the clothing sector Chinese businesses have influenced production and markets, with mixed fortunes for Africans. Drawing on detailed research at a factory in Zambia, the workers' experiences of employment in a modern Chinese-managed clothing factory producing for global markets are documented, showing the opportunities and risks presented by China's new engagement in Africa. Following on from this, the impacts of mass imports of used clothes to Africa are investigated, which leads on to a chapter on Mozambique and a discussion of the livelihoods of traders like Mario.

Second-hand clothes are not just found in poor African countries; they are retailed around the world. Vintage fashion is a growing trend in the global North; case studies from some of the world's fashion hotspots – London, New York and Tokyo – show how the retro clothing and vintage sectors are linked to the new fashion industry. Other examples from middle- and low-income countries, including Bolivia, India, Papua New Guinea and the Philippines, provide further evidence of the flourishing of used-clothing markets and detail some of their diverse social and economic impacts in the global South. Next, some of the myths and realities surrounding the production and consumption of ethical fashion are investigated. New green and socially responsible garment sectors, which are intended to improve labour conditions and be more environmentally friendly, are being promoted by clothing brands. Ethical consumption and sustainable fashion are emerging trends; some of the contradictions and opportunities presented by alternative methods of manufacturing and retail are investigated, using different examples of fashion, from the mass-produced Toms shoes to the exclusive collections of Vivienne Westwood.

The business of making, selling and buying clothes affects everyone in the world. Apparel is a multibillion-dollar industry and one of the cornerstones of economic and cultural globalization. Western consumers have a huge amount of choice over what they wear, because poor people across the developing world grow cotton, dye materials and sew fabric, and are paid low wages, which keep clothes cheap for those consumers to buy. These low wage levels cannot allow cotton farmers and factory workers to consume the garments they help make, and so a global division in consumption has emerged. People in the global North have grown used to the ever-changing supply of garment styles and the instantaneous and relatively effortless consumption of clothing. Rapid cycles of predominantly East Asian manufacturing and retail in the global North subsequently determine the onward sale of unwanted used clothing to Africa and elsewhere. The international used-clothing trade is a countercurrent to the flow of new garments; it only makes sense when it is considered in tandem with new clothing production and what has come to be known as *fast fashion*. To understand how and why hundreds of pairs of jeans end up on Mario's stall, first it is necessary to learn exactly how the new fast-fashion clothing system of provision has developed and explain why different countries have become winners and losers in the global economy.

'Fast fashion' is a term coined by retailers to encapsulate how trends move rapidly from the catwalk to the store. Manufacturing is quick and cheap and consumers can easily take advantage of affordable collections in shops like Gap, H&M and Zara, and get involved in current fashion crazes. In order to appreciate how our shopping for fast fashion makes us complicit in a system which is denying people in the global South the chance to escape poverty, we need to begin by thinking about where our clothing comes from. Next we have to consider how, as the affluent minority in the global North indulges in the rapid consumption of clothing, the disposal of old garments has a knock-on effect and sets in motion the international second-hand clothing trade. Flows of used clothing reach the poorest of people in the global South and lock them into another relationship of dependency. The boom in fast fashion and the little-known second-hand clothing trade it has produced have shaped lives and determined patterns of dress around the world. Divisions of labour in the clothing sector play their part in keeping places of new clothing consumption rich and areas of production and second-hand consumption poor. This book looks beyond 'Made in China', or whatever label is found in your clothes, and explores the hidden story of both where clothes come from and where they end up. The relationships and case studies drawn from around the world and across different periods of human history illuminate and contextualize gross injustices at the heart of contemporary globalization. The concluding chapter offers insights from new research on the pressing global environmental impacts of fast fashion and discusses radical alternatives which could challenge the inequality embedded in global clothing systems of provision.

A BIOGRAPHY OF JEANS

Jeans are one of the most popular items of clothing. From their humble origins as the quintessential American workwear to their present status as among the most ubiquitous garments, denim is worn every day around the world by women and men, young and old, rich and poor. Most people own a pair of jeans or at least one related article of denim. Jeans therefore provide a good universal case study that it is easy to relate to. However, a T-shirt, a sweater or a pair of socks could equally be scrutinized. This chapter maps new clothing production and explores where jeans are designed, where cotton is grown and denim is woven, and where jeans are sewn together before being marketed and retailed; it is a biography of jeans. Starting with design in San Francisco and cotton fields in India, travelling via factories in Bangladesh and Mexico, to retail in New York and London, this narrative illuminates how an everyday clothing item has a rich history and passes along a geographically diverse commodity chain.

The aim of this biography is to understand the 'systems of provision' which bring jeans to consumers. This means charting how jeans have become a default clothing choice for millions of people, and understanding where manufacturing takes place and who profits from – and who is exploited by – the global denim industry. The economist Ben Fine coined this approach as a way of understanding why people buy certain goods and how choices are shaped by history, culture and geography. The system-of-provision approach maps the 'chain of activity that attaches consumption to the production that makes it possible'.[1] So, before discussing the manufacturing process, we examine the social history of jeans, to reveal how they became such a popular clothing choice. Complex relationships linking people around the world are involved in the manufacture of a simple pair of jeans. A brief account of the different work of farmers, factory workers and shop assistants shows what is involved in making jeans. The production process, or system of provision, is divided into six main stages: origin, design, cotton growing, denim milling, manufacturing, advertising and retail. This biography examines different labour processes from across the globe to provide a broad description of trade patterns, rather than following the same raw cotton from farm gate to department store rail.

JEANS: A SOCIAL HISTORY

The birthplace and early heritage of denim jeans are disputed. France and Italy as well as the United States lay partial claims to their origins. Sailors from Genoa (from which the name 'jeans' is supposed to derive) were said to have spread hard-wearing Italian cotton fabric. Alternatively, the name 'denim' can be translated as *de Nîmes*, 'of Nîmes', the Roman city in the south of France famous for its textiles. Where there is consensus is that the history of modern blue jeans began with the weaving of denim fabric and the use of indigo dye, a natural colour easily fixed to cotton. Blue jeans material is made from weaving cotton threads: the diagonal weft thread passes under two or more dyed warp threads. The characteristic blue jean colour and diagonal pattern are produced as the warp threads are coloured blue and the weft left white, which makes for a strong twill fabric and also gives the inside of jeans their lighter colour. In the 1870s Levi Strauss made the critical contribution of riveting the denim, which prevented tearing, and subsequently

added five pockets and belt loops. These early models inspired the standard jean style, elements of which
are seen in most contemporary designs. Levi Strauss's
developments were so influential because they
brought together a range of useful parts: copper rivets provided long-lasting toughness; rugged twill fabric offered robust protection; the blue denim colour
was simple to reproduce, first using indigo and later
synthetic dyes; blue also proved a popular neutral colour; and finally the five-pocket design was functional
and later augmented by various combinations of belt
loops, buttons and zippers to aid fit.[2]

The hard-wearing nature of jeans meant they
became the trousers of choice for the American working man and were readily adopted by the iconic
cowboy. Later, they provided part of the uniform of
industrial workers during the emergence of mass-
manufacturing industry in the early twentieth century.
In the 1950s and 1960s jeans became more than utilitarian workwear. Denim offered a casual and subversive
mode of dress for women as well as men. Screen icons
like Marlon Brando, James Dean and Marilyn Monroe
adopted jeans as part of a costume which exuded
characteristics such as youth, freedom and sex
appeal. Hollywood colour films projected aspirational images of blue jeans, and young people in

America as well as overseas imitated these dress styles. Denim gained both popularity and notoriety in youth culture. However, jeans were not just passively taken up by other societies imitating America; they have grown to have their own local meanings and significance. In the United Kingdom they were associated with transgressive and rebellious youth. Further east in Poland they became politicized garments. Behind the iron curtain jeans were a symbol of rebellion in communist societies. Brazilians have modified the basic design to reflect desires for a particular body image. In Japan jeans have a unique social history, which is discussed later. Towards the end of the twentieth century jeans began to lose their subversive qualities in most of Europe and the Americas and became something closer to a default wardrobe item. What you chose without thinking about what to wear. Wearing jeans has become a way to escape making a decision, and putting them on is an act of conformity. They no longer demark a particular social group and instead offer anonymity. Wearing jeans is part of an entrenched clothing system of provision. The previously rebellious connotations of denim have disappeared and they are a part of mainstream society. Buying and wearing jeans means participating in the market and they are retailed at every price point from designer lines to bargain basement. Jeans are the dress-down uniform of presidents and prime ministers as well as the street outfits of punks and protesters.[3]

Blue jeans have spread across the world and are worn in nearly every country. In many places they are among the most common item of dress. Although the USA is the largest market, with up to half a billion pairs sold each year, sales in Asia, particularly China, Japan and India, are also huge and expanding. Jeans have become a default item of clothing because they can be easily manufactured and meet the practical and cultural needs of modern lives. Their popularity is not simply due to customers' desires nor demand stimulated by producers. Rather, production and consumption influence one another.[4] They both also shape the 'use value' of jeans. *Use value* means the worth of a thing in relation to what humans both *need* and *want*. The 'usefulness' is influenced by their original design as the garments for American agricultural and industrial workers. Hard-wearing denim trousers were practical, reliable and very useful. Mass-manufacturing made the trousers affordable and they satisfied basic needs. As they grew in popularity various social groups – from movie stars to teenagers – found that these robust and affordable garments could be tailored to convey different cultural messages. New denim styles emerged for women and men around the world. They became something that people wanted. Jeans are a product of early US industrial development and in turn have shaped how globalized culture developed, leading to the emergence of jeans systems of provision.

Denim has a life and lives with the owner. If wearers stretch to climb over fences the fibres will be pulled as they extend their legs; if they work bent over fitting carpets or scrubbing floors the knees will thin out and split; if they sit cross-legged the denim will stretch across and pull around the thighs. These daily movements will exercise the twill fabric and leave the imprint of the rhythms of each wearer's life. Old jeans can induce powerful feelings of warmth and reassurance. When someone wears their own familiar clothes they can rekindle memories of past events, soothe, and provide emotional as well as physical protection. Despite the lively nature of denim any associations the owners might have are a result of the social relationships that the jeans embody, and this only has meaning in a given social context. When used jeans are transported somewhere new and taken up by a second owner they will be valued differently depending on the local culture.

Think about the ways in which ripped jeans are valued and excluded in different places. This idea is important to understand in the context of the second-hand clothing trade and does not concern just our individual relationships with jeans, but also how they are perceived in a broader cultural context in a particular society. As anthropologist Daniel Millar has discussed, 'the first core semiotic marker was the association of jeans with the United States. But this is now seen as merely historical. People do not wear jeans in London today to appear more American even if that association is essential to understanding how jeans first became ubiquitous.'[5] America played a vital role in establishing denim systems of provision, but now wearing jeans is a global phenomenon. There is a world market in which the United States is one of many players.

At the level of individual garments, the same pair of jeans will affect people differently. When a second-hand buyer re-wears someone else's old jeans they will feel differently about them. Just as their body will move in a different manner and stretch and work the threads in new ways, so will they also form new associations with the jeans, born of their own social interactions.

DESIGNING DENIM

Today, Levi Strauss designs jeans in San Francisco, drawing upon the heritage of the brand and the early connection with frontier livelihoods, like raising cattle in the Old West. The advantages of this location are not just historical; the proximity to an important contemporary core customer base – a hip youth market in a leading financial and cultural centre – allows designers to innovate and introduce fresh design details to the basic jean formula and target new consumers. For instance, Levi's launched a 'commuter' series after observing the popularity of jeans among cyclists in the Bay area and then promoted this design nationally and internationally, demonstrating the web of feedback between producing for an established market, and cultivating new patterns of consumption. After a new design has been decided upon, a product developer, also in San Francisco, picks up the ideas and works out the details. They make prototypes, fit the jeans to mannequins and models, check denim finishes, communicate the final design to manufacturers around the world, and liaise with merchandisers so the product will have its correct home within the Levi's brand.[6]

Elsewhere, Italian designer brands like Armani, Gucci and Prada have their headquarters in Milan, where the couture fashion sector can influence the designs of jeans. Milan also serves as a commercial hub connecting fashion houses to advertising agencies, distributors and the fashion press. Catwalk styles can be incorporated into denim designs and rapidly transmitted to overseas producers. Trend spotters and fashion bloggers are found on the high streets of London, New York and Paris identifying what is on-trend among key groups. Fashion scouts either purposefully or indirectly feed in to the creation of new and modified styles that will later be found in malls and on Main Street. These specialized professions also have an important role in determining how vintage clothes influence new trends and designs, which is discussed towards the end of the book. What all these activities in London, Paris, Milan, New York and San Francisco have in common is a location in the global North; this is skilled, technical, metropolitan work, undertaken at trade fairs and in design studios and downtown loft workshops. All the labour processes associated with this type of work are relatively well paid, often graduate-level jobs, which stand in stark contrast to the low-skilled, poorly paid and sometimes dangerous production work in the global South. The design process is physically separated from the manufacturing enterprise in a way which would be totally unrecognizable to Mr Levi Strauss, who in the 1870s produced jeans in San Francisco to clothe the Californian working man.

Despite the differences in design and the dispersion of manufacturing activities, the basic pattern of jeans is still fairly faithful to its early origins. A single design language is common to thousands of product lines drawn up around the world, and a whole lexicon of jean styles has emerged: baggy, boot-cut, boyfriend, carpenter, classic, cowboy, drainpipe, flared, hipster, low-rise, relaxed, skinny, straight. Each new subcategory has become established as a different genre of jeans with associated cultural values that wax and wane across social contexts. Details also matter in denim design; these include the type of stitching and the colours of thread, the use of a belt loop, the number and cut of pockets, the fly and stitching of the yoke. Jeans can be embellished with embroidery, glitter, rhinestones, bleaching and buckles. Some of the more minute details are only ever seen by the wearer, but a successful designer knows it is important to furnish jeans with the right stylistic notes to complement the familiar denim blueprint. Designs can allow you to be noticed or provide you with anonymity. Denim designers work to effect a balance between providing uniform and individual looks, which reflects societies own tensions between social liberty and conformity to prescribed patterns of behaviour. Aspects of design also live on to influence how jeans are valued in secondary marketplaces, like Mario's stall in Mozambique.

One of the distinctive properties of contemporary jeans is the way in which millions of pairs are deliberately distressed. Bleached-out, faded and ripped denim is visible when one visits any branch of Gap, Macy's or Topshop. Denim is given effects to show a worn-in look, which is the output of particular types of labour activity, discussed below. This designer's trick establishes values of authenticity, which can relate back to earlier popular cultural history and a sentimental version of the past. Jeans can be made to look like the worn workwear of cowboys from the turn of the twentieth century or have the tears and fraying of mid-1970s punk style. Vintage fashions influence design; yet the designer is also trying to build a more personal association between the customer and the jeans. Designers play upon the 'lived-in' aesthetic, which can make denim more comforting and appealing. The clothes industry attempts to replicate the physical relationships our bodies forge with jeans, such as stretching, thinning and tearing them, to try to stimulate shoppers to buy them. The role of the designer is important in forming the symbolic value of jeans.

It is true that there is some correlation between relatively objective notions of quality and price, but the association rapidly falls away as the retail price point climbs towards $100. Differentiation then becomes increasingly important. Designers in all price brackets play a vital role, increasing the social value of jeans, so that the retail price no longer represents the cost of the labour and materials involved in manufacturing. Consumers buy jeans unaware of the conditions of production, and the most fashionable jeans become a major source of desire. Buyers covet new trends or styles, and the yearning to consume becomes a form of control. In fact, control is central to everyday life in capitalist societies. The market for goods and services is always expanding. People have to be compelled to buy more and more things. Both designers and advertisers play key roles in provoking people to purchase *authentic*, *fashionable* or *luxurious* jeans. Part of the design process in the global North is the stimulation of the market. Successful businesses depend on forming aspirational images. Brands including Levi Strauss, Lee and Wrangler have achieved this by attaching themselves to the values of authentic, original and honest Americana. The designers play a key role in systems of provision by creating visual formulas that can be cultivated to emerge as part of sophisticated advertising and marketing strategies which cast a spell on the consumer.

Designers shape systems of provision for all jeans; this is most apparent with luxurious high-end fashionable jeans, but the same is true for the more mundane, affordable and less dramatic styles. Just as Diesel, Gucci and Victoria Beckham jeans are 'designer', so are those found in Primark, Walmart or Target. Each pair of trousers still has to be designed and the production process mapped out, even if this is a piecemeal replication of the basic five-pocket blue jean pattern.

Alongside aesthetics, culture is a diffuse yet powerful force that surrounds the production of distinctive values in different jeans. It also influences how we buy and wear denim. In Brazil there is a specific style of jeans which grew in popularity in the 2000s, where this distinctive domestic design born in the 'funk balls' of Rio de Janeiro became known locally as *calça da gang*, or more widely as 'Brazilian jeans'.[7] The design uses elastane within the weave to produce thinner denim with both horizontal and vertical stretch. Popular first among young women and associated with dance culture in the *favelas* of Rio where the design was appropriated and given meaning, these tight pants have developed local notoriety and given rise to some lurid analysis. They 'are often described as a "bra for the bumbum", that it is actually giving lift to the buttocks, although in practice it is more that it holds and reveals rather than lifts'. These designs spread from the *favelas* and were taken up by clothing firms catering for the middle classes; using the 'edgy' aspects of Brazilian culture and their relation to sensuality and sexuality, they went on to influence international fashion and designers based in California and Paris.[8]

GROWING COTTON

Wads of fluffy white cotton are the fruit of the shrubby, grey cotton plant. They are native to tropical countries, but cotton is grown around the world from Ukraine in the north to Australia in the south, in deep, well-drained soils with good nutrient content. The ideal climate is a constant temperature of 18–30 degrees Celsius (64–86 degrees Fahrenheit), sunshine, dry conditions and long periods (175 to 225 days) without frost. Sometimes known as 'white gold', cotton is a natural fibre mostly composed of cellulose; cotton strands are formed by twisting these smaller ribbon-like fibres together. After food crops, cotton is comfortably the world's most farmed plant. It is widely used in industry to make items such as bandages and bank notes, while the seed provides feed for cattle, can be pressed to make cooking oil, and used in cosmetics and soaps.

Farmers who grow cotton are faced with management decisions that include seed choices, crop rotations, irrigation strategies, and they increasingly have to consider the environmental impacts and sustainability of their work. Cotton growing covers around 2.4 per cent of global agricultural land, yet accounts for 24 per cent of insecticides and 11 per cent of pesticides.[9] Proportionally cotton uses a far greater degree of chemical input than most food crops because there is less concern over consumers' health (as they are not ingesting the product), but this can have disastrous impacts on agricultural environments and workers' well-being. A study from Punjab, Pakistan showed the potentially serious health consequences of pesticide use by cotton growers. High exposure risks resulted from pesticide spills, faulty sprayers and using the chemicals in inappropriate weather. Farmers reported irritation of skin and eyes, headaches and dizziness. In India mild to severe poisoning has long been observed following interactions with pesticides. This includes extremely serious neurotoxic effects in 6 per cent of spraying sessions.[10] In addition to the widespread use of pesticides, cotton is very dependent on water consumption, requiring an incredible 11,000 litres of water for every kilogram (or 1,320 US gallons per pound) of cotton grown, picked, produced, packed and shipped to make jeans. This 'virtual water' – the invisible agricultural and industrial consumption of water that goes into the production of goods – far exceeds the water requirements of food crops such as rice (3,400 litres per kilo) and wheat (1,300 litres).[11] Much cotton is grown in water-scarce environments; our thirst for new jeans and other cotton apparel is part of a broader pattern of trade which also involves the rapid consumption of other water-hungry goods such as coffee, beef and leather. Demand for these products is often driven by overconsumption in the global North, which threatens precious water resources, particularly in tropical and semi-arid environments. Environmental damage is occurring on a wide scale; for example, water extraction from the Amur Darya and Syr Darya rivers in Central Asia for cotton irrigation has led to the near disappearance of the Aral Sea.[12]

Agricultural workers in the cotton sector have been treated in an abhorrent way for centuries. In the United States the history of cotton growing is inextricably linked to slavery, and in Africa is connected to colonial labour abuses (discussed in Chapter 4). What is clear, from both historical and contemporary perspectives, is that cotton has always been grown at great human cost. Among the particularly upsetting aspects of cotton farming are the many reports on the abuse of child labour in cotton-growing regions, including Egypt, India and Uzbekistan.[13] Labour exploitation is found throughout the global South. The international NGO Oxfam has detailed the tough life of a cotton grower in Peru:

> Lily Arteaga Cabrera, 47, also grows cotton in Pisco. She gets up at 5 in the morning to prepare food for the family and then goes to the cotton field at 8, where she stays until 6 in the evening. The cotton they grow earns them just enough to feed the family – but not very well. It is hard work but they are locked into a cycle of debt – they borrow to plant and then work eight months caring for the crop until they harvest and earn enough to pay the debts: They rarely have any extra left over. Lily looks after the family money and has to budget carefully.[14]

This report was prompted by a change to the trade relationships between Peru and the USA, which posed a threat to the vulnerable livelihoods of cotton growers such as Lily Arteaga Cabrera. Research by Oxfam has highlighted how demand for cotton is keeping peasants, smallholders and agricultural workers in poverty across the global South and especially in the West African countries of Benin, Burkina Faso, Chad and Mali. Oxfam highlights how relationships of dependency with international cotton markets and trade regulations are structured against poor producers and have negative effects on farmers' livelihoods. The role of international trade agreements and cotton farming in Africa is discussed in greater depth in subsequent chapters. It is also important to note how Oxfam has been advocating for change, while also being embroiled in the second-hand clothing trade. This book later explores the impacts of second-hand clothing exports.

In general, cotton growing provides a poorly paid livelihood; furthermore, environmentally harmful approaches to agriculture are implemented throughout much of the global South. Unfortunately, the exposure of these travesties rarely translates into practical action. The barriers to a politics of radical social change, and how they relate to our addiction to fast fashion, are themes explored throughout this book. This is not to neglect the fact that some limited attempts have been made to address the pressing human and environmental costs of cotton agriculture in middle- and low-income countries, namely via accreditation schemes for clean, green and Fairtrade cotton. Turkey has been at the forefront of organic cotton agriculture, and jeans made from Fairtrade cotton are beginning to reach some department stores, like Marks & Spencer in the UK.

After China, the United States is the largest producer of cotton in the world, where much investment has gone into the development of high-yielding cotton varieties and efficient production techniques. The USA and other producers in the global North, such as Australia, grow cotton in less socially and environmentally exploitative ways. Cotton production is now mechanized and the environmental impacts are regulated, but this is only commercially viable as the sector is heavily subsidized in the global North.

GINNING, SPINNING AND WEAVING

Harvested cotton is processed at a ginnery, usually in the same region as the cotton fields. Bales of cotton are then taken to a spinning plant to form thread, before being woven into denim. Ginning, spinning and weaving can occur side by side or be spread across continents. At the Mulungushi Cotton ginnery in Kabwe, Zambia, cotton used to supply a local factory, but is now processed for export to China, the world's largest importer of ginned cotton (this factory is discussed further in Chapter 5). After fluffing and drying, the cotton is opened to remove dirt and leaves, and then is processed by ginning to further remove fragments of stalk, seeds, soils and other waste from the fibres. Labour standards can be as low in the ginneries, as in the cotton fields. Child labour has been employed in Indian ginneries, where workers are paid just over $2 a day for a 12-hour shift in dangerous conditions.[15]

Mapping out where the cotton fibres that make up a particular pair of jeans come from is very difficult; this is partially due to the type of cotton used in denim. Jeans do not generally require high-quality cotton. Short cotton fibres can be used, whereas long ribbons of fibre are needed to make fine and delicate garments such as dress shirts and underwear. In Zambia the low-quality B-grade fibres are more likely to be used locally for hard-wearing twill fabrics such as denims, whereas A-grades are exported to China.[16] At the spinning plant, tens of thousands of cotton fibres are spun and twisted together by centrifugal force to produce strands of yarn. It is not unusual to combine fibres from different areas to produce thread. Rachel Snyder notes that 'a single foot of thread might contain fibres from farms in Texas, Azerbaijan, India, Turkey and Pakistan', and at 'a spinning plant in Italy bales of cotton from countries across Africa, America, Asia and the former Soviet Union can all be spun together'.[17] Labelling can also be inaccurate; for instance, Uzbekistan has an established reputation for producing high-quality cotton, which means that cotton from neighbouring states such as Azerbaijan is sometimes fraudulently labelled as Uzbek cotton to give it a higher value.

To make denim, the warp yarn is dyed in synthetic indigo dye and then woven with the weft thread into denim. The dyeing process involves strong chemical compounds. Even most organic cotton is dyed in this manner. Weaving combines different weights of fabric, and flexible yarns such as lycra or the elastane in Brazilian jeans can provide stretch. Industrial laundering techniques create different effects and looks; staples are used to gather fabric and allow graduated colouring and bleaching, just like tie-dyeing a T-shirt. Pumice stones are used to create stonewash. Glasspaper and brushing techniques create shine on fabrics. These activities are very water-intensive, which contributes to the high volumes of virtual water involved in the production of jeans. Laundering processes use toxic combinations of chemicals, including formaldehyde, and appropriate safety equipment, such as boots, gloves, masks and eyewear are required to protect workers, though are often missing in developing-world factories. The side-effects of these chemicals go beyond the workers and can harm local communities. Denim plants have a heavy ecological footprint; for example, in Lesotho a factory owned by the Taiwanese firm Nien Hsing Fashion Group, which supplied Gap and Levi Strauss, was discharging deep blue wastewater polluted with chemicals, which contaminated the water table and a local river.[18]

Local environmental controls are often poorly enforced in the global South, but in manufacturing, spinning and weaving, cotton factories are held to exacting international standards to produce denims with minimal faults. Tracing the origins of cotton is further complicated by standards such as those put forward by the American Society of Testing and Materials (ASTM), which leads to the production of uniform cotton threads:

A brand in Japan can buy cotton from Mexico and Turkey and have it made into cloth in France and North Carolina and sewn into a garment in China and Bangladesh and sell it on store shelves in Tokyo and Madrid and have the constituency and quality be exactly the same for each garment in every country.[19]

At the Zambia China Mulungushi Textiles in Zambia, where the ginning, spinning and weaving processes, as well as the garment-making, were all carried out together, ex-employees reported that a consignment of jeans sent to the USA were returned due to the poor quality of cloth. Japan, in contrast, is known to be the home of the highest quality premium denims used in many top fashion brands. The expertise that has developed in Japan is linked to the country's social history and its access to American second-hand denim in the post-war era (discussed in Chapter 8).

The blending of different patterns of agriculture and manufacturing makes it difficult, if not impossible, to audit the multiple relationships between farmers, ginneries, spinners and fabric weavers that constitute the production of denim cloth. Throughout global jeans systems of provision denim is usually produced in one factory and by one contractor and then sent onwards to garment factories where it is cut and sewn. Across the linked chain of transactions there is a co-dependence between the designers, retailers, garment sewers and denim manufacturers. Designers and advertisers find inspiration from producers, especially those who adapt and modify the traditional blue jean appearance through processes such as textile laundering. Despite these patterns of co-dependence it is normally either the designers at the beginning of the chain or the retailers in the global North who monopolize the most valuable activities and extract the greatest overall surplus, or profit, from labour, rather than the firms and individuals in the middle of a system of provision.

MANUFACTURING JEANS

Manufacturing jeans involves transforming woven denim into final designs. Flat rolls of denim are transformed by the input of labour and the addition of different design details. Subdivision of labour is a hallmark of production systems in today's factories. The trousers will pass through many hands as workers are allocated specific tasks; patterns are drawn and the two legs will be cut by different operators; each seam is sewn by someone dedicated to that job; one worker may rivet the right pocket, while their partner takes care of the left. Sewing machines form long lines across huge warehouse-like workspaces. Jeans pass from one employee to another at a relentless rate, following well-rehearsed movements of the type popularized in the time-and-motion studies of Frederick W. Taylor, which led to the scientific management of factories in the early twentieth century. Once jeans have been sewn they might be cleaned and laundered to produce a particular type of finish, such as fraying or bleaching, or workers can grind, sand-blast and scrape jeans to give them lived-in looks. Further down the line, labels are added and jeans are inspected. Substandard garments are discarded for local retail or reuse, and finished trousers are finally packaged before leaving the plant. A detailed case study of labour standards in a clothing factory will later discuss some of the horrific conditions found in garment industries.

Some recent broad trends and developments have affected jean manufacturing. Clothing production is no longer a major industry in Europe, and jeans man-ufacturing has long since expanded away from its origins in the United States. In Europe, even Italian fashion brands like Armani, Gucci and Prada have moved their manufacturing to Asia. Luxury labels have managed to sustain desirable brands, which stem from their couture heritage still being controlled by designers, like those in Milan. The movement of clothing manufacturing out of Italy is related to the recent changes in the quotas and tariffs found in the global clothing industry (discussed in Chapter 2). Italy itself only became inundated with foreign jeans at the start of the twenty-first century; imports rose dramatically – by 260 per cent between 2000 and

2005 – as the market opened to Asian-produced fast fashion.[20] The undermining of Italy's clothing industry, along with other elements of its manufacturing base, is one of the reasons why the economy suffered so badly in the 2007–8 financial crisis.

It is often argued that Americans who complain about the decline of national industry readily purchase foreign-made jeans at Sears, JCPenney and Walmart and therefore are themselves the cause of the problem. This argument is over simple and gives the consumer too much autonomy and responsibility in decision-making. Consumers are like deer caught in the headlights when faced with jeans systems of provision. They are led in their decision-making processes by designers, retailers and social pressure, rather than basing their choice on concern for whoever produced the jeans, or feeling patriotic concern for national industrial strategy. American brands have relocated and it is unrealistic to expect shoppers to audit supply chains. Levi Strauss, although still headquartered in the USA, has gone through a process of de-verticalization, licensing the manufacturing to foreign firms. Much of the company's production is now carried out in Mexico. This buyer-driven, decentralized approach allows Levi's to move production to different factories around the world and take advantage of variation in labour prices and other associated manufacturing costs, rather than being tied to the comparatively high wages of the working classes in the United States. Meanwhile the highly profitable design and marketing processes are protected and retained by Levi's, in places such as San Francisco and New York. Manufacturing processes are not tied to the production of component parts and often take place in countries which do not grow cotton, weave denim or produce buttons, rivets and zippers. For instance, many of the component jeans parts are exported from China to Cambodia, another centre of manufacturing, where denim is cut and the finished articles assembled.

The term 'fast fashion' does not just encapsulate the rapid changes in trends and styles found in the global North and the pace of retail sales, but also the speed at which designs can be transmitted around the world and orders turned into garments. Digital pattern designs, subcontracting and flexible ordering are advanced production management approaches that the fast-fashion industry utilizes to enhance profitability. Efficient use of labour is fundamentally important; workers are not always employed in sweatshop conditions. Sri Lanka has made improvements in working environments and prides itself on being socially and environmentally accountable while maintaining a competitive position in global supply chains.[21] Torreon in Mexico has good working conditions for jeans and many firms have clustered together to service the North American market, in an industrial area just four hours by road from Texas, producing denim trousers and jackets for brands including Calvin Klein, Old Navy, Sears and Target.[22] China is by far the world's largest producer of jeans. Most garment workers are female, although there is often a gender division in tasks. Work such as loading and unloading materials and truck driving is more likely to be performed by men, whereas the static production tasks are primarily undertaken by young women in their late teens, twenties and thirties. Work in garment factories is a classic example of global patriarchy. Women pay the price for decisions made by men, as factory ownership in clothing manufacturing as well as senior management positions in international clothing firms are overwhelmingly male.

Labour standards vary around the world and there are countless cases of worker abuse. Chapter 5 provides a detailed case study based on testimonies from garment workers. Three brief examples among thousands are: migrant workers from South Asia going missing from factories in Jordan while sewing jeans for Walmart; the violation of workers' right to association by G-Star jeans suppliers in India; 52 deaths and over 1,000 workers suffering lung and respiratory problems following the sandblasting of denim in Turkey to give it the 'lived-in' appearance that consumers love. Atrocities have been documented by advocacy organizations including the Institute for Global Labour and Human Rights, the Clean Clothes Campaign and Labour Behind the Label. In 2013 the horrific collapse of the Rana Plaza garment factory in Bangladesh is one of the worst examples of exploitation in jeans production, and resulted in the loss of over 1,100 lives and caused 2,500 serious injuries. Rana Plaza contained multiple garment factories which produced jeans for retailers, including Primark in the UK. Akter Rojina, who was injured in the collapse, earned just $65 a month as a sewer's assistant, which, although above the $37 minimum wage for Bangladesh's garment workers, still left her poor. 'We entered the factory because we needed to be paid. But the government should have overseen the construction of Rana Plaza; it was built on marshy land.' Rojina noted that the top three floors were added illegally.[23] Stories such as this rarely receive much attention and are quickly forgotten when people go shopping for jeans. Researching labour conditions is very difficult; academics and investigative journalists have problems gaining permission and access. Likewise there are many barriers to practical action. National policies on labour are likely to be defeated by a lack of local political will, but even if there are robust regulations the lead design and retail firms from the global North are prone to see out their short-term contracts and relocate to another country where labour costs are lower. Policies put forward to protect workers' rights often show a complete lack of ambition in addressing global inequality and are at best tokenistic. The struggle to improve labour standards in garment manufacturing is explored in the concluding chapter.

ADVERTISING AND RETAIL

Typically consumers in the USA say they spend approximately $35 on a pair of jeans and own on average 6.7 pairs. Jeans ownership in the USA is actually down from a historical high of 8.2 pairs per individual in 2006.[24] The trade body Cotton Incorporated argues that the fall in ownership has been associated with economic pressure, as well as the fast-fashion phenomenon, which has compelled clothing retailers to reduce quality and cotton content. There is also a steady rate of discard as people get rid of old jeans.

In the short term clothing prices are generally likely to rise. At the same time, American shoppers have become concerned with declining quality and the reduced value jeans represent. Jeans suffered a similar setback in the 1980s with the rise of polyester and the popularity of tracksuits and joggers. Yet, despite the recent decline in the USA, the global market for jeans is booming, currently estimated to be worth around $60 billion, or an eighth of the total clothing sector. Jeans are not going away any time soon.

How we buy jeans is changing. Online retailers are growing in popularity, either as digital storefronts for established names like Gap and Zara, or as solely e-retailers like ASOS and Mr Porter, the latter often specializing in rapidly bringing new fashion trends from the catwalk to the customer. For many jeans shoppers either the mall or the supermarket is at the heart of their retail experience, and this is where globalization, consumption, identity and cultural politics collide. Supermarkets have been the leaders in bringing ever cheaper denim to consumers. In the UK sales of jeans increased in the 2000s as unbranded jeans retailed in supermarkets, including Asda (owned by Walmart), brought very cheap denim to market. While firms like Walmart primarily generate profit on the basis of exploiting cheap Chinese labour, they are also efficient organizations able to set themselves apart from competitors through their effective distribution networks and, like many supermarkets, the paying of low wages (the legal minimum wage is currently £8.21 ($10.75) per hour in the UK, whereas many workers in the USA earn under $10 an hour). When jeans are purchased as an impulse or routine buy alongside the grocery shopping they become an unreflexive part of life going on as normal. Daniel Miller and Sophie Woodward even argue that this type of banal shopping for 'denim is special, being as much a refusal as an acceptance of capitalist pressures such as fashion'.[25] However, this type of zombie-like shopping is not, in my view, in any way a rejection of capitalism and shows compliance with rather than rebellion against this economic system.

Within malls specialist jeans retailers can be found alongside fashion stores. Both are distinctive spaces engineered for consumption, and prime examples of how place is a source of potent symbolism, infusing jeans with imagined values, depending on how the garments are presented and the ways in which the store itself is dressed. Levi's is one example of a company that has extended its activities at the consumption end of the system of provision through their carefully branded stores. Levi's stores around the world emphasize their association with Americana culture, and denim is expertly presented in clean shops with an industrial aesthetic, making use of exposed steel and seasoned timber. Having its own stores allows Levi's to control the merchandising activity and shape how its jeans are presented to the customer. As the lead firm in a complex system of provision it controls this key node which provides the most profitable business opportunity. Behind the branded storefronts and the neat displays of carefully folded denim is a whole complex of advertising. Studios in the heart of New York's garment district support Levi Strauss's marketing strategies and provide a stimulating environment to foster creative ideas. Advertisers work in close collaboration with designers and must perform the trick of convincing the consumer they have free choice instead of having their desires stimulated by marketing.

Advertising and merchandising contribute to establishing value in expensive jeans. Very few pairs of jeans cost more than $20 to manufacture, in rare cases $50; but even $500 designer jeans cost only marginally more to make than an average pair of Levis.[26] Designer brands invest in establishing advertising and marketing strategies. Capital is expended on renting the best retail space, fitting out shops in chic and minimalistic styles, buying glossy advertising space and employing top models in advertising. These costs are added into the retail price and the brand owners extract a surplus from all these different types of labour activity as well as the previous manufacturing process to amass a profit.

TODAY'S JEANS SYSTEMS OF PROVISION

The label sewn in the back of jeans, which may read 'Made in China', actually tells the consumer very little about the origins of their garment. Starting from the cotton (which could originate anywhere from Alabama to Zimbabwe) onwards, the production of jeans is nigh-on impossible to audit. They are not made in one place, but are constructed as a commodity with a particular set of social values through a whole web of relationships. Consumers do not only pay for the item, they also pay for advertising, design, transport, packaging, wastage and profits. The fruits of production are unevenly distributed. Diverse people involved in the growing of cotton, or the weaving of fabric, or the marketing of jeans receive different wages; meanwhile the managers, owners and investors, who control the means of production, extract surplus from both manufacturing and retail. Consumers' obsessions with the relationships between commodities – how the jeans relate to other clothes on sale, how they are advertised and marketed as part of a lifestyle, and how they are priced – obscure the relationships between the people who labour to produce them and their employers. Understanding the detail in such a journey is very difficult, but if we step back from looking at individual jeans the bigger picture is clearer. In the international clothing trade the most profitable activities are concentrated in segments with the highest barriers to entry. This can mean formal protection via trademarks or patents, or softer barriers such as a close relationship with the fashion press or a nuanced understanding of styles in rich consumer markets. Identifying and forming trends are enabled by the cultural influence of designers in London, Paris and New York. Access to the market is also very important, and large chain stores as well as supermarkets have an entrenched position in the retail sector. In some jeans production systems, especially for higher-value jeans such as Armani or Levi's, a lead firm plays a key role even though they may be a long way away from the actual production of trousers in the developing world. A lead firm monopolizes the highly profitable activities and can be a producer/designer and/or a buyer/retailer. This alone does not stop successful companies emerging in the global South, but it does make it difficult. The global economy is getting more complicated.

The rise of China, the emergence of new economic powerhouses like Dubai and Singapore, and the spread of transnational corporations across both the global North and the global South, means the old power centres of the global fashion industry are losing their dominance. In the future new denim designer brands are likely to emerge from the global South. Indeed there is already evidence of this, such as the rise of the Mavi fashion brand from Turkey, as well as the influence of Brazilian jean styles on designers in the United States and Europe.

The mega-consumption of fast fashion reflects and reinforces socio-economic inequality while simultaneously degrading the environment. The quest for cheap new jeans has led to the migration of industries from the (more expensive) global North to the (less expensive) global South, and to the depression of inflation-adjusted wage rates for many workers. There is more than just a human cost, as pressures on farmland and water-scarce environments has ratcheted up.[27] Consumption has become an incredibly important force in defining identity. Increasingly people are what they buy, which in particular places enormous financial and psychological pressure on the young to participate in what one might call a 'consumption arms race'. Teenagers have to buy the latest style to take part in distinction-making so they can simultaneously subscribe to current norms of behaviour and try to narrate their own identity.

But there is a second volume to this biography of jeans. Consumers in Europe and North America are involved in another concealed chain of activity, where the relationships between people and profit are even more obscure than those that are hidden from view within the new jeans system of provision. Used jeans and other second-hand clothes are internationally recycled and traded from the rich to the poor. This second life cycle also stretches across continents and unequally connects diverse people. The story of jeans continues after the wearer has grown tired of them and donated them to a charity or recycler for reuse. From here they are resold to a commercial operator, processed, packaged and exported, resold again, and can be retailed in a market like the one in Mozambique seen in the Introduction. Alternate trajectories for used jeans and other garments are picked up and discussed alongside the broader impacts of fast fashion throughout this book.

THEORIZING PRODUCTION AND CONSUMPTION

There are two important lessons to learn from this chapter. The first is simple: there is a spatial division of labour in the clothing sector. Tasks are undertaken in places where it is cheapest or easiest. Design takes place in studios in rich cosmopolitan cities. Cotton is grown where climate, landscape, workforce and technologies enable profitable farms. Historical uneven development has resulted in the divisions between high- and low-value work in the global North and South. The reasons for this pattern of inequality are explored later through evidence from across the globe.

The second lesson is that jeans and their constituent parts – like any commodities – are not just 'things', but are also a set of social relationships: a link between a farmer and a cotton trader, a connection between a factory owner and a sewing machine operator, or a cultural symbol purchased by a teenager. The social relationships, which are positions of power and dependency in economic transactions, are in no way *natural*. To explain this we must examine how we use jeans. Jeans, have a basic *use value*: on the one hand, they are worn to provide warmth and protection; on the other hand, various types of jeans are more or less stylish, depending on the cultural context. Frequently, the exchange of money which accompanies the sale of jeans in a supply chain is not directly associated with a labour activity that would make jeans *more physically useful*. In fact, social relations in market exchange are not connected with the material transformation of goods. People get paid not for making jeans, but for making them into a commodity. It is wrong to take the production of jeans at face value. If we focus on the roles of different types of workers in transforming materials, we miss the other aspects through which value is produced. Value is socially determined and affected by factors such as advertising, fashions and trends, and not derived from the basic usefulness of a thing. Value arises from both contemporary and historical conditions. A simple example would be to consider the different values which have been attached to flared or skinny jeans at various historical moments (this will become important to bear in mind when we consider the development of vintage fashions). People involved in the jeans system of provision, like designers, stylists, models and sales assistants, all play a social role in creating *symbolic value*, and the work they do is a product of culture.

The arguments presented in this chapter are informed by a critical, political economy approach. The discussion of commodities as social relationships in the previous paragraph is derived from Karl Marx's analysis of commodity fetishism. In *Capital*, Marx illuminated how the veil of market exchange hides the social relations of production from consumers.

Producers and consumers are thereby alienated from one another. As Ben Fine succinctly puts it, 'whilst capitalism organizes production in definite social relationships between [women and] men, these relationships are expressed and appear as relationships between things'.[28] This book is an attempt to investigate connections between different types of clothing, consumers and producers and thereby heeds the call of the radical geographer David Harvey to 'get behind the veil, the fetishism of the market'.[29] People buy clothes not knowing how or where they are made; the fetishism of the commodity is such that it even appears as if things exert control over people.

Studies of connections between production and consumption have proliferated across a range of disciplines – including anthropology, business studies, cultural studies, economics, geography and sociology – and scholars have attempted to research how commodities move between different places. Journalists and documentary makers have also tried to map connections between production and consumption. This type of work stretches between the developing and developed world and has contributed to surveying the different contours of globalization; for example, newspaper exposés of labour conditions in mobile phone factories in China or documentaries on pesticide use on banana plantations in Nicaragua. Yet this type of research tends to be American- or Eurocentric, in so far as consumption in the global North is usually the starting point. What is ignored is the consumer in the global South. This book begins to redress the balance through case studies from Africa and elsewhere in the developing world.

This biography has sketched out the form of new jeans systems of provision. However, there are also other systems of provision that determine the flow of second-hand jeans around the world, and bring denim to Mario's stall in Mozambique. Second-hand clothes are the mainstay of many markets across the global South; Chapters 3 and 6 explain how these little-known trade patterns have emerged. Mario's small business and his struggles to provide for his family, as well as the livelihoods of millions of other people involved in the making and selling of new and second-hand clothes are much more important and socially interesting than the particular origins and lifespan of a pair of Levi's 501s.

In that respect this is a book not about clothes but about people. To explore the full effects of the fast-fashion industry on billions of people it was necessary to think first about the manufacturing and retail of a new clothing commodity. The next step in understanding the relationships between clothes and poverty is to look at how and why the unequal geographical relationships in garment production and consumption have emerged. This necessitates a brief history of clothing and capitalism.

CLOTHES AND CAPITAL

BRA WARS

Economic globalization has transformed the world. Making, trading and selling commodities like jeans is part of a dynamic global market system that shapes everyone's lives. What can be thought of as 'the official' or mainstream story of globalization begins with the line of argument that Britain – soon followed by Europe and North America – first adopted liberal free-market and free-trade policies in the eighteenth century to promote world economic development.[1] Liberal or laissez-faire approaches to trade involved removing barriers that constrain the free flow of goods and investment. Barriers to trade include duties (payments levied on goods), quotas (fixed numbers of imports) and protectionism (shielding domestic industry from foreign competition). According to popular history, liberal reforms by the early English pioneers of commerce removed trade barriers, freeing the market and enabling capital and products to circulate around the world. It was the superiority of these policies that led to the spectacular success of the global North. Free trade is commonly seen as the mechanism by which economic growth and prosperity are derived.

One of the main means by which laissez-faire approaches to trade policy are promoted today is the World Trade Organization (WTO). This global body represents 164 member states and both supervises and liberalizes international trade. A key function of the WTO is to resolve disputes between member states. Recent examples of quarrels include some curious-sounding cases: China and the European Union (EU) disagreed over duties relating to X-ray machines; Turkey banned imports of Hungarian pet food; South Korea disputed Japanese quotas on dried and seasoned laver (seaweed); and Costa Rica complained about Trinidad and Tobago's anti-dumping measures relating to macaroni and spaghetti. Among the varied disputes associated with barriers to trade are many examples relating to clothing products, including American textiles, Argentine leather, Australian boots, Egyptian apparel and Indian cotton. WTO dispute settlements are designed to ensure trade flows smoothly and so play an important role in governing the global circulation of clothing.[2] China was a relative latecomer to the WTO, joining in 2001 following difficult negotiations. In 2005, China and the EU were involved in a major trade dispute over clothing. This clash garnered much greater public attention than their disagreement over X-ray equipment and exposes how, rather than promoting free trade and open markets, European states have actually hidden behind protectionism and long benefited from uneven terms of trade.

The so-called 'bra wars' were a dispute that erupted after quotas under the Multi-Fiber Arrangement (MFA), which restricted the imports of Chinese textiles and clothing to Europe, were removed on 1 January 2005. Contrary to the official version of globalization, European clothing and textile industries have always been safeguarded by trade barriers such as the MFA; indeed the long-term development of European economies has been preceded by centuries of protection for important industrial sectors, as will be expanded upon later. Many of the barriers to garment imports were finally phased out in 2005 and the full costs of free trade were suddenly to be borne by European factories. However, across the continent manufacturers were not prepared for the increased competition. Following their urgent complaints some

80 million Chinese-made garments, including 48 million pullovers, 18 million pairs of trousers and 11 million bras, were blocked at European ports by new barriers to trade. In a gift to headline writers the dispute was soon christened 'bra wars', as clothing piled up in warehouses and customs checkpoints across the continent. The flood of cheap garments was temporarily stemmed, but many of the shipments had already been paid for by retailers, who were enraged and faced the prospect of empty shelves. Scare stories of a 'run on bras' soon circulated in the tabloid press. Across the Atlantic, the administration of George W. Bush imposed similar barriers restricting the import of bras and other garments.[3]

This was not how free trade was meant to work. Wealthy developed countries were implementing politically expedient protectionism. Free-trade advocates saw this as kicking away the ladder to prosperity – removing the steps up to industrial progress that enabled the Western economies to develop. The theory that free trade would enable civilization to flourish and prosper via their comparative advantage was not being put into practice. European intransigence meant that China was being prevented from utilizing its huge modern factories and vast pool of cheap labour to drive forward development.

European governments may have been united in the EU common trade bloc, but were politically divided. France, Italy and Spain, all with significant clothing sectors, called for protection, whereas the more ideologically committed northern European governments, especially Denmark and the UK, opposed barriers to trade. The neoliberal (or 'new' liberal) right called for the EU to refocus on developing industries that could be globally competitive and retraining former textile workers when their jobs disappeared. They argued that short-term protection of dying industries would only harm low-income European consumers. Caught in the middle was the EU trade commissioner, Peter Mandelson, a divisive British politician whose instincts led him to the liberal right of centre. Following the customary 'gruelling all-night negotiating session' Mandelson and his Chinese counterpart, Bo Xilai, brokered a complicated fix, which led to the bras and other garments reaching the shops. The message which came out of their meeting in Beijing was that the 'Textile wars have been blown out of all proportion', in Mandelson's words, and that moving forward the two parties would work to build stronger ties as one another's first or second largest trading partner.[4] This was a victory for globalization.

But who are the real winners and losers of a globalized economy and free trade? Wages in China are a fraction of those in the EU. Modern garments such as bras have complicated designs made of 40 or more different component parts and are labour-intensive to produce, as delicate sections of fabric, elastic and fasteners must be sewn together. Labour costs make the difference in this relatively low-tech sector. The truce that came out of the bra wars offered only temporary relief for European manufacturers; since then jobs have been lost throughout the EU clothing sector, while production in China has surged forward. Governments play a key role in facilitating globalization as they negotiate the liberalization of markets. The bra wars dispute was a transitional step towards freer trade. Removing barriers to trade enables the further spatial advance of capitalism, which must be understood as the greatest force for transforming the world. Capital and commodities such as clothing are the lifeblood which flows through the body politic. Liberal economists and their proponents on the political right would lead us to believe that barriers to trade are deeply unhealthy for the global economy, and that eliminating them will have an effect akin to coronary surgery to remove fatty deposits on the walls of arteries; dangerous blockages are avoided, and after convalescing the patient is restored to health and vitality. While offering a seemingly logical diagnosis, when we look at how tension is globally built up and released, we see that there is something diseased at the heart of capitalism; rather than moving towards an even and stable status, inequality and catastrophe are the unavoidable prognosis. The bra wars were a painful episode on the road towards a major crisis.

CRISES OF CAPITALISM

One threat every business faces is the challenge of the falling rate of profit in established markets, for instance when clothing shops spread and saturate a territory.[5] So when people make money they look for new places in which to invest. Successful businesses are inherently expansionist. Clothing manufacturers look for low-cost locations to make garments and new marketplaces in which to sell their brands. Investors want to circumvent constraints on trade and compete in new regions. There have long been tensions between the state and business in controlling access to labour and the market, but the outcome persistently results in governments being overridden by the political rule of capital. Despite attempts to fence in production through protectionist measures, in the long run capitalism breaks free and companies search for new territories to conquer. Daily life has come to depend upon the production of commodities through a system that has profit-seeking as its principal and socially accepted goal. Central to the vivacity of capitalism is the need for new investment opportunities to maintain profit growth. When too much capital is accumulated in one place it must be reinvested in a new area and therefore seeks out what is known as a 'spatial fix'.[6] Driven by the logic of maximizing profitability, investment spreads to occupy and seek a 'fix' in new spaces. It is this expansionist urge which has pushed bra production out of Europe and pulled Chinese factories towards the pre-eminent position in the global garment trade.

The need to expand and grow is at the centre of the capitalist mode of production and is linked to another important feature: the crisis-prone nature of capitalism. When we look back at the past two centuries we see clear evidence that capitalism is inherently ridden by crises. At a global scale these manifest as episodes of severe financial crisis, which occur when there is devaluation or a drastic loss of capital. Mega-events include the banker-led financial crisis of 2007–08, the oil crises of 1973–74 and 1979–83, the Wall Street Crash of 1929, the Long Depression of 1873–96, as well as the Panic of 1825 when the Bank of England was on the brink of collapse. In between the large worldwide systemic crashes, smaller crises occur on a regional scale.

This happens when tension builds as capital encounters limits and barriers, such as protectionism, labour problems, technological failings, environmental limits and a lack of effective demand, which can slow down or disrupt capital flows. There are multiple ways in which different crises can form; the efforts of capitalism to overcome these barriers have become part of the history of economic development and change.[7]

In the short term investors can avoid the impacts of crises by taking advantage of the 'spatial fix', and flows of capital can be switched between places. Relocating factories enables businesses to temporarily overcome the falling rate of profit. Moving manufacturing to new lower-wage locations mitigates the chance of a crisis of production in sectors such as clothing; hence garment manufacturing moved from Europe to Asia. Crises, though, can only be temporarily avoided. The spatial fix is not a real solution to the internal contradictions of capitalism; it merely moves the crises around, producing, as David Harvey explains, 'an uneven, unstable and tension-packed geographical landscape for production, exchange and consumption' that periodically erupts as a major global crisis.[8] Tensions build through unequal geographical development and bring about disruption and destruction to social and ecological systems, which are felt at particular places and times. The bra wars constituted one of countless historical moments when the switching of labour and capital resulted in a minor crisis, and were also a harbinger of the general global financial crisis of 2007–08.

Minor crises of capitalism have real human impacts. The bra wars did not cause long-term disruption to overall production and consumption of clothing, but had major social effects in particular parts of Europe. Following the bra wars, employment in EU fashion manufacturing fell from 2.9 million to 1.9 million between 2004 and 2009, affecting some of the less prosperous regions of southern Europe, including Italy and Portugal.[9] Meanwhile, labour conditions in China involve the large-scale exploitation of predominately female workers. Crises have diverse social impacts and amplify uneven geographical development.

In spite of the many crises, the global markets continue to expand. Accelerating cycles of purchasing and disposing of fast fashion has severe environmental effects. The inherently expansionary logic of capitalism means profit growth in the clothing sector is based upon more and more consumption. Shopping for fast fashion is relentlessly prompted. For instance, retailers, somewhat unrealistically, suggest bras have a life expectancy of just 6–9 months and must be regularly replaced.[10] Bras are made of materials such as nylon and polyester, produced from petrochemicals that do not biodegrade; spandex, which is energy-intensive to manufacture; and latex, which, although a natural material, is often produced using methods that result in deforestation and biodiversity loss.

The long history of economic change and the global spread of trade are examined through the prism of the clothing sector in this chapter. We start with the development of weaving in early societies, then move on to explore the role of textiles and clothing in feudal kingdoms, colonialism, the Industrial Revolution and the expansion of capitalism up until the early twentieth century. Focusing on the social impacts of economic change, evidence will demonstrate how barriers to trade, including protectionism, were utilized in the textile trade to enable the economies of Europe and North America to grow. Uneven terms of trade helped produce the different levels of development in the global North and South, but protectionist measures in clothing production are now being overcome by economic globalization. Following the brief history of clothes and capital, the more recent story of twentieth-century globalization, including the negotiation of the MFA, and the growth of today's fast-fashion systems are discussed. Given the vast sweep of human history covered, the material offers an overview of massive shifts in political economy. Later in the book, as the hidden world of clothes unfolds, in-depth case studies of specific clothing systems of provision provide the story with far more nuanced human detail and give further examples of the crises formed by globalization.

THE ORIGINS OF CLOTHES AND UNEVEN DEVELOPMENT

A history of early clothing begins with the origins of society and culture. People worked collectively in social groups to make garments that protect, cover and decorate. Like all 'stuff', clothing comes from the environment and could only be made once humans had mastered the ability to produce a permanent social surplus – that is, reliably generating more food, drink and shelter than is needed to sustain life from the soils, water, flora and fauna. In the long run, by extracting surplus, people also irreversibly changed the environment. Over time the expansion of human activity has transformed the planet, leading to global environmental change. Humankind has transgressed planetary boundaries, most notably causing mass bio-diversity loss, disrupting the global nitrogen cycle, polluting rivers and oceans and transforming the global climate, to the extent that there no longer exists a natural world outside of human interference.[11]

In ancient times, with the emergence of early societies, the production of surplus enabled the division of labour. Some people came to live from the excess produce others generated, presenting new possibilities to organize communities into hierarchical social structures. Increased social diversification accompanied growth in production and population. New groups of people not directly involved in producing surplus food and other goods for subsistence emerged, including teachers, rulers, priests, artisans and warriors. They engaged in new social, cultural and political activities, sharing knowledge, exercising power, forming religions and making art and war, while others became specialist craftspeople producing new goods such as weavers and tailors who made cloths and garments.[12]

Throughout most of human history clothing has been difficult to access. Most people had few garments, as the overall surplus produced was small. There were constraints to human activity and clothing production was in essence ecologically sustainable. In societies where surplus production grew and social organization further diversified, production for exchange developed. Commercial activities and a market grew to facilitate complex exchange transactions. Crucially money emerged to mediate the exchange of different types of commodity. Money enabled farmers to sell their produce on the market, save up, and then later purchase a shirt from a tailor using the cumulative surplus earned from many harvests. The tailor could then return to the market and purchase cloth with the money earned to make new shirts, as well as buying bread to satisfy his own hunger.

The theory behind the development of the market is universal, but different environmental and cultural conditions enabled varied types of clothes-making. Early societies across the world independently developed woven fabrics and used animal products to make clothing. The cultivation of clothing fibres accompanied the emergence of early cereal-based agriculture between 9500 and 2000 BCE, which originated in many different major cultural regions around the world. Early domesticated fibres included flax for linen grown in the Middle East and southwest Asia, hemp in China, and cotton in the Andes, Amazonia, India, Mesoamerica, West Africa and the Sahel.[13] Environments were important in enabling the development of plant agriculture and also animal husbandry, for hides and wools. However, one must not fall into the trap of environmental determinism and think that the physical environment alone, such as geology, landforms or climate, determines patterns of human culture and social development; the environment may set possibilities, but does not define culture. Rather, culture is defined by the opportunities presented and the choices people make in dealing with limits. There is no one habitable place or group of people innately more inventive in growing crops, rearing animals or making clothes, as all human beings share the same basic psychological capabilities.

Equally, agricultural systems and clothes-making did not 'diffuse' between places, like a contagious disease emerging outward from some permanent centre that represents a source or innate 'cultural hearth'; a place where land-use changes led to creativity and invention. Yes, ideas spread between neighbouring villages and tribes and endemic species were traded from their native areas, but at the scale of major cultural regions there was the independent invention of early technologies, including agriculture, money, sail, wheel and clothes-making. There is no innate 'modern' core and peripheral 'traditional' sectors to the world. Diffusionist beliefs, which predominate in popular environmental determinist accounts (like those of the widely popular Jared Diamond), stem from a colonial view of the world. Although colonialism itself *is* a diffusion process, diffusionism is misused to justify the subjugation and oppression that accompanied European colonialism as somehow 'normal, natural, inevitable, and moral' because it bestowed 'civilization' on areas of the world considered 'savage'.[14] Societies transitioned from hunter–gatherer communities to feudal kingdoms and later to capitalist nations. Evidence points to the development of various capitalisms in merchant and maritime urban centres in dispersed cultural regions from Western Europe to eastern Asia and southern Africa. Yet there was not a straightforward teleological march through history from a less developed 'primitive' stage to today's globalized economy. Instead the interaction between communities and the differential levels of affluence and impoverishment experienced by varied groups across space led to patterns of uneven development, and ultimately to the geography of production and consumption in the global clothing trade.

European nations came to drive forward globalization and dominate world trade, including the clothing and textile sector, over the last 500 years. Differing theories explore how Europe came to dominate global trade, but one of the most convincing arguments is that an economic factor gave Western Europe an advantage. The injection of gold and silver from the

New World after 1492 provided resources in the form of valuable currency that propelled European merchant capitalists towards political power. Once emboldened by the power of transatlantic trade, merchants wrested political control from Europe's feudal masters – the centuries-old dynasties of kings and queens which had monopolized legal authority – and then later destroyed political power and social groups elsewhere in the colonized world.[15]

CLOTHING IN ANCIENT SOCIETY

The background history detailed above is important for understanding uneven development. However, as the political economy has got ahead of the social and cultural story of clothes, some infilling needs to be done to account for how garment production and consumption changed on a human scale.

Early people, 100,000 years ago, probably did not wear clothing at all. It was only when humans migrated from East Africa to colder (or possibly hotter) climates that people first came to clothe themselves using animal skins for protection. The origins of clothing remain speculative as there exists little evidence from the Palaeolithic (Stone Age) period. However, archaeological finds do show how Stone Age people used flint knives and bone needles to butcher mammals and to sew hides and leathers. Tools found in southern Africa for working hides have been dated to at least 61,000 years ago.[16] Weaving has been dated to around 27,000 years ago, significantly pre-dating the earliest records of cereal agriculture and sedentary farming societies. Textiles themselves do not survive, but impressions of woven twill plant fibre fabrics have been found on clay artefacts in the Czech Republic from the Upper Palaeolithic period. Archaeologists hypothesize that weaving using gathered plant fibres may date even further back and be found elsewhere.[17]

Wool was also woven to produce garments by early humans. Producing yarns from animal hairs enabled people to reduce the weight of clothes, in comparison to using hides. Tufts of sheep wool were likely collected from thorny bushes and experimented with; people could play with the hairs, spinning yarns between their fingers and later carded wool to form fibres more easily. After the development of permanent set-tled agricultural societies, sheep were domesticated. Grasses and leaves could be woven together. Flax underwent beating to separate the better fibres, which enabled linen yarns to be spun. With the production of permanent social surplus, the development of hier-archical societies provided an emphasis for clothing as it denoted status within tribal groups. In early history, garments made from plant fibres, skins or wool were likely highly prized as production was costly and laborious. Ancient garments were not poorly made; good-quality articles were produced making the most of carefully collected resources. Ötzi, a well-preserved natural mummy from 5,300 years ago discovered in the Alps between Austria and Italy, was found clothed in a cloak of woven grass and wearing items made of different leathers, including a coat, belt, leggings, loincloth and shoes. Petr Hlavacek, a footwear expert, re-created Ötzi's shoes, observing that 'because the shoes are actually quite complex, I'm convinced that even 5,300 years ago, people had the equivalent of a cobbler who made shoes for other people', suggesting he lived in a socially diverse community.[18]

With social development in early civilizations, different labour roles emerged for women and men. Yarn-making became a prized skill undertaken by females at the household level in the Middle East, as is eulogized in the highly gendered language of the Old Testament:

Who can find a virtuous woman? For her price is far above rubies ... She seeketh wool, and flax, and worketh willingly with her hands ... She layeth her hands to the spindle, and her hands hold the distaff [a tool for spinning yarn] … She maketh fine linen, and selleth it; and delivereth girdles [wraps of clothing] unto the merchant.[19]

Hebrews as well as Babylonians, Celts, Egyptians, Greeks and Romans, along with other cultural groups around the world, developed different styles of dress that often involved variations on long tunics, togas, robes, wraps, kilts and trousers, the last of which were particular to northern Europe. Finding evidence of early clothing is difficult as natural materials break down with age. Only in rare arid, waterlogged or frozen conditions can well-preserved garments be found. Examples from Europe include items of Bronze Age clothing found in oak-log coffins in Denmark; pre-Roman and Roman-age garments preserved in acidic bogs in Denmark, northern Germany, the Netherlands and Sweden, in villanovan tombs from Italy, and in Roman burials in France. Elsewhere there are frozen mausoleums in Central Asia and the Andes and arid tombs in the deserts of the Middle East.[20] The examples discussed above are rather European- and Middle Eastern-centric, reflecting the balance of research that has been carried out in the field of ancient clothing. Elsewhere other patterns of dress and networks of exchange developed. Some of West Africa's early history of clothing production and trade is explored in Chapter 4. Detailing the changes in costume, the different materials used throughout the ages, and the styles of dress found across the whole world would involve a cultural history of every social group. Rather than offering the socio-cultural story of different local clothing systems of provision found in, say, the Inca Empire, Moorish Spain or the Khmer kingdom, the subject of the remainder of this chapter is the change from local and regional patterns of trade to the international circulation of clothing commodities, which was part of the transition to, and expansion of, capitalism.

PROTECTED TRADE IN THE FEUDAL ERA

This chapter opened with a contemporary case study of trade protectionism, yet barriers to trade are not a recent phenomenon; governments have long attempted to defend and promote special interests and indigenous clothing and textile sectors. One of the earliest well-documented examples of regulation comes from alliances between garment and fabric guilds and the Crown in England. Guilds were membership societies paid for by subscriptions that afforded their patrons specific benefits. Funds raised by the medieval weavers' guild of London were used to make a contribution to the royal treasury, in exchange guild members were granted exclusive rights and privileges by the king. The first recorded payment was in 1130, and thereafter guild members were able to exercise powers such as punish defaulters in their own court who failed to pay subscriptions, or other weavers that encroached upon their trade. By the mid-twelfth century the guild had established a cartel and was very powerful as the cloth trade was the basis of England's economy throughout the Middle Ages. Their monopoly frustrated consumers, who were faced with high prices, as well as prospective producers outside the guild, some of whom moved overseas.

In 1321 the situation changed and freemen were allowed to set up looms and sell cloth, so long as the king received his tax. Edward III enabled expanded production as he realized the broader value of a managed cloth trade to the English economy. The weavers' guild lost its pre-eminence and other textile guilds developed, including the mercers, drapers, merchant tailors, haberdashers and clothworkers; descendants of many of these guilds survive today as the livery companies of the City of London. The king forbade the export of unprocessed wool and the import of foreign cloth, yet at the same time recognized the value of skilled immigrants. Flemish weavers, discontented with conditions in Flanders, were encouraged to bring their skills to England.[21] Additional protectionist barriers imposed by Edward III included restrictions on what normal people could wear, which remained in place until at least 1571 and the reign of Elizabeth I. Aside from the upper classes, everyone had to wear English-made woollen cloth. Dressing in purple, scarlet, crimson or blue cloth was prohibited as these fabrics were coloured with imported dyes. Constraints on trade and costume were also found in other feudal societies. Elsewhere in Europe, German towns such as Strasbourg enforced similar ordinances requiring people to wear local cloth, while in France there were attempts to control imports such as fabric from Flanders, lace from Milan and materials from China. Outside Europe, in seventeenth-century Japan efforts to control dress restricted ordinary townspeople to plainer cottons and silks, and the Ming, Qing and Manchu dynasties in China all had official styles of dress that signalled acquiescence to imperial authority.[22] These historic examples from feudal eras all share some basic similarity to the way that pre-2005 the EU market was protected from Chinese competition by the MFA.

Protectionism was important in developing clothing and textile sectors. The transition from artisanal making to industrial cloth manufacturing centred on Europe, and in many ways this progression is archetypal of the continent's rise to the pinnacle of global power from the sixteenth century onwards. Especially significant in spurring the expansion of manufacturing were the colonial projects, which brought new raw materials and markets under European control. Colonial missions were initiated to further satisfy the personal desires and political appetites of feudal rulers. Before the Columbian exchange era was launched, luxury clothing for the elite was already traded over vast distances. Exotic fabrics from distant lands denoted wealth, power and status. The silk roads stretching from Europe to China via the Middle East and Central Asia became conduits for the exchange of ideas, goods and culture. Trade networks were also sources of conflict and tension, which prompted explorers to investigate new oceanic routes. Christopher Columbus's voyage to America was infamously motivated by a desire to find a new passage to Asia to access valuable goods, including luxury silk and spices as well as satisfy the hunger for precious gold and silver.

At the same time as Columbus's great discovery other Iberian adventurers were voyaging out of Spain and Portugal. Key was the rounding of the Cape of Good Hope and the southern tip of Africa by Portuguese explorer Bartolomeu Dias in 1488 and later voyages by his compatriot Vasco da Gama, which opened up trade links with the Far East. Maritime exploration led to new forms of interactions between Europeans and the rest of the world and the era of colonialism began. Sustained contact in the long term meant new relationships in one of three modes: as relatively privileged foreign traders in new lands (Jesuits in China and Portuguese in Japan), as conquerors and dominators of existing societies (French in West Africa and British in India), or as invasive land clearers who decimated and supplanted aboriginal communities (British, French and Spanish in the Americas). The three types are a simplification; in reality different combinations, varieties and forms of interaction took place depending on context. China, for instance, although never formally colonized, was subservient to European mercantilist interests, especially after the British victory in the Opium Wars, which removed protection and opened up China to trade. European traders then benefited from a series of unequal treaties during the nineteenth and early twentieth centuries. Chapter 4 provides a detailed account of how formal and 'modernizing' colonialism worked in different parts of Africa, including the repugnant transatlantic trade in slaves. One of the most significant outcomes of the early colonial period was that it introduced the cotton trade to Europe. The international circulation of cotton and cotton products, while not the only material that played an important role in clothing and textile economies, became key to catalysing the Industrial Revolution in the north of England.

CAPITALISM AND THE INDUSTRIAL REVOLUTION

The Industrial Revolution conjures up images of brick-built factories, billowing tall smokestacks, heavy kinetic machinery and an army of industrial workers toiling away weaving textiles, none of which existed before the late eighteenth century. Like every major revolution it represented a qualitative and fundamental transformation in society. Arguably it is the most important global event since the establishment of hierarchical societies based on a permanent social surplus, and was certainly wider ranging than the more evocative American, Chinese, French or Russian Revolutions. The large-scale movement from handicraft tools to mechanized devices, which took off from about the 1780s with the increased use of machines like power looms in northern England, transformed not only cloth production but social relations across industrialized societies. Machines began to perform work formerly done by self-employed artisanal labour, leading to massive increases in productivity. For instance, a human cotton spinner could operate one spinning wheel and use just one spindle to form cotton fibres into thread, whereas the invention in 1764 of the spinning jenny in Lancashire helped revolution-ize production so that eight or more spindles could operate in concert. Pivotal during this epoch was the transition of women and men from being sources of skilled motive power to machine operators. Labourers spent hours in dimly lit factories, listening to the con-stant clatter of machines and diligently watching woven material appear, then correcting mechanisms and mistakes. As Frederick Engels records in *The Conditions of the Working-Class in England*,

The consequences of this were on the one hand, a rapid fall in the price of all manufactured commodi-ties, prosperity of commerce and manufacturing, the conquest of nearly all unprotected foreign markets [by British made cloth], the sudden multiplication of capital and national wealth; on the other hand a still more rapid multiplication of the proletariat, the destruction of all property-holding and of all secu-rity of employment for the working-class, demorali-zation, [and] political excitement.[23]

Factory employment necessitated widespread changes to work patterns, which redrew social hierarchies. Society became polarized between two classes: the wage-earning, hard-working proletariat and the vampire-like capitalist class of bourgeois industrialists. One sucked *surplus value* from the other in the form of profit. Now, it is worth briefly considering how wage labour is exploited to produce profit by capitalists. An hour's labour has, like any commodity, a value equal to the cost of its purchase; if one works for £10 an hour one's labour-power is a commodity that costs one's employer £10 per hour. In any profitable business the contribution made by labour-power to the value of a product is greater than the wage received for that work. All surplus value (or profit) is created by the *exploitation* of labour. This is best demonstrated by example. Suppose you work eight hours a day weaving cotton and make 100 yards of cloth, which sell for £160. The necessary labour to produce your wage is half a day's work as 50 yards of cloth is equal to £80 or eight times your £10-per hour wage. Now assume the cost of maintaining the means of production – the cost of the cotton yarn and pro-rata investment in weaving machines and factory – amounts to a further £10. Therefore, for three hours each day you work for 'free' for the capitalist and they extract £70 of surplus value from your labour in the form of the profit they realize when they sell the 100 yards of cloth (£80 Wage + £10 Means of Production + £70 Surplus Value = £160).[24]

Rates of exploitation continue to increase as long as the socially accepted imperative of capital is to expand and generate ever greater profit. Competing and expanding firms seek to drive profits forward. There are two means to maximize the exploitation of labour. The first is by brute force: using existing work processes and technology, more surplus value can be produced by increasing the length of the working day or simply cutting salaries. Second, via technological change the cost of labour-power can be reduced.[25] This was kick-started in the Industrial Revolution as labour was more finely separated into specific tasks, new machines and factories were used, and the pace of work increased. Technology was not the only leverage for increasing profitability, as brute force was also applied. Textile workers' wages were relentlessly suppressed in the eighteenth and nineteenth centuries. This was socially and culturally justified by the emerging bourgeoisie as low pay was deemed to increase productivity. As an English businessman of the time observed, extending working hours and suppressing wages could go hand in hand with crude attempts to justify social modernization:

The manufacturer who can subsist on three days' work will be idle and drunken the remainder of the week ... The poor in the manufacturing counties will never work any more time in general than is necessary just to live and support their weekly debauches ... We can fairly aver that a reduction of wages in the woollen manufacture would be a national blessing and advantage, and no real injury to the poor. By this means we might keep our trade, uphold our rents, and reform the people into the bargain.[26]

At the heart of the Industrial Revolution, and its defining characteristic, was the factory-based system of provision, which facilitated exploitation and generated goods in such vast quantities and at diminishing costs that they formed their own markets for cloth products. But why did these factories emerge? The simple answer is profit; buying cheap and selling dear was the incentive. Yet why then? And why there? How were countless early British entrepreneurs to know that a radical shift in social organization would deliver great profits? Well, the Revolution did not have a definite beginning or end; nor did it have a revolutionary leader or grand architect. What came to be known as the Industrial Revolution occurred in northern England because of the particular political context,

and not due to a single event, intellectual refine-
ment or technical innovation. Although technologies
were a precondition, some industrial manufacturing
approaches preceded the Industrial Revolution, and
neighbouring France and Germany had made comparable scientific advances. Rather, the political context
was the ultimate causal factor: Britain was ready and
primed for an exponential growth in the capitalist
mode of production as it was an expansionist nation
where money talked and governed. The political system had long been influenced by commercial powers
(like the earlier trading guilds), coupled to which maritime Britain was already the major colonial power.
The political rule of capital propelled the Industrial
Revolution. The late Marxist historian Eric Hobsbawm
recognized that two fundamental preconditions were
required in addition to the political context: 'first an
industry which already offered exceptional rewards
for the manufacturer who could expand his output
quickly, if need be by reasonably cheap and simple innovations, and second, a *world* market largely
monopolized by a single nation'.[27] The combination
of political context and specific preconditions applied
to Britain alone and most importantly in one industry: textiles. The cotton sector had developed with
British colonial expansion overseas. The inhuman

slave plantations of the West Indies first provided the bulk of raw cotton for industries in Manchester, Liverpool and other cities; thereafter English cotton cloth exports went to West Africa and the North American colonies. The colonial trade in cloth as well as garments proved to be highly lucrative and overseas markets expanded in a rapid and unpredictable manner, without ready limits. While individually the colonized areas of Africa, Asia and South America provided small markets for textiles and other British goods, collectively a huge customer base was held in a near monopoly by the early nineteenth century. With the support of the British government the colonial market boomed. Expansion of trade was facilitated by policies such as those implemented in India, where the mercantilist interests of the East India Company systematically deindustrialized and underdeveloped the subcontinent and produced a captive market for Lancashire woven cotton cloth. At the same time protectionist laws enacted in Britain in the 1700s banned the import of textiles made in India.

The scene was set for social transformation and the expansion of capitalism around the world. To capitalize on the expanding foreign market early English industrialists had to use new technologies and were tempted to take risks to adopt revolutionary techniques in organizing labour, spurring the development of factories. Colonialism helped form the demand which pump-primed the emergence of industrial capitalism; once up and running, the age of industry gained its own momentum.

CAPITAL AND COLONIAL EXPANSION

Developments in English textile manufacturing had global impacts and helped propel British industrial supremacy in the nineteenth century. Once Britain had shown the way and demonstrated the profitability of the factory system, the approaches were rapidly imitated and skills and capital were imported by neighbouring countries. English experts and investment travelled to continental Europe and also moved across to North America, spreading the ideas and enabling factories to be developed in societies that shared some of the preconditions. Factories would later multiply out from New York across the 'Rust Belt' of the USA. Elsewhere in America, cotton sales influenced the trajectory of economic growth in the Southern slave states, including North and South Carolina, Georgia, Alabama and Mississippi. Raw cotton imports to the UK grew from less than 5 million pounds in weight in 1771 to 528 million pounds by 1841.[28] Ginned cotton from the South also became an important input into early industrialization in the northern United States and exports of cotton were sent elsewhere in Europe.

The effect of the emergence and expansion of capitalism and the factory were inherently spatial; while what would become the global North experienced economic development, the rest of the world paid the price. Colonized territories were drawn into the service of industrial economies. Africa, Asia and South America were underdeveloped as local artisan production declined in the face of competition and people were forced to supply raw materials for the industrial powers, which established the patterns of uneven development found across the world today. Marx, writing in 1867, observed these processes at first hand and merits quoting at length:

> On the one hand, the immediate effect of machinery is to increase the supply of raw material in the same way, for example, as the cotton gin augmented [stimulated] the production of cotton. On the other hand, the cheapness of the articles produced by machinery, and the improved means of transport and communication furnish the weapons for conquering foreign markets. By ruining handicraft production in other countries, machinery forcibly converts them into fields for the supply of its raw material.

In this way East India was compelled to produce cotton, wool, hemp, jute, and indigo for Great Britain. By constantly making a part of the hands 'supernumerary', modern industry, in all countries where it has taken root, gives a spur to emigration and to the colonisation of foreign lands, which are thereby converted into settlements for growing the raw material of the mother country; just as Australia, for example, was converted into a colony for growing wool. A new and international division of labour, a division suited to the requirements of the chief centres of modern industry springs up, and converts one part of the globe into a chiefly agricultural field of production, for supplying the other part which remains a chiefly industrial field.[29]

While textiles and clothing were not the only industrial sectors structuring the uneven development of the global economy, they clearly played a major role. The history of capitalism is bound up in the progress of textile and apparel production in Europe and North America in the eighteenth and nineteenth centuries. As the great nation-state powers of the colonial era expanded overseas, new territories were drawn into the capitalist mode of production, and market integration gradually drew nearly all society worldwide into one economic system. The Industrial Revolution brought the world's first global clothing systems of provision into operation.

Away from Europe and North America the influence of colonial powers – principally Britain, France, Germany, Italy and Portugal – alongside the cultural, political and economic weight of the United States, and the spread of Christianity, projected Western patterns of dress onto the colonized world. Not just cloth but also finished clothing was exported from the metropoles: key European industrial cities like Manchester and Paris to colonial capitals such as Delhi and Saigon. Colonial elites and assimilated populations purchased male buttoned dress shirts, cotton khaki trousers and leather shoes, alongside long ladies' dresses and embroidered lace. Native employees were dressed in formal service dress or industrial uniforms of caps, jackets, overalls and dungarees. In different regions the adoption or rejection of European styles of dress demonstrated acquiescence to or confrontation with different forms of authority, as people aspired to equality with, or exerted their autonomy from, the Western world.[30]

Later, dress became a key terrain for opposition to British rule in India. Foremost was Mohandas Gandhi's role as an anti-colonial leader and the pattern of dress he adopted in response to British oppression. For two centuries weavers throughout the Indian subcontinent had been driven out of business and into poverty by the expanding trade in English textiles. British business had even conspired with the colonial authorities to cut off the fingers of Bengali weavers and break their looms to create captive markets. As Jeremy Seabrook documents,

> The future champion of free trade destroyed the fabrics industry in Bengal before Britain attained pre-eminence in textile manufacturing ... As a result, the spinners and weavers of Bengal fell into the greatest penury. Dacca [Dhaka], centre of muslin production, became a deserted city: tigers and leopards roamed once-prosperous streets, and by the 1820s the city of men had become a city of animals. Weavers' dwellings were overgrown, the thatch alive with birds, snakes and insects ... The first great de-industrialisation of the modern world had begun. The population of Dacca fell from several hundred thousand in 1760 to about 50,000 by the 1820s. By this time, Manchester's rise had become irresistible. Bengal's abandonment of ancient crafts appears in Britain as a fable of our progress and entrepreneurial genius. To the desolate weavers, it meant the

collapse of their world; and Bengal, famine-stricken, impoverished, reverted to agriculture.[31]

Capitalist expansion had brought crisis to India, transforming the economic geography and impoverishing the populace. India exported raw cotton to Britain where it was manufactured into clothing and then exported back to India; this process was effectively paid for by the export of other raw materials and created a relationship of structural dependency. British protectionism and trade policy blocked Indian industrialization in a process repeated across the colonized world.[32]

Gandhi recognized the tyranny at the heart of British Imperial policy and would come to play a foremost role in the independence struggle. Having previously adopted Western-style clothing when he studied law in London, Gandhi later became associated with a dramatically different costume. After graduating, and when working in South Africa, he engaged in radical politics. Gandhi began speaking out against minority rule and swapped his English suits for simple white cotton attire. On returning to India in 1915, Gandhi adopted his iconic loincloth and shawl, despite hailing from a prosperous merchant family. His style of dress was not widely imitated as he led the struggle for Indian nationalism; it was too closely associated with social egalitarianism and did not unite Muslim, Hindu and Sikh groups. However, Gandhi's costume formed part of a powerful cultural and economic protest movement. The loincloth was made from *khadi*, traditional homespun, undyed cloth, woven on a hand loom, which became a symbol for the independence struggle. Nationalists were encouraged by Gandhi to spin *khadi* daily for half an hour, partly as meditation and partly to provide competition for imported machine-made cloth. Boycotts of foreign goods became a core strategy of the Indian independence movement alongside non-violent protest. *Khadi* cloth cut in different ways, such as the Nehru jacket, would become de rigueur for Indian leaders for decades to come.[33]

CAPITALISM ADAPTS IN THE TWENTIETH CENTURY

The twentieth century was an age of extremes that saw rapid and fundamental changes to society in every corner of the world, from the cottonfields of rural India to the declining industrial towns of northern England, to the rising suburbs of Middle America, and the booming industries of eastern China. Rather than summarize the myriad transformations, some reflections on the reorganization of the global economy and changing patterns of dress are presented here.

At the turn of the twentieth century a major development spread across the industrialized world of North America and Western Europe. 'Fordism' was a term popularized by the Italian Marxist Antonio Gramsci to refer to a new approach to organizing industry for which Henry Ford's car factories provided the model. New production-line techniques were developed drawing on the ideas of Frederick W. Taylor, which promoted the scientific management of workers, who had to repeatedly perform static and standardized tasks.[34] Workers were assigned set roles in manufacturing processes to enhance the efficiency of production. A division of labour emerged between workers performing unskilled repetitive tasks and those in middle-class skilled and managerial roles. Ford and other industrialists began to recognize that they needed to stimulate markets for their products, to try to overcome the internal contradictions of capitalism. A link was established between production and consumption, and labour exploitation was relaxed as workers were paid salaries sufficient to enable them to consume the goods they were making. Life improved for labourers. The working day was shortened to eight hours, to create efficient workforces with stable family lives. Mass-manufactured, uniform, affordable garments, like Levi Strauss's five-pocket blue jeans, provided a new type of consumable clothing for the working classes. Capitalism could profit by creating standardized patterns of dress; new modern clothing systems of provision emerged.

It is instructive to look back at photographs and film from the first half of the twentieth century that show such relative uniformity in the way different sets of people dressed according to their place within a broader social system: for example, rows of English working-class men at football matches in flat caps and dark woollen suits, white cotton shirts and knotted neckties; Parisian bourgeois women parading along the Champs-Elysées in stiff long dresses in muted blacks, whites or subtle pastels with parasol shades; American factory workers emerging from plants in the Midwest in blue denim dungarees and shirtsleeves. Standardized costume denoted social class. For the poor this was partly due to the limited number of garments they owned; but it was also because Fordist patterns of production and consumption helped regulate and dictate dress and were forged through a particular system of provision that was part of the rise of modern ways of organizing society – modern in the sense that society followed centralized patterns of social and political control and accepted scientifically rational norms. Progress occurred within limits and was stabilized by the factory system of industrial production and employment, and the operation of the market economy. Control was exerted by the nation-state and mass democracy, although the latter was only applied selectively in the global North; elsewhere the colonial ideology was enforced by a specific and racialized idea of modernity. The social practices of modernity set the tone for the European-dominated world, which until after 1945 saw the culture of the continent as the central axis around which the rest of the world revolved.

During the post-war era the structure of the world economy was steadily rebuilt. For around 30 years after the Second World War the problems of capitalist expansion were solved through the development of mass consumption in the global North. A modern consumer class emerged as surplus extraction further relaxed. People were organized in nuclear families, with car ownership, televisions, refrigerators and of course affordable new clothes. Alongside the rising living standards in Europe and North America, a global shift began to occur in manufacturing as economies in Asia, the Middle East, South America and to a lesser extent Africa were transformed.

A mass migration of capital to the global South began to take advantage of these countries as sources of cheap labour for industry, rather than simply being suppliers of raw materials and captive markets for goods from the global North. Clothing was one of the first manufacturing industries to spread as increasing wage levels in Europe and America and improvements in communication motivated capital to move clothing production to economies where costs were lower, enabling greater exploitation and accumulation of profits. The partial industrialization of some of the former underdeveloped countries provided a spatial fix for capitalism and further opportunities for capitalists, old and new, international and local, to expand the extraction of surplus value from wage labour.

Decolonization in Africa and Asia was important in stimulating industrial expansion. Beginning in the 1950s, many governments in the global South promoted basic manufacturing as a means to develop and modernize their economies, foremost among which were China and South Korea. A new international division of labour led to the long-term migration of factories from the old industrial heartlands of the global North to the developing world. Eventually some of the early clothing and textiles production regions, like the northern English cities of Liverpool and Manchester that had led the Industrial Revolution, would decline as they became uncompetitive. Clothing and textile industries took off in the global South. As poor countries gained political independence they adopted, first, import substitution approaches to industrialization (ISI), protecting their infant domestic industries from competition by foreign clothing, before progressing to export-orientated manufacturing. The technologies employed in clothing production up until the 1970s were similar to techniques that had been used for the previous century and a half. Within the global South labour conditions often echoed those found in eighteenth- or nineteenth-century Britain, rather than the Fordist mode of production. Workers were employed on low wages and for long hours – 12 to 14 hours a day were not uncommon. Exploitative labour regimes in China are explored further in Chapter 5.

THE MULTI-FIBER ARRANGEMENT AND THE GROWTH OF FAST FASHION

Over the past 50 years there has been a realignment in the geography of global clothing production, but this has not spread development to the world's poorest countries. Equalization in the levels of development between the global North and South has partially been blocked by the inherited patterns of international business established in the colonial period and enforced through measures such as trade protectionism. Clothing trade patterns have primarily been structured since 1962 by the Long Term Agreement (LTA) regarding international trade in cotton textiles, and then from 1974 to 2004 by the Multi-Fiber Arrangement (MFA). Both agreements placed import controls, or quotas, on clothing and textiles, protecting certain markets. The LTA and MFA were intended to allow for steady and controlled development of clothing industries and provide benefits for countries in both the global North and the global South. Access to European and North American markets was limited; it increased at around 6 per cent a year, as developed markets were partially protected. Bilateral arrangements between pairs of countries were negotiated to control the imports of specific types of clothing and textiles. Rather than liberalizing market access, this system constrained trade and was repeatedly renegotiated (in 1977, 1982, 1986 and 1991). The constraints on clothing imports benefited the rich countries as they were slowly able to adjust, rather than experiencing a 'shock' to their economies.

The quotas and controls relaxed further as part of market liberalization in the 1990s and early 2000s, bringing more affordable new clothing to the global North. The spread of fast fashion accelerated when the MFA expired in 2005, triggering the bra wars. European and American manufactures failed to compete with more efficient Asian producers who paid lower wages. As the clothing market has been increasingly liberalized, developed markets were inundated with affordable fashion imports. Clothing prices fell dramatically in the 2000s: by 26.2 per cent in Europe and 17.1 per cent in the USA. At the same time consumption boomed, with the number of items sold in the UK increasing by a third, leading to over 2 million tonnes of clothing being consumed every year.[35] Exports of Chinese clothing to the USA increased by 18 per cent per year, and to the EU by 21 per cent per year, between 2000 and 2007, and these economies went into trading deficits in clothing, standing at around $81 billion per year for the USA and $60 billion for the EU in 2007. This resulted in local crises in clothes-producing regions.[36]

While in economics the world was undergoing a major restructuring through the second half of the twentieth century, there were also social and cultural challenges to the modern ways of organizing society. In the global North this happened across the full spectrum of cultural life, including art, architecture, film, literature, music and fashion. Old prescribed patterns of dress were destabilized through both cultural and social movements, such as the sexual revolution, anti-war protests and the end of segregation in the USA. In the 1960s and 1970s cheaper popular fashion first became accessible for youth markets. On the media scene female personalities like Jacqueline Kennedy Onassis, Jean Shrimpton, Audrey Hepburn, Twiggy and other fashion icons became household names, famous in part because of the way they dressed; as such they inspired new demand for clothing styles. Change, though, was not always 'radical' in the sense of a shift to the political left. Socio-cultural development often served the market as it was consonant with developing new modes of consumption that depended on expanding the exploitation of labour in the global South to bring cheap clothing into the market.

Fashion firms such as Sears and Marks & Spencer found new opportunities for growth by increasing the speed at which stimulated tastes and fashions change. Allied to clothing manufacturing is the influential fashion press and entertainment industry. Glossy magazines like *Elle* and *Vogue*, as well as advertising, fashion shows and later social media, promoted new trends, while celebrity culture supported the system of provision. Developments in transport and communication technologies, the spread of flexible production techniques, the breakdown in traditional autumn/winter and spring/summer fashion collections, and the increasing sophistication of advertising imagery have transformed the consumer landscape. New clothes are designed that are positional and will shortly become obsolete. In the 1990s the Spanish chain Zara pioneered a fast fashion production approach based on short batch orders with a two-week turnaround from design to retail. Zara's business model is built upon producing a 'scarcity value'; the company launches 11,000 new items a year in comparison to the 2,000–4,000 of rivals like H&M and Gap. Zara's business model inspired online fast fashion labels.[37]

This chapter has briefly demonstrated how clothes-making moved from pre-modern artisanal production to the emergence of the fast-fashion system of provision. Across the long arc of human history the global circulation of cloth and clothing has been a key force in human development and economic globalization. As apparel is traded around the world it has contributed to the enrichment of the global North and the poverty of the South. Uneven development is a testament to humans' ability both to transcend and to despoil nature. The spatial impacts of industrial progress are irregularly distributed as concentrated patches of affluence and spaces of impoverishment. Rather than spurring equality between places as posited by classical liberal economics, uneven development is the defining characteristic of the spread of capitalism around the world. Some places are becoming ever richer – London, New York and parts of Beijing and Delhi – while billions remain impoverished as the gap between winners and losers in the global economy widens.

Governments, be they run by medieval feudal kings, colonized tribal leaders, imperial powers, democratic parties or the supranational EU, have long been pressured and drawn into disputes around access to the market due to the great tension between state and capital over who and what exerts political power.

Protectionism has served the development of clothing- and textile-based capitalism, most notably in the Industrial Revolution, but has also constrained free trade. The advance of capitalism and its pursuit of a 'spatial fix' led to the eventual deindustrialization of the global North and the relocation of clothing industries to China and elsewhere, as barriers to capital flows have been surpassed or crushed. One important question left unresolved in this chapter is why clothing production is concentrated in the emerging Chinese economy and other parts of Asia rather than the more impoverished societies of Africa? For one might expect the lowest labour cost to be found in the world's poorest continent, and the logic of the market to dictate that capital would relocate production there. The reasons behind the absence of clothing production in Africa are explored in later chapters.

In the present fast-fashion sector the rhythm of purchases far exceeds the tempo of fabric dilapidation. Much sound and light is focused on the continual cycles of new clothing purchases, which generate an increasingly large volume of old waste clothing as garments are discarded before they are worn out. Yet there is a counterpoint to the trade in new clothing, a dim silhouette that has escaped attention. Throughout history there have been other secondary hidden systems of provision that have clothed a significant proportion of the world's population. The next chapter draws attention to the neglected, yet globally important, shadow trade in used clothing.

THE SHADOW WORLD OF
USED CLOTHING

CLOTHING IN PAPUA NEW GUINEA

For as long as clothes have existed, they have been borrowed, exchanged and swapped. One can easily imagine prehistoric people bartering used animal skins and furs for meat and flint tools. There is nothing new about second-hand clothes. Garments were likely shared between early people, as this is observable among present-day hunter–gatherer communities and other isolated tribal groups. Papua New Guinea is a remote country; a mainland of mountainous rainforest surrounded by scattered tropical islands, located between the Indonesian archipelago and the north coast of Australia. The main island of New Guinea is home to some of the world's most inaccessible communities, many of which have had limited contact with the modern world. Although notions of present-day tribes of 'stone age people' are inaccurate and unhelpful, many New Guineans do live in subsistence societies; as well as tending vegetable gardens, they have livelihoods that include elements of the hunter–gatherer approach – shooting birds with bow and arrow, and collecting plants from the bush.

Communities in the remote Western Highlands province can only be accessed by hiking for days or taking a flight in a cramped Cessna light aircraft. Flights pass over steep mountain valleys and ravines and the small planes touch down on grass landing strips in forest clearings. To reach the most isolated groups visitors must continue by foot and trek over the Bismarck mountain range. In remote villages clothing is very basic. Many men wear stretched and stained shirts and long trousers that have been ripped or worn down to shorts. Others have pieces of fabric knotted around their waists like loincloths. Women may wear *lap-laps*, simple wide pieces of fabric tied around the midriff, and maybe a *meri* blouse, a basic dress or top introduced by missionaries to encourage them to cover up. The material is often old, little more than rags, worn down by hard wear in tropical conditions. Everyday clothing for most rural Papua New Guineans consists mainly of second-hand items which have come from Australia and the United States. Some even show logos from their earlier lives, ranging from the dress shirt of an officer in the Australian Royal Air Force, to the T-shirt of a waiter at Chili's Grill and Bar (a fast-food chain originating in Dallas, Texas). Imported modern clothing is hard to come by; the few items held in rural communities may be shared around, because people have so few material possessions. However, during *bungs* (tribal celebrations) everyone dons intricate ceremonial costumes which combine feathers, wood, bark and animal skins using techniques that are in all likelihood millennia old. Men wear fur headdresses, dyed grasses bound to their arms, and wraps around their waists woven from fine jungle vines; women wear seas shells traded from coastal regions threaded on necklaces and garlands of flowers; children have leaves tied to their elbows and feathers in their hair. Faces are painted red, white and black. Some people add to their traditional outfits with plastic beads and dayglo nylon fabric, precious new items that have been purchased in towns and carried back to near inaccessible rural areas.[1]

Furs, feathers and face paints are not everyday wear, but such dress patterns are a key part of cultural life. Isolated tribes cherish their limited clothing resources as modern garments are precious and difficult to obtain. The previous chapter showed how the clothing industry developed and spread around the globe. Across the world clothes manufactured using modern production techniques have largely replaced outfits made from materials like animal skins and vines. In Papua New Guinea, however, remote rural communities have little connection with the global economy. They are partially isolated from the capitalist market and therefore many traditional approaches have persisted. The few modern clothes that reach the Western Highlands province are mainly imported second-hand clothes from the global North. Used clothes are found throughout the developing world, from the Mozambican markets, introduced earlier, to the mountain communities of Papua New Guinea. Later in the book more examples from Africa, as well as Asia and Latin America, are introduced. Trade networks spread around the world, reaching even some of the most isolated corners, and there is a vast unseen circulation of second-hand garments from rich to poor countries. This chapter explores how used clothes have been shared, exchanged and traded between various communities at different historical moments, and how and why second-hand clothes are collected in the global North for resale to communities across the global South. An in-depth case study in the second half of the chapter uncovers what happens to clothes after they are donated to a charity or a textile recycler in the UK and shows how there is a hidden world of commercial, and even criminal, activity involved in the trade of used clothing.

SECOND-HAND CLOTHING IN HISTORICAL CONTEXTS

For most of history clothes-making has been time-consuming and garments difficult to acquire for all but the richest people. The rewearing of clothes has existed for as long as humans have stitched together materials. Strong social bonds in close-knit communities meant that clothes were likely shared between people who had little, as they are sometimes in Papua New Guinea today. Limited evidence remains, but there is every reason to believe that rags and torn old fabrics were also recycled. The British Museum has a Roman doll filled with textile rags, found in Egypt, dating back to between the first and fifth centuries CE. Used clothing has also been traded commercially for many centuries; in the medieval period old clothing was taken from rich cities to be sold in poorer rural regions at markets and country fairs. In Europe the value of second-hand clothing changed from the preindustrial era to the post-modern contemporary era, as the tunics and breeches of the past were more readily re-worn than the T-shirts and board shorts of today. Good-quality second-hand clothes were prized, even being valuable enough to have served as an alternative to currency. Throughout pre-modern history wearable used clothes would never have been discarded, but instead passed between different social groups.[2]

Early accounts of second-hand clothing markets are hard to find, especially prior to the improvements in communication (literacy, newspaper printing, photography) that accompanied the Industrial Revolution. As is often the case, the history of the poor is fragmented; consequently the surviving record of how clothes were reused often focuses on the circulation of higher-end luxury garments. One example from Italy, in 1407, shows there were guilds concerned with the trade in high-quality clothes and other used goods in Florence. Formally established trading guilds dealt with items such as second-hand silk gowns and velvets, and lower-class, often female, itinerant vendors worked the street buying and selling old clothes of any quality from different classes of household.[3] Used clothes were also gifted between different tiers of society and passed from European feudal masters to their serfs, domestic staff and the local poor. Societal norms or formal laws, like those imposed by Edward III in medieval England, meant that lower-class servants were often unable to re-wear the same clothing as the aristocratic masters, so they resold luxurious garments. One main customer was theatre companies. For centuries travelling troupes of actors provided entertainment for the masses. In the Elizabethan period, Shakespearean plays were widely performed across England. Plays included a cast of rich and colourful characters such as Romeo and Juliet, Oberon and Prospero, for which actors would depend upon second-hand clothes for costumes. Bodices, cloaks, ruffs and stockings made of taffeta, silks and even garments with gold effects would be put to use to embellish thespian performances and create fashionable and fantastical outfits. Old clothes were readily sold on across Europe. Beyond the Western world examples of used-clothing markets are harder to find, which is not to say they were not traded elsewhere. One well-documented illustration from pre-modern Japan is the vibrant trade in used silk kimonos. These elegant garments with delicate and intricate detailing and flowing sleeves were as much objects of crafted art, which were – and continue to be – re-worn, and hence have encapsulated different values in specific times and places.[4]

The scarcity of clothes among preindustrial societies ensured their careful safe keeping, whether it was actors looking after their costumes or the working poor preserving their best church-going clothes. Many people were what the French call *bricoleurs*: skilful or creative individuals who carefully reused textiles in clever ways. Clothes were repaired in the home; for example, women would spend hours darning, and tailors would let out trousers that had been outgrown. These domestic and local patterns of preservation and reuse continued until the development of cheap new clothing in the twentieth century.

Articles of used clothing have long had an ambiguous status as they are, on the one hand, items that are often given away as charitable gifts, while at the same time being commodities traded on the market. Recognizing this peculiarity, the Scottish economist Adam Smith wrote in 1776 of how the poor would receive the 'charity of well-disposed people' and that a 'beggar' would exchange gifts of clothing for more suitable garments or other items, or even sell them: 'the old cloaths [*sic*] which another bestows upon him he exchanges for other old cloaths which suit him better, or for lodging, or for food, or for money, with which he can buy either food, cloaths, or lodging, as he has occasion.'[5] Old clothes were often easier to obtain than any other form of charity, but the good intentions of donors were sometimes exploited. Organized beggars like the so-called 'shallow coves' – rascals who would go around English cities affecting shivers while exaggerating their poverty – visited homes half-naked asking for clothes. Barefoot 'limpers' specialized in collecting shoes. Donated old boots, shirts and waistcoats would then be sold on for a few pennies to the 'dolly shops', which, like today's thrift stores, sold old apparel, rags and other junk.[6] With the expansion of the Industrial Revolution new clothing gradually became more affordable and the value of second-hand clothes shifted as they became less desirable. In Charles Dickens's Victorian England it was common for out-of-fashion styles, worn clothes and stolen garments to be traded in open-air markets. For instance, when left with nothing but the clothes on his back, Dickens's most autobiographical character, David Copperfield, sells his waistcoat in desperation and struggles to secure a fair price. In *Oliver Twist* the infamous real-life Field Lane marketplace in London is described in detail as

a commercial colony of itself: the emporium of petty larceny: visited at early morning, and setting-in of dusk, by silent merchants, who traffic in dark back-parlours, and who go as strangely as they come. Here, the clothesman, the shoe-vamper, and the rag-merchant, display their goods, as sign-boards to the petty thief; here, stores of old iron and bones, and heaps of mildewy fragments of woollen-stuff and linen, rust and rot in the grimy cellars.[7]

In parallel with the development of industrial production of apparel, used clothing was gradually becoming something that was considered deviant, associated with crime and morally ambiguous processes on the fringes of society.

Damaged and deteriorating clothes that could not be re-worn were recycled, providing an input for early industrial processes. Marx discusses how female workers were exploited in the rag trade:

One of the most shameful, the most dirty, and the worst paid kinds of labour, and one on which women and young girls are by preference employed, is the sorting of rags. It is well known that great Britain, apart from its own immense store of rags, is the emporium for the rag trade of the whole world. They flow in from Japan, from the most remote States of South America, and from the Canary Islands. But the chief sources of their supply are Germany, France,

Russia, Italy, Egypt, Turkey, Belgium and Holland.
They are used for manure, for making bedflocks, for
shoddy, and they serve as the raw material of paper.
The rag-sorters are the medium for the spread of
small-pox and other infectious diseases, and they
themselves are the first victims.[8]

The nineteenth-century rag networks had a transnational geographical extent, which is paralleled in
today's second-hand clothing systems of provision.
Used clothes – including rags as well as re-wearable
garments – have been traded around the world for
more than a century; the emergence of these networks
was both an outcome and a response to the changing
nature of industrial garment manufacturing and the
rise of capitalism.

With the growth in clothing manufacturing and the
rapid development of North America and Europe in
the nineteenth century, the availability of new clothing improved and second-hand distribution became
increasingly formalized as a type of charitable hand-
out. Old clothing passed down the social gradient
from rich to poor as charitable donations. The ladies
of the New York Clothing Society for the Relief of the
Industrious Poor gave away 1,742 garments in 1837.[9]
This type of gift-giving was often mediated through

religious groups, which provided the urban middle classes with a virtuous outlet for unwanted clothing. By making donations to churches, respectable house-wives had a way to get rid of clothing, avoiding direct contact with the undesirable underclass and criminal elements associated with the rag trade. Put simply, donors could feel good about themselves. The history of the second-hand clothing and rag trade as both a dirty and a deviant sector, and as a socially impor-tant means of charity, has influenced the development of contemporary systems of used-clothing provision, just as the social history of jeans influences how they are designed, manufactured and retailed today.

The advent of Fordist production and the 'golden age' of capitalism filled marketplaces with consumer goods and provided people with disposable income for consuming new clothing. This socio-economic system depended on people's ability to maintain a continuous cycle of consumption. In the modern world repair and reuse of clothing was discouraged, as conveyed in Aldous Huxley's dystopian modernist novel *Brave New World*. The protagonist Bernard Marx overhears elementary pupils rhythmically reciting: 'I do love having new clothes, I do love ... But old clothes are beastly ... we always throw away old clothes. Ending is better than mending, ending is better than

mending, ending is better.'[10] People's relationships
with clothing began to change. Business recognized
that retaining clothes and wearing them out does not
drive free-market development. There is an underlying need for capitalism to reinvent and constantly
bring new products, often with simulated demands, to
the marketplace. As B. Earl Puckett, a leading clothing
retailer in the United States, said in 1950 when addressing 400 fashion experts in Manhattan:

> Basic utility cannot be the foundation of a prosper-
> ous apparel industry ... We must accelerate obso-
> lescence ... It is our job to make women unhappy
> with what they have ... We must make them so
> unhappy that their husbands can find no happi-
> ness or peace in their excessive savings.[11]

Clothing consumption was heavily gendered, pressur-
izing women to conform within patriarchal societies.
Manufactured obsolescence, promoted by migrating
fashion trends and endless cycles of new production,
brought more and more clothes to market, which transformed how women and men related to used clothing.
Clothes were less likely to be used again in the household. In American cities like Chicago and Philadelphia,
prior to the Second World War, used clothing was

traded away by hard-working housewives and domestic staff. Ragmen exchanged unwanted clothes for new commodities such as pins, pans and needles. These merchants made sophisticated calculations of the monetary value of used clothing and weighed this against what they paid in hardware. Ragmen sold clothes to other, poorer, households or in street markets, and ripped and torn garments were wholesaled as shoddy for use in industrial processes, where they became machine wipers or recycled, for instance in furniture stuffing.[12]

The formalized culture of donating clothing for reuse also grew, and organizations such as the Salvation Army developed extensive networks for collecting and distributing second-hand clothes, providing an outlet for consumers who wanted to clear out their wardrobes. Later, in the second half of the twentieth century, charity and thrift stores like Good Will and Value Village in the USA and Oxfam and YMCA in the UK spread, retailing used clothes at cheap prices. Throughout the twentieth century this served as a system of provision of clothing for the urban poor, providing low-value apparel to impoverished people on the margins of modern society. One of the particularities of the market is that everyone has the ability to consume something; there is differentiation in consumption and people become socially defined by their shopping habits. The purchasing of pre-consumed used clothing at charity shops, thrift stores and yard sales is perceived negatively as undesirable, acceptable only for the impoverished and countercultural groups in Western society. Despite the current popular rise in household recycling and vintage fashion (discussed in Chapter 8), those who take an active role in the disposal and consumption of 'waste' are still normally viewed as outside the mainstream of society, as were the rag-and-bone men, the 'disease ridden' female rag-sorters, the rascals, the vagabonds and the thieves found in Smith's, Dickens's and Marx's time.

WASTE AND CLOTHING CONSUMPTION

By the end of the twentieth century the ways in which people in the developed economies thought of used clothing were transformed. Old clothing became a form of rubbish, often consigned to the dustbin alongside food waste and empty packaging. In the UK an estimated £12.5 billion ($16.4 billion) or 300,000 tonnes of clothing goes to landfill each year.[13] Generating household waste is integral to the economic system as it helps drive consumption forward. The growth of markets for new commodities depends on the disposal of old stuff. Purchasing and discarding objects are forms of freedom which override saving and repair. While old clothes are viewed negatively and past fashions often ridiculed, the new clothing sector and the fast-fashion system are positively associated with youth, independence and even female emancipation, although as the above quote from Puckett suggests this has been manipulated by business. This is a charade. Fashion, by its very nature, is effective in restricting social mobility and places consumers, particularly young women, in a never-ending contest of purchases which contribute to expressing their identity. Indeed, everyone has some adherence to culturally constructed norms of dress, which evolve over time. Conspicuous consumption is not restricted to those who follow the latest fashions. Garments get ripped, stained and outgrown – all processes which diminish value. Clothing is often considered outdated or unwearable in the global North when it is still useable, because social pressure dictates the perceived obsolescence of clothes, ensuring that it becomes imperative to consume new garments regularly to maintain social status. Throughout the global North superfluous consumption has grown, driven by the falling real price of goods manufactured in China and elsewhere. Garments are priced far too low to reflect their true social and ecological value as capital mobility and excess global labour supply enable clothing firms to depress wages and avoid paying environmental costs. Consumers have responded to clothing availability and an environment of competitive consumption by purchasing increasing numbers of artificially cheap goods, and getting rid of old garments, in rapid cycles of acquisition and discard.

The continuous purchase of clothing is interlinked with the idea and practice of disposable fast fashion. Concurrent with conspicuous clothing consumption is the downgrading and throwing out of existing wardrobe items. As clothes age, they lose their aura of newness, becoming unfashionable or worn out in the eyes of the owner. Data suggests that up to 70 per cent of garments in home wardrobes may be inactive.[14] Clothes are purged periodically from the wardrobe, passed on to relatives or friends, placed in charity collection sacks, casually sold on eBay or at car-boot sales, or, most commonly, discarded with household rubbish. Disposing of things and creating wardrobe space for the consumption of new commodities is central to the maintenance of the fashion sector. Meanwhile, in the global North the market for second-hand clothes has shrunk in volume in the last three decades relative to the mass increase in new clothing sales. However, the highly lucrative vintage fashion sector is booming.[15] The demand among the American and European poor for second-hand clothes fell away with rising affluence and the boom in affordable low-end value fashion sold by retailers such as Primark, Target and Walmart that encourages mass production by low-paid labour in the global South and continues to drive down real-term prices.

As more and more clothes are consumed, greater volumes of textile rubbish are produced. Old clothing waste does not just go away; it goes somewhere. New clothing consumption creates the preconditions for second-hand clothing systems of provision. The new and used clothing sectors are woven together. New purchases are interconnected to disposal; indeed imports of new apparel are a significant predictor of the export of used clothing from the United States to the rest of the world.[16] Transient clothing ownership produces a mass of used clothing, which is recycled in a second system of reproduction and consumption. Clothing donated to charities and textile recyclers enters a new economic network. Labour activities are undertaken and profits are accumulated by charities, firms and individuals as used clothes are traded to places like Mozambique and Papua New Guinea. But how does clothing go from the First World wardrobe to a Third World market? The remainder of this chapter explores how clothing is collected and processed in the developed world using a case study from England.

SECOND-HAND CLOTHING CHARITIES IN THE UK

Staines is a commuter town on the outskirts of London. Long the butt of satirical jokes, it is a dull, grey town that epitomizes Western suburbia. The high street has branches of chain shops along with a few small independent stores; away from the centre there is the Two Rivers Retail Park, which includes a Gap, a large Tesco Homestore and the discount trader TK Maxx, three shops which represent mass market clothing retail. The YMCA shop in Staines is on a quiet end of the main street and has the typical appearance of a charity store, a slightly dilapidated retail space, with rails of random used-clothing items hung in a disorderly way, and some crockery and toys scattered around the shelves alongside well-thumbed Dan Brown and Jackie Collins paperbacks. The YMCA is a Christian charity which supports young people; it has over 150 charity shops in Britain and programmes around the world. Clothing-collecting agencies like the YMCA receive donations from households, which first select, sort and bag up clothes that can be worn again. Giving away used clothes does not fit within rigid definitions of materiality such as 'commodity', 'gift' and 'rubbish', yet donors expect their clothes to go on to make a difference somewhere. Some people find it hard to let go of their clothes, but charities like the YMCA are perceived as a good home.

Charities use promotional material to stimulate the donation of second-hand clothing. Some of this recalls the earlier social history of clothing being donated between different groups as well as emphasizing the environmental benefits of clothing reuse. Oxfam, the leading charity which fights global poverty, connects international development and environmentalism in publicity materials, with slogans such as: 'Having a clear-out? Reduce landfill and raise funds to fight poverty by bringing your unwanted items to Oxfam' and 'Save lives. De-clutter yours'.[17] Different ethical narratives and images are used in doorstep collection materials to stimulate donations. Sustaining this picture is an integral part of the system of provision and the material culture which surrounds the donation and consumption of used clothing. Charities such as the YMCA and others operating in the USA, like Goodwill Industries International, have become relatively effective in monopolizing collections for the specific historical cultural reasons that normalized the gifting of used clothing from the affluent to the impoverished in the nineteenth and twentieth centuries, and even earlier. However, this is not the full story: there is a darker side to clothing collections.

Used-clothing collection leaflets continually arrive in letter-boxes across the UK. Many come from small local charities such as hospices and others from national NGOs like the NSPCC (National Society for the Prevention of Cruelty to Children). One leaflet distributed in Nottingham is a green and yellow flyer that shows an image of an Asian child in the aftermath of a disaster. Although the photo has no caption, an online image search reveals that it was a doctored picture of an earthquake in Sichuan, China. The text states 'All clothes are shipped to under-developed countries to improve their lives and welfare', but there is no mention of how this will be achieved or of the names of any charities or organizations linked to the Chinese earthquake.[18] The only identifications are false company registration and mobile phone numbers. Another example from Nottingham is a leaflet with pictures of helicopters, which gives the casual observer the impression that donations will benefit a local air ambulance charity. Careful inspection of the small print reveals that this collection company has no direct connection to any air ambulance service. Private organizations employ imagery that falsely suggests that donations will go to charity. There are many other examples of deceitful practices in the used-clothing trade, including unlicensed collections by Ragtex in neighbouring Leicester.[19] In Richmondshire, Yorkshire, householders have been warned about the rise in 'bogus' charity collections by Councillor Jill McMullon:

> These leaflets are often worded to encourage people to assume that the items are collected for charity … Unfortunately, these anonymous 'bogus' collectors try to exploit our generosity for their own gain. They may also steal donations left for collection for genuine charities.[20]

Research shows that, when alerted to the widespread illegal practices, donors are seriously concerned about the use of collection sacks and leaflets that imitate legitimate charities' brands: 'I think that [the use of the pink ribbon] is … deliberately done to make you think you are donating to breast cancer.'[21] This problem is not restricted to the UK. It has also been reported in Canada, as a donor in Ontario expresses in disbelief: 'This bin is here and it's leading me to believe that it is part of a charitable organization. It almost even says so on it. So when I find out that it doesn't go to charity,

I'm just flabbergasted that this can happen in my community.'[22] In California executives from Goodwill, the most established US clothing collection charity, have raised concerns about commercial operators using colours that evoke their branding of collection bins.[23] Brian Lincoln, regional manager of the YMCA, expressed anger about how many companies imitate charitable branding and expressed his belief that such operations are commonplace. The motivations for deception and theft stem from the large profits that can be made from exporting second-hand clothes.

THE COMMERCIAL TRADE IN SECOND-HAND CLOTHING

Leaving aside the 'fake' charity collections, many honest organizations, such as the YMCA and legitimate commercial companies, operate across Europe and North America running clothing banks, carrying out domestic collections, and accepting donations directly to stores. These donations are then transformed into marketable goods. Second-hand clothing is big business in the UK, although measuring the size of the sector is difficult and up-to-date statistics are hard to obtain. The most recent estimates from WRAP (The Waste and Resource Action Programme) show that 650,000 tonnes of used-clothing items were collected in 2014 by the secondary textile industry. In 2016, 1,130,000 tonnes of new clothes were consumed, suggesting around half of clothes are recycled.[24] The total volume of clothes collected is estimated to have since increased due to further government recycling initiatives. Similar processes occur in many countries in the global North, including Australia, Canada, Germany, the Netherlands, Spain and the United States.

Donated clothes are transformed from waste into resalable commodities by collecting charities and commercial recyclers in the global North that sort and grade used clothes for onward sale. This process begins, for example, in a back room at the YMCA shop in Staines. Labour processes (sorting, unpacking, sometimes cleaning) and pricing and marketing are undertaken by waged or voluntary workers. This work activity is needed to turn the gift into a commodity. High-quality second-hand clothes are retailed in stores like the YMCA in Staines, although local shoppers are more likely to be found at Gap, Tesco or TK Maxx in the nearby Two Rivers Retail Park. The YMCA shop generates only a small amount of revenue through retail sales, although such high street stores do have the additional purpose of raising the organization's profile. Due to the weak local demand in Staines, Brian Lincoln's colleagues sell on the surplus stock to a textile merchant, Choice Textiles, which deals with all their unsold shop waste (including bric-a-brac, electronic items and furniture). There are significant price fluctuations. For example, in 2001 the 'market almost collapsed' and went 'down to 10p a bag'; in contrast, by 2009 rag merchants' purchases were a 'very important revenue' source.[25] Brian said he was unsure exactly what happened to the majority of the wholesale used clothing, but was sure 'most of it ends up in the Third World'. Choice Textiles sells wearable used clothing to overseas markets and worn-out items for recycling.

This pattern is replicated across the country. A far greater volume of clothing is donated than is actually retailed in the UK's 9,000 charity shops. Obtaining exact national figures is not possible, but estimates indicate that only 10–30 per cent is retailed in the UK; this is similar to the situation in Canada and the USA.[26] The largest clothing collector in Britain is the Salvation Army, which accounts for approximately 15 per cent of the total volume of used-clothing collections.[27] They also have a large presence in Australia, Canada and the USA. They are major suppliers to both Mozambique and Papua New Guinea. Most of the clothing they collect is for export or for sale as recyclable material, with only a very small proportion being sold in their 50 or so UK shops, or is used to support their local programme work – that is, it is provided free to homeless people. Despite accounting for only a small segment of the total used-clothing market, charity shops are important as the public face of the second-hand clothing trade. They are an influential, symbolic part of the image and material culture of the used-clothing system of provision, which encourages people to associate clothing donations with local charitable retail.

Many charities also operate in partnership with commercial operators who pay a royalty fee to use the name of the charity and collect second-hand clothing donations directly from the public. Licensing charitable branding allows companies to expand their involvement in the system of provision and increase their profitability. The UK charity Help the Aged operates two different models of collection. In total they distribute 30 million collection bags per year: 13 million from an internal business run by Help the Aged staff and volunteers to stock the Help the Aged shops; while 17 million bags are distributed by Precycle, which uses the Help the Aged name as a licensed operator, and pays 50 per cent of profits to the charity.[28] In the latter model, clothing donations are collected from the doorstep and taken to the Precycle depot in Reading; they then go by road to grading and sorting plants in Poland where they are categorized: A-grade items are sold in Polish shops; B grade are exported to Africa; C grade are exported to Iran, Iraq, Syria, Jordan and Pakistan; and other grades are recycled for industrial use. As with the tracking of new jeans production, tracing the transactions is difficult since the donations go through processes of amalgamation and separation from other used-clothing collections.

There is controversy around the activities of some companies that operate entirely for-profit collection schemes, or that make 'token' donations to charities, as well as NGOs that have little positive social impact. In the USA Planet Aid, which has clothing banks in 80 cities across 20 states, is nominally a non-profit organization. Planet Aid has been heavily criticized in newspaper reports for a lack of transparency and insufficient spending on programme services:

> the most recent federal tax return from non-profit Planet Aid, which operates donation bins across the country, shows that just 28 per cent of its $36.5 million in spending went to its international aid programs in 2011. The bulk of its spending went to collect and process clothes for recycling.[29]

The lines are becoming blurred between charity and commerce in the second-hand clothing sector. In another example, typical of small British charities, the Rainbow Hospice entered in an agreement to receive a minimum of £40 ($67) for every tonne of used clothing collected by its commercial partner, when the market value of collected used clothing was £600–900 ($1,000–1,500) per tonne.[30] The British Heart Foundation has estimated that 'in some cases as little as 5 per cent is paid to a charity who is working with a commercial company'.[31] There is also competition between charities and commercial collectors. Brian Lincoln claimed that the YMCA had had 'problems from other charities' stealing their collections and that 'Great Ormond Street Hospital just blanket an area' with collection bags.[32]

A long-standing issue in the second-hand clothing sector is the outright theft of used clothing. Steve Wooldridge, head of property and stock operations at Help the Aged, said that when the price for used clothing is high, at around £900 ($1,500) per tonne, there is a problem with the theft of donation bags. Their drivers have been threatened, demands made for maps of their routes, and collection vehicles followed by unmarked trucks, to enable theft of donated clothing. Help the Aged suggested that those acting illegally are frequently Eastern Europeans. Similar problems have been experienced in Canada, where violent attacks have been reported in turf wars between clothing collectors. As an industry insider reported, 'People are getting beat up because these things work as a territory [different organizations control certain areas] … We have orders from the company, like don't let competition around you.'[33] This is not a new phenomenon; criminal elements have long been associated with the used-clothing trade. In 1939 in the United States, for example, the Salvation Army complained that bags from door-to-door collections were being 'kidnapped' and 'hijacked'.[34]

The profits accumulated by legitimate commercial operators can also be viewed negatively as they violate the 'spirit' of the gift and distort donors' intentions. Shea and Brennan, who carried out focus group research with UK households, found that the majority of households were 'unaware that all goods collected door-to-door do not necessarily go straight to charity shops … When made aware of commercial partnerships with charities and charity shops, many respondents' initial reaction was negative/ unhappy with the idea.'[35]

Partnerships formed between charities and textile merchants because they recognized that as the established market in the global North was becoming less profitable, developing countries offered more profitable new markets in which to expand. A used-clothing system of provision which connects charitable donations to efficient commercial operators has emerged to maximize profit generation from the second-hand clothing trade. The actions of clothing-processing charities and companies can be understood within the free-market social relations Adam Smith mapped out in the eighteenth century, described earlier. Both the companies' and the charities' objectives are to realize the latent value in used clothing and sell them for the maximum price, even if this is not achieved through using the donated clothing in the manner intended by the donor. Paul Ozanne of the Salvation Army believes that people are quite comfortable about giving clothing to the Salvation Army knowing that only a small proportion will directly be worn again by people in need (e.g. the homeless) or sold locally, and 'makes no bones about' the fact that the majority is sold overseas to generate profit.[36] However, the evidence from Shea and Brennan suggests otherwise.

Charities are responding to the transformations in the clothing sector. On one hand, in the global North demand for good vintage clothing has increased and charity shops and retro stores are raising the prices

of fashionable vintage items to levels that are proving unaffordable even for some consumers. On the
other hand, overall demand in volume terms for
the much larger amount of lower-quality donated
garments has fallen away as average incomes have
risen and more and more affordable new clothes are
available. This has led to new markets being identified in the global South, which have provided
expanded business opportunities. Second-hand
clothes have long been exported on a small scale;
the 1980s saw supply grow as a disaster relief measure. Organizations such as the Red Cross shipped
donations of clothes to provide warmth and protection following catastrophes such as earthquakes or
wars. This was the case in Mozambique where used
clothes are still known as *roupa da calamidade* (clothing of the calamity). Elsewhere the fall of the Berlin
Wall and the collapse of the USSR opened up new
second-hand markets as Czechs, Poles, Lithuanians
and others in former communist countries grew hun-
gry for the styles of the West; as they could not afford
new clothing, used garments began to flow east. The
broader-scale demand and need for clothing and the
potential for a commercial market in poorer countries were recognized and the trade developed as
the supply grew. Once the trade shifted from a local

scale to international export, charities were unable to connect supplies and markets; they thus built relationships with commercial traders. In the 1990s, on an ever expanding scale commercial operators began exporting clothes to Africa, Eastern Europe, Latin America, the Middle East and Asia in what has since become a highly lucrative wholesale international trade. Globally the second-hand clothing trade was valued at over $4 billion in 2017, according to published UN statistics, which likely underestimate and undervalue the total trade due to the prevalence of smuggled and stolen clothing. The scale is more effectively demonstrated by the official total volume: 4.1 million tonnes of old clothes were recorded as being exported globally in 2017, which is equivalent to 7.9 billion pairs of jeans or 33.4 billion T-shirts.[37] This total does not include domestically traded second-hand clothing, such as the worn garments and vintage fashions resold in American thrift stores or British retro stores.

International traders connect used-clothing supply in the UK to demand in countries that include Lithuania, Nigeria, Pakistan and Poland. Migrant communities often play a key role as they possess the entrepreneurial skills and contacts which charities lack and are able to amalgamate and split supplies to achieve critical economies of scale. The UK is the second largest exporter in the world. In 2017 it exported $508 million (or 371,000 tonnes) of used clothing, the top five destinations for which were, Ghana, Poland, Pakistan, Ukraine and Nigeria. In the United States, the world's largest used clothes exporter, items are collected by small, often family-owned, firms. In all there are nearly 3,000 such businesses, in what is a very competitive industry.[38] Clothes worth $632 million (or 789,000 tonnes) are exported, the main destinations being Guatemala, Chile, Honduras, Canada (primarily for sorting and re-export) and India.[39] Karen Tranberg Hansen, who worked on tracing second-hand clothing exports from North America to Africa, found that diasporas play an important role. Many players are 'recent immigrants who know the potential of the second-hand clothing trade from their former homes in Third World countries', including people of 'Jewish and Middle Eastern background with long-term involvement with the textile and clothing trade, and more recently established firms with backgrounds in south Asia, particularly India and Pakistan, some of whom are recent immigrants to Europe and North America from Africa'.[40] The importing of second-hand clothing to Africa is explored in depth in Chapter 6.

OXFAM WASTESAVER: PROCESSING
CLOTHES FOR EXPORT

Clothing is processed before being exported to the global South. Sorting, grading and packaging is undertaken in large industrial units. Oxfam is the second largest collector (accounting for approximately 3 per cent) in Britain, and retails used clothes through 700 charity shops. It differs from most charities and has its own processing plant, Wastesaver, which is, as general manager Tony Clark says, 'Oxfam's rag merchant in crude terms'.[41] Located in Huddersfield in the north of England, Oxfam Wastesaver is at the heart of one of the largest used-clothing export networks in Europe. The Wastesaver plant receives 200 tonnes of unsold goods from Oxfam shops per week, which accounts for 74 per cent of all the charity's donations.[42] Wastesaver sorts and grades clothing for export (60 per cent), recycling (25–28 per cent) and niche product lines for retail in the UK (8–10 per cent), with the remainder being waste.[43] Different categories vary dramatically in value. Recycling grades are worth £25 ($42) a tonne, whereas the UK retail category includes high-end vintage fashions valued as high as £20,000 ($33,000) or even £30,000 ($50,000) a tonne.[44] The plant has the appearance of a factory; there are conveyor belts dictating the tempo of work, time cards regulating employees' working days, and gantries and offices for managers overseeing the labour process. All are features of modern factory architecture, long exploited by capitalists in new clothing production to enforce discipline and enhance systematic production. The main labour activities of sorting and packaging are comparable to static work in new clothing production lines. Oxfam workers carefully sort clothes into 200 different categories, such as men's white T-shirts, ladies' button blouses, silks and fancy-dress outfits. Matching articles are weighed, labelled and bound into tightly packed bales. These bales are new commodities produced from a labour process that harnesses the material value still embodied in waste clothing. Wages are paid (although some work is done by volunteers), new labour costs that are contained within the final price for consumers in developing countries.

Oxfam has two different models of clothing export; the majority is channelled through normal market exchanges. Clothing is sold in 40 ft or 20 ft shipping containers. Each 40 ft container holds approximately 550–600 45 kg (100 lb) bales. This is standard practice throughout the used-clothing trade, including by exporters in North America as well. Clients in the global South purchase a container with a mix of different bales, as Clark explains: '35 bales of men's T-shirts, 2 bales of bras and so on'. They sell to African companies, which are relatively small, 'what you would call an entrepreneur'; each importer takes between four and 20 containers a year. Dealing with African customers has created challenges for Oxfam; it now requires 'payment in advance', as it 'used to have people walk through the office with £20,000 in cash in an envelope'. Oxfam ships mainly to West Africa where 'markets are more stable and governments are more stable ... [in] Ghana, Togo, Benin, Gabon, Senegal'.

Oxfam also exports a 'second pick for Eastern Europe'. This comprises items not suitable for the African market, rather than secondary in terms of quality. Lower-quality items go to the Middle East, from where they are exported on to Central Asian countries, including Afghanistan and Uzbekistan. Oxfam's role as a campaigning organization advocating for change in the cotton sector sits uneasily with its position in the second-hand clothing system of provision. Clark commented that '[i]t was quite an eye opener for me' speaking to colleagues within Oxfam who are campaigning against US cotton subsidies and promoting fair-trade clothing. 'Oxfam was reluctant to talk about clothing ending up in countries they worked in ... which could affect local industry.' Aloysius Ihezie, the Nigerian director of Choice Textiles, explains that there 'are two schools of thought. One is that it is killing the local economy' by destroying clothing industries, and the other is that it has benefit of creating local jobs. These debates are explored further later.

In an effort to address some of the ethical issues that surround the trade, Oxfam has started exporting by means of a second method, which attempts to provide more local jobs and create income-generating opportunities. Large 450 kg bales of 'tropical mix' are sent to its own sorting plant in Dakar, Senegal. This commercial social enterprise, which aims to support Oxfam's in-country programme, sorts and grades used clothes and sells them to local traders. It employs 25 or so people. Oxfam is trying to link the operation to its work on livelihoods. There are difficulties in Senegal, however, as Clark further explained: 'We can't shift everything from a commercial basis to an ethical basis because the risk is too great ... it's not easy ... [we] invested £300,000 [$500,000]; you've got to have that level of investment ... [we are] paying full duty, putting us at a commercial disadvantage in-country.' The disadvantage is in relation to unethical commercial operators who may pay bribes to avoid duties: 'African markets [have] got a [reputation] for bending the rules' (the smuggling of used clothing is discussed further in Chapter 6). Oxfam is proud of its Dakar operation: 'that's our unique selling point.' It is 'sustainable' and 'as ethical as you can get these days. We're leading edge.' However, this is a small part of the charity's business, accounting for only 10 per cent of exports. Clark added: 'There is the international division which spend the money [Oxfam programme staff who work on international development projects] and others which support it [Wastesaver and the Oxfam shops].' Each is 'specialist'; 'they get on with what they need to do and I get on with what I need to do.' This shows the disconnect between Oxfam's campaigns and advocacy programmes, and the impact of its own commercial trade in used clothing.

One of the largest markets for British used-clothing exports is West Africa, mainly Ghana, Benin and Togo, because, as Ihezie explains, 'the West African market has been in the trade for years, since the 1950s and 1960s'. Imports from the UK are found across the continent. Despite the large scale of African markets the British branch of the Salvation Army chooses not to export used clothing to Africa. It has a limited number of large buyers in Eastern Europe, including Bulgaria and Estonia. Multiple reasons were given for not trading with African merchants. There is an issue with clothing types, as 'overcoats and puffer jackets [are] unsuitable for the climate', a problem which has been accommodated by Oxfam, which has a different product line for Eastern Europe. Ozanne from the Salvation Army argued that, if they are not handled correctly, imports could damage local manufacturing in Africa. He believes Africa suffers from 'political unrest' and there are ethical considerations with providing 'financial incentives for senior officials', which 'is an issue for an organization with Christian values'. The Salvation Army had made an exception and exported bras to Africa, when they responded to a need identified in Malawi for women's underwear. They campaigned to collect additional bras in the UK. But there was a conflict between the Salvation Army's Christian values and the local cultural context. Malawian women were utilizing the bras not as undergarments in the service of modesty, but ostentatiously to display the figure and flaunt female sexuality. Unhappy with this, the Salvation Army halted the export programme.

Exporting second-hand clothing raises different ethical concerns for some NGOs. UK-based charities like Help the Aged and the YMCA are concerned with raising funds as part of their domestic charitable work and to enhance their local reputations, and do not focus on the downstream impacts of the second-hand clothing trade. As Clark observed, 'The difference between [Oxfam and the] YMCA is that the rag trade isn't going to impact their work.' Oxfam had prioritized fundraising, but was beginning to engage with the ethical impacts of the trade, especially as it potentially contradicted the charity's recent core programme work, including campaigns on trade justice, because imports can out-compete locally produced goods. As a large international development NGO, it occupies a broader geographical space than many other UK national charities and so is responsive on a different scale of accountability. The Salvation Army also took a broader-scale approach to morality. But, as the example from Malawi illustrates, its actions were ultimately informed by 'Christian values' rather than the immediate needs and desires of people in the global South.

THE SECOND-HAND AND NEW CLOTHING TRADES IN GLOBAL CONTEXT

This chapter has traced how the history of the second-hand trade has been important in structuring the contemporary systems of used-clothing provision. The long traditions of donating and gifting used clothing and today's cultural pressures in the global North that compel people to dispose of wearable clothing provide the preconditions for a highly particular and well-organized global circulation of used commodities that is not paralleled in other sectors, such as second-hand books, furniture or other household goods. There is a hidden professionalism to the used-clothing trade. UK-based second-hand clothing organizations such as Choice Textiles, Oxfam Wastesaver, the Salvation Army and the YMCA, and their counterparts in the USA like Goodwill and Planet Aid, have highly organized corporate business models, of which donors are frequently unaware. Second-hand clothing is sold as a commodity in market-based transactions and primarily bought by the poor in the global South. Consumption is served by the market.

In the used clothes market, the position and activities of those involved in producing clothing commodities is concealed. Social and economic relations are hidden from view. Ben Fine discusses how the market conceals relationships: 'money provides a common measure across commodities … [it] seemingly sets aside the underlying social relations, structures and processes by which use values [goods] are made available for consumption. The fashionable trainer does not display the child labour upon which it depends.'[45] Equally the clothing collection bank or used jeans do not show what happens to donated clothing. The labour activities associated with the collection, processing and export of second-hand clothes and the complex interactions between waste-making, donations and environmental acts are hidden. Across the global North and South the linkages between new clothing consumption and used-clothing origins and markets are therefore often unknown by those who donate, purchase and wear used clothes, as patterns of capitalist exchange obscure and confuse the connections.

New clothing production is dominated by the marketplace in the developed world. Retailers maintain cycles of production by manipulating demand for unnecessary goods. The excessive consumption of new clothing in the global North provides a vast surplus of used clothing. By disposing of clothes through donations, people in the global North reinforce a series of connections. How second-hand clothes end up in the global South and what impacts they have on local economies and culture will be examined in Chapters 6 and 7 using case studies from Mozambique and elsewhere in Africa. To fully explain the diverse impacts, it is necessary first to understand the African clothing sectors, which are themselves interlinked with the affluence of the global North. The next two chapters present, first, an in-depth analysis of why the cotton sector is connected to poverty in Africa, followed by an investigation of how the rise and fall of clothing industries and the increasing engagement of China in Africa have affected economic development in the world's poorest continent.

COTTON IS THE MOTHER
OF POVERTY

AFRICA AND GLOBAL MARKETS

The great Zambezi river flows across southern Africa, draining parts of Angola, Botswana, Malawi, Mozambique, Tanzania, Zambia and Zimbabwe. A delta at the mouth of the river opens into the Indian Ocean in northern Mozambique. Moving upstream, the Lower Zambezi receives the Shire river, bringing water from the majestic Lake Malawi. Further west the powerful channel is dammed at Cahora Bassa, a massive hydroelectric project built by the Portuguese during the turbulent era of decolonization to calm the waters and modernize the Mozambican state. Passing through spectacular scenery and wondrous wildlife, the middle river extends back, forming the border between Zambia and Zimbabwe. Water thunders over the Victoria Falls near Livingstone, the tourist centre named after the Scottish explorer who was the first European to set eyes upon the world's greatest waterfall. The Upper Zambezi curves round eastern Angola and the river rises in north-west Zambia in marshy woodland near the border with Congo. Along the river's course, tributaries fan out as the catchment area forms some of southern Africa's most valuable agricultural land.

On a Friday night in central Zambia, at the heart of the vast Zambezi basin, Pieter, a heavy-set white South African, relaxes after work, lounging in Tuskers bar. He calls over to the waiter: 'My friend, tonight the beers must flow like the waters of the mighty Zambezi!' Pieter manages a large cotton estate and needs to slake his thirst with cool Mosi lager after a long week delegating tasks and shouting orders on the farm. South Africans throughout the continent often fill managerial roles in the service of foreign businesses, helping them make profits in agricultural and natural resource sectors. Cotton has become an important crop in Zambia, attracting new investment. It draws on water from the Zambezi catchment. Water is important in cotton growing and hydrological resources have to be carefully managed. Local agricultural labourers also need to be supervised; they work hard sowing seed, growing the shrubby plants and harvesting the cotton balls. Pieter explains how many of the short fibres from these plants are exported to China and go to make the thread for khaki and denim fabrics.

Across Africa, the warm climate and fertile environments offer good conditions for growing cotton. North of the Sahara, cotton is cultivated along the banks of the Nile. Egyptian cotton cloth, woven using local and imported fibres, has become a byword for fine, high-quality fabric. In francophone West Africa, cotton is found in Benin, Burkina Faso, Chad, Côte d'Ivoire, Mali and Senegal, and is a key export in all these states. Some East African economies have important cotton sectors, such as Tanzania, but other agricultural products, including tea in Kenya, and coffee in Uganda, play a greater role in countries with cooler, high-altitude farmland. Moving south, cotton has been important in the economic histories of Angola, Mozambique and Zimbabwe as well as Zambia. Today in Malawi some farmers are switching from tobacco to cotton crops as the market for cigarettes contracts. International cotton markets remain buoyant, driven by demand from Chinese and other Asian textile manufacturers, and ultimately retail markets in the global North. African cotton is woven into clothes that are sold around the world, after travelling though the complex systems of provision encountered earlier in the biography of jeans.

Malawians and Zambians, alongside other African farmers, are currently expanding production, but there is nothing new about cotton agriculture or textile and clothing production in Africa. Cotton is endemic and has been grown south of the Sahara since at least 3000 BCE.[1] Large-scale artisanal clothes-making was to be found across Africa prior to the arrival of Europeans. In the east, Mogadishu had a weaving industry in the twelfth century that produced coarse cotton goods and camel-hair cloth, which was traded in Egyptian markets thousands of miles away. Further south in 'Bantu Africa' – roughly the present-day southern African region and Congo basin – production was less established and cotton cloth was found only in towns and around gold mines at the time of the first Portuguese contacts.[2] The story is very different in West Africa. Vibrant trade networks involving textiles and indigo dyes, as well as iron tools, were part of the culture of the Upper Guinea coast prior to the arrival of European traders. Cloth was both imported overland from Sudan and North Africa and manufactured in Guinea and Yorubaland (southern Nigeria). Interestingly, cotton cloth was even used as a form of currency known as *panos*. As historical geographer

Linda Newson explains: 'A *pano* was a piece of cloth measuring about one by two metres ... Cloth money was used in many parts of Africa in pre-colonial times, notably in eastern Africa, the Congo, and the savanna area south of the Sahara.'[3] Clothing trade networks extended from urban centres to small villages. Later, when intercontinental trade first took off in the sixteenth century, Portugal initially imported textiles from West Africa to sell in Europe, a pattern which would be reversed in the following centuries.

Coastal societies around the Gulf of Guinea were gradually challenged and changed by European mercantilism, the economic system where national strength was maximized by exporting goods and restricting foreign imports. Slavery formed part of this trade pattern. Local leaders succumbed to economic pressure and a manipulative African ruling class collaborated with the Europeans in exploiting the African masses through the transatlantic slave trade.[4] The discovery of the Americas and the demand for labour in Brazilian gold mines and Carolina cotton plantations forced African feudal leaders, kings and merchants to provide more and more enslaved people on a horrific and insatiable scale.[5] West Africans were skilled and experienced in tropical agriculture and mining, and superior to European workers in equatorial climates.

In the seventeenth century, enslaved African labour was exchanged for imported manufactured goods – cotton cloth, metal hardware and guns – produced in Britain, France, the Netherlands and Portugal, often using raw materials from the new American colonies. Portuguese traders led the way, practising methods that brought 'order and clarity to complex sets of transactions', as a precursor to modern capitalism.[6] Trade between West Africa and Europe developed and textiles were increasingly imported to ports around the Gulf of Guinea. Yet the process was not as straightforward as European goods entering captive markets, as Newson observes:

> The importance of cloth and clothing indicates that commercial relations between Africans and Europeans in the early seventeenth century did not consist of a simple exchange of imported goods for slaves, but rather that both parties participated in an active trade in local products. It also demonstrates that far from being dependent on Europe for textiles and clothing, as has sometimes been argued for Africa in general, the demand for these commodities in Upper Guinea in the early seventeenth century, at least, was largely met by its vibrant local textile industry.[7]

Locally produced fabrics and other manufactured commodities were exported from Africa in the seventeenth century, but eventually the balance of trade would shift decisively. European engagement in West Africa increased as new powers followed in the wake of the Portuguese. As the Industrial Revolution took hold in Britain in the early eighteenth century, there was a co-evolution in the expansion of factories in northern England and the extension of colonial rule. The emergence of capitalism and the business mentalities it produced in the form of autonomous enterprise, and the separation of ownership and management in joint stock companies, enabled Europeans to dominate more profitable trade networks. Cheaper mass-manufactured imports emerged from textile factories in Britain, France and elsewhere that undermined local African production. This European head start restricted the further development of local artisan manufacturing such as fabric weaving, explaining why industrial capitalism failed to develop in West Africa.

Independent African feudal leaders across the continent were subsequently supplanted. Superior arms, communications and other technologies, along with capital for investment and new business approaches, enabled Belgians, English, French, Germans, Italians and Portuguese first to establish and grow trading networks, and later to extend administrative and governing powers across Africa. Authority gradually extended across the continent through the diffuse and exploitative influence of colonialism. Foreign sovereign powers spread out from port cities and co-opted local chiefs and kings or violently wrestled executive powers from rulers. Some former feudal leaders held on to authority under colonial protection, enabling them to maintain rule over indigenous communities. Revenue was raised by both taxation and new foreign-owned business that specialized in exporting minerals and tropical agricultural products. The culmination of the nineteenth-century 'Scramble for Africa' was the Berlin conference in 1884, when the continent was carved up by German chancellor Otto von Bismarck and representatives from the other European powers. Eventually nearly all of Africa fell under European control, if not formal colonialism, as was the case with Liberia and Ethiopia. Colonization transformed Africa as local societies built on tribute payments and tribal loyalties were forcibly integrated into a global, European-dominated capitalist economy.

Colonialism had different effects on women and men. Cash crops such as cotton, as well as cocoa, tea, palm oil and rubber, were often cultivated by women, but they did not control the income generated from their work. Meanwhile men were more likely to undertake waged employment in colonial economies. As well as this gender division of labour, all Africans encountered racism and discrimination when serving the interests of Europeans. Exploitation was based on cultural difference, and through cruel new practices surplus value was extracted from the hard work of native people. Colonial rulers paid low prices for crops, provided low wages for workers or enforced high taxation on Africans, which left the continent severely impoverished.

Cotton was just one of many African goods produced for the colonial powers. Cocoa in Côte d'Ivoire was processed and retailed as chocolate bars in France; Eritrean coffee was roasted, ground and brewed to make Italian espressos; Ghanaian gold, Kenyan tea and Nigerian palm oil have all been exported to Britain; and Congolese rubber went to Belgium to be moulded into tyres under one of the most brutal colonial systems. Such patterns of trade were established in the colonial period and although the companies and nations involved have changed patterns of exploitation continue. Many tropical products and minerals have long been exported from Africa, and profits accumulated in Brussels, London, Paris and New York. Beijing can now be added to this list as Chinese investment in Africa booms. Export trade is not in and of itself a problem – indeed it is vital for growing economies – but the flow of commodities out of Africa has long been of low-value primary goods. African minerals and tropical plants are manufactured into more complex consumable goods elsewhere, some of which are obvious, such as jewellery (gold), furniture (tropical hardwoods), cotton (jeans), and others less so, like oil (plastics), soaps and beauty products (palm oil), and mobile phones (coltan). Value is added in downstream industrial and service sectors outside of Africa. Labour in the global North enjoys higher wages; for instance Italian waiters earn more than Eritrean coffee growers, although both work to bring the espresso to the customer. The African labour that goes into producing primary products receives only a tiny proportion of the final sale price, whereas shareholders and managers gain far more from these enterprises. Surplus value is extracted from African labour by the firms which make the more complex goods, as well as transport and warehousing companies and final retailers, all of which take a slice of profit. Merchants in particular make money by purchasing commodities at below market value. Large American and European supermarkets are particularly adept at making money. They buy tropical products such as fresh bananas, canned pineapples and freeze-dried coffee at very low prices and sell them cheaply to their customers, who rarely question why goods like imported bananas cost less than local apples.

Extensive and complex networks of international trade are involved in the supply chains that bring cotton jeans and other goods to markets. Agricultural workers in the global South are structurally abused throughout many trade networks. Exploitation is a product of history. In nineteenth- and twentieth-century colonial Africa, cotton farming involved horrific labour practices. Agricultural communities were transformed by imperial greed, leaving a scar that is still visible in present-day societies. As Marx argues,

> [Women and] Men make their own history, but they do not make it just as they please; they do not make it under circumstances chosen by themselves, but under circumstances directly encountered, given and transmitted from the past. The tradition of all the dead generations weighs like a nightmare on the brain of the living.[8]

Understanding the historic role of colonized peoples in production helps explain why cotton farming remains an exploitative labour practice. Unequal exchange is embedded within the 'historical materialism' of cotton production and normalized global inequality. The former southern African Portuguese colonies of Angola and Mozambique, among the poorest countries in the world, had some of the worst examples of colonial labour abuse.

COTTON IN COLONIAL MOZAMBIQUE

Prior to Portuguese colonialism, Mozambique was home to layered and complex societies. East African culture was not simple and uniform. There were different patterns of productive work; the past was not a pre-capitalist paradise. Indigenous societies had their own injustices, but colonialism led to a new level of severe oppression.[9] Portuguese engagement in Mozambique began with the voyages of Vasco da Gama and the golden age of lusophone exploration in the early sixteenth century, but impacts were minimal until after the Berlin conference of 1884. Colonialism began to expand markedly as each European power felt the need to demonstrate and prove that they were the 'legitimate' rulers of their agreed African dominions. Imperial expansion grew in Mozambique with the arrival of greater numbers of Portuguese settlers, more conflict and warfare, the establishment of government legislative power and the creation of new taxes. The impacts of Portuguese colonialism were especially severe, as Portugal was a relatively poor European country, whose desire to prove its right to occupy vast areas of Africa led to harsh and punitive demonstrations of authority. As the Portuguese state lacked capital, it could not fund the initial investment required for economic colonization. Therefore the Portuguese established large chartered companies, including the Nyassa Company and the Mozambique Company (similar to the British East India Company), that were allocated administrative jurisdiction over vast swathes of territory. Charter companies were mainly funded by non-Portuguese investors; although mandated to develop regions, their primary motivation was to make profits.

Portugal and her colonies were ruled by the autocratic Prime Minister António de Oliveira Salazar from 1932 until 1968. Salazar stated that colonies must 'produce raw materials to sell to the motherland in exchange for manufactured goods'.[10] Mozambique produced cotton, which was exported exclusively to Portugal until the early 1970s. Cotton prices were fixed and production patterns dictated by the colonial government through a marketing board, the Junta de Exportação de Algodão Colonial (Colonial Cotton Board).[11] Cotton was sold to the concessionary chartered companies with monopoly rights below the world market price. In 1930 Mozambicans were legally obliged to grow cotton. Every man between 18 and 55 and his family were expected to cultivate at least 2.5 acres of cotton, and each single woman and man aged between 56 and 60, 1.5 acres of cotton. Commercial agricultural production was expanded and the proportion of agricultural goods used and consumed in Mozambique reduced. The colony got poorer and poorer to support Portugal. Rural life deteriorated as food production fell and famines occurred. By the mid-1950s between half a million and a million women, men and children worked in the sector, producing 140,000 tons of cotton and receiving an average income of only $11.17 per year. Portuguese administrators ensured that cotton was grown to sell to the chartered companies and farmers were not allowed to take their crops to alternative buyers. Police harassed families and ensured that men, women and children were all out tending cotton crops every day throughout the cotton season. Cotton farmer Gabriel Mauricio Nantimbo recalls life on the cotton farms in the 1960s:

The time of cotton growing was a time of great poverty, because we could only produce cotton; we got a poor price for it, and we did not have time to grow other crops. We were forced to produce cotton. The people didn't want to: they knew cotton is the mother of poverty, but the company was protected by the government. We knew that anyone who refused to grow it would be sent to the plantations on São Tomé where he would work without any pay at all.[12]

Rebellious peasants were exiled to São Tomé on the fringes of the Portuguese colonial empire, but the valuable cotton they produced was at the heart of the European economy. Angolan and Mozambican cotton provided 82 per cent of inputs for the textile factories of Lisbon and Porto. Portugal successfully developed an industrial clothing sector, which in the 1960s employed a third of the industrial labour force and accounted for a fifth of Portuguese exports.[13] This helped grow the Portuguese economy throughout the twentieth century. Portugal has developed from being a poor state in the 1930s to a high-income country today. Growth in the Portuguese clothing sector was dependent on having a secure supply of cheap cotton and colonies also provided a captive monopoly market for Portuguese clothing production. Meanwhile, peasants in Mozambique were forced to grow and sell cotton in a brutal and exploitative system of production.

Economic life in Mozambique served the metropolitan power throughout Salazar's rule.[14]

COTTON AND STRUCTURAL ADJUSTMENT
IN CÔTE D'IVOIRE

One of the key policy instruments of the colonial state in Mozambique was price control. The price paid for cotton was below the world market rate; thus local people were structurally exploited by the colonial state. Despite this history, state price controls of agricultural products have not always been exploitative. In the post-independence era many African states inherited agricultural marketing boards that set prices. Once free from French colonialism, successful early economic development in Côte d'Ivoire was based on expanding export crop production, predominantly of coffee and cocoa, but also cotton. The state marketing boards (Caisses de stabilisation) extracted surplus from smallholders, who made up 70 per cent of the population. The differential between the lower national price and the global value of agricultural export products provided half of government tax revenue in 1980.[15] The Caisses surplus subsidized government wages, social investment in urban areas and industrial development, but also facilitated rural agriculture through providing trading,

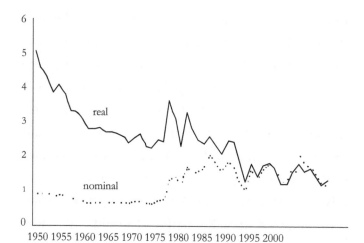

Figure 1 Cotton prices, 1950–2000 (US$/kg)

Source: John Baffes, *Cotton: Market Setting, Trade Policies, and Issues*, World Bank, Washington DC, 2004, pp. 62–3; www-wds.worldbank.org/servlet/WDS ContentServer/WDSP/iB/2004/06/03/000009486_20040603091724/rendered/ PDF/wps3218cotton.pdf, real prices have been adjusted and deflated to 2003 prices.

support and subsidized farm inputs, such as fertilizer. Additionally, marketing agencies could accumulate surplus funds to support the prices paid to farmers when the global market value of agricultural goods dropped.

Cotton and other export crops were providing revenue to help government development strategies in many independent African nations in the 1960s, 1970s and early 1980s, but growing tropical agricultural commodities did not lift African countries out of poverty for two interconnected reasons. The real price of cotton declined throughout the second half of the twentieth century from an inflation-adjusted $5.05 per kilogram in 1950 to $1.34 in 2000 and prices were also volatile (see Figure 1). Commercial agriculture was susceptible to fluctuations and crashes in international prices.[16] The dual problems of declining and fluctuating agricultural commodity prices were part of the reason for persistent poverty not just in Côte d'Ivoire but throughout Africa. However, a further shock imposed upon the continent would have widespread and devastating impacts.

In the 1970s, Côte d'Ivoire had been undertaking unsustainable government spending maintained by expanding borrowing, based on inaccurate future export crop revenue predictions. Côte d'Ivoire and other African nations had been encouraged to borrow money from global markets. A funding crisis developed and Côte d'Ivoire struggled to keep up with debt repayments. In 1981, under pressure from the international community, structural adjustment programmes (SAPs) were implemented based on a World Bank stabilization loan that was tied to reduced investment and a freeze on government salaries. The SAPs had calamitous effects. Sadly this blow to development was not unique to Côte d'Ivoire. Across much of the global South in the 1980s and 1990s, SAPs were widely imposed on highly indebted countries and these programmes had a very negative effect on social and economic development. Drawing on the liberal traditions of Adam Smith and David Ricardo – hence the term *neo*liberalism – the theory was that freeing economies from the control of the state would enable growth. A naive faith in 'the magic of the market' was projected upon already impoverished nations as a condition for restructuring loans. SAPs were designed to limit government expenditure, remove state intervention in the economy, and promote liberalization and international trade. Conservative neoliberal leaders such as Margaret Thatcher and Ronald Reagan inspired these programmes. Throughout much of Africa the impacts were great, bringing hardships to some of the most vulnerable communities, including the urban poor, who faced increased prices for basic necessities. African nations could not compete on the world market and SAPs hampered agricultural and industrial development as domestic markets for locally produced goods lost protection. These crude programmes provided a shock to fragile economies, leading to stagnation.

In Côte d'Ivoire, SAPs were implemented through the 1980s and 1990s.[17] SAPs liberalized markets for agricultural products, removing marketing board price controls and exposing farmers to market price fluctuations, compounding the effects of a sharp recession. Development gains were lost and social impacts included a reduction in investment in rural health care. In the mid-1980s new SAPs aimed to shift economic policy in favour of export crop producers, but the policies were only partially implemented, and occurred against a background of further recession, followed by drought in 1983. Under SAPs the promotion of export crops was purely an economic policy, not supported by extension services or subsidized farm inputs. Technical assistance for farmers declined, and after 1990 there were mergers and redundancies at extension agencies. The costs of SAPs were increasingly borne by export farmers whose produce entered a world market beset by overproduction and declining prices. The tendency for profit to fall under competition in an increasingly liberalized market required producers to cut labour costs and sack workers. This created a process of de-proletarianization in some areas. De-proletarianization meant that landless and unemployed farm workers who lacked opportunities to work in other sectors or the mobility to search for jobs elsewhere took positions as unpaid forced labour in a form of 'modern slavery'.[18] Life worsened for most Ivorians, as increases in the cost of living easily outstripped any growth in income that resulted from liberalized crop prices. For example, the costs of insecticide rose faster than increases in cocoa and coffee prices.[19] Smallholders producing cotton in the savannah region of northern Côte d'Ivoire suffered some of the steepest declines in income. Tensions with local cattle herders also escalated.

The examples from Mozambique and Côte d'Ivoire illustrate some of the economic hardships Africans faced in the twentieth century. Throughout most of European rule the development of industry was deliberately restricted. African dominions served as suppliers of agricultural and mineral products for their colonial masters. European economies gained a head start in their industrial development at the expense of Africans, who were doubly disadvantaged – receiving low prices for their primary goods and being denied the opportunity to develop clothing factories and other manufacturing sectors. At the time of independence, inherited marketing boards, which had been used by colonial governments to extract wealth from colonies, enabled some independent African nations to generate revenue, yet declining terms of trade and the erosion of the value of tropical products limited this opportunity. Crucially, global recession in 1979–83, triggered by the oil crisis, led to the growth of indebtedness in Africa as another crisis of capitalism amplified uneven development. In exchange for further borrowing, African governments were forced to accept the SAPs championed by the World Bank and the IMF (International Monetary Fund). The conditions associated with lending involved a suite of policies which further inhibited national development: state companies were privatized, public spending reduced, currencies devalued, public-sector pay cut, and subsidies and price controls removed – all in the name of increasing economic liberalization. The punitive impacts of SAPs on cotton farmers and other smallholders were harsh, social crisis spread and, critically, the decline in price support reduced rural incomes as protection was lost when the volatile world market price for cotton fell.[20]

ECONOMIC LIBERALIZATION AND COTTON SUBSIDIES

Conditions in the 1990s and early 2000s improved for some farmers in West and Central Africa, which led to reductions in poverty. Despite the positive trends, concerns were raised about the continuing volatility of cotton prices, which are heavily influenced by US subsidies as well as the long-term downward trend in commodity prices. Oxfam raised these issues in regard to Mali, Africa's second largest cotton producer and one of the poorest countries in the world. Trade-distorting subsidies and pressure from the World Bank and the IMF to increase the role of the market destabilized rural livelihoods. Reforms centred on the continuing liberalization of price-setting:

> While reform may create economic opportunities for cotton producers, such as the chance to negoti-ate a higher share of the world price and participate in the management of the sector, producers cannot manage the risks associated with depressed, vola-tile, and generally declining prices. Transferring the risks of a highly volatile world market down to the bottom of the chain may benefit the ginning companies and exporters, but only at the expense of poor farmers. It also begs the question of why those least capable of managing these risks are increas-ingly expected to pick up the responsibility. At the very least, price risk should be shared between the farmers, the ginning companies, and the traders.[21]

This example illustrates how other parties involved in the clothing system of provision, including ginning companies and traders, extract surplus from cotton production as vulnerabilities to price fluctuations impact upon impoverished Malian cotton farmers.

Economic liberalization and the removal of price controls are policies promoted by decision-makers in the global North, especially bureaucrats in Washington, who advocate free trade as a solution to the problem of poverty in Africa's rural communities. Price controls are viewed as market distortions. The argument follows that once free from the constraints of state interference, entrepreneurial farmers should be able to expand their agricultural businesses. In principle this libertarian approach is appealing, yet it is a policy prescription based on the principle of 'do as I say' not 'do as I do'. The inconvenient truth is that the USA was until recently the world's largest dispenser of cotton subsidies and price support. Large industrial farms are the primary recipients of US government subsidies, which shield them from price volatility. US subsidies distort the world cotton market, deflating international prices and enabling American farmers to maintain their position as the largest exporter of cotton. World cotton prices are reduced by an estimated 10 per cent due to the effect of US subsidies.[22] Developing countries have applied through the World Trade Organization (WTO) to reform the programme, and the WTO twice judged US subsidies to be illegal, but the US government failed to act. Domestic US political pressure as well as lobbying from Brazil tried to change these policies. But now a new nation is set to dominate the world cotton markets and their subsidies and policies will determine the livelihoods of African farmers.

Beijing is becoming increasingly dominant in controlling world cotton prices. In 2009–10 China overtook the USA as the largest dispenser of cotton subsidies; China is also the world's largest importer of cotton, accounting for 36 per cent of all imports (followed by Bangladesh, Turkey, Indonesia and Vietnam), and holds half the world's stockpile. Cotton production in Africa is increasingly influenced by Chinese market dominance: China is the primary destination for African cotton. The International Centre for Trade and Sustainable Development argues that Chinese trade regulations negatively affect African cotton farmers as China 'imposes import duties from 5 percent up to 40 percent on cotton imported outside of the annual 894,000-ton import quota related to WTO obligations. If China were to allow entry of African cotton free of duty, such cotton would therefore gain some competitiveness versus other origins of cotton.'[23] As the global significance of US cotton production declines, both in volume terms and as a payer of subsidies for cotton production, China's role in the sector is expanding. China's ascent in cotton mirrors the broader-scale rebalancing of the global economy as we move further into a Chinese-dominated twenty-first century. China now takes centre stage in clothing and other major economic sectors, whereas African countries are often on the margins of global trade. Taking the long view brings a different perspective. Rather than being peripheral to world economic affairs, Africa has played a pivotal role in the emergence of international trade patterns. Prior to the encounters with Portuguese and other explorers in the sixteenth century, there were flourishing clothing sectors in some parts of Africa, which attracted European interest. The establishment of trade between West Africa, Europe and America in slaves, cloth, cotton, gold and other commodities set the conditions for centuries of exploitation. Trade centred on the Atlantic enabled the emergence of mercantilism, or merchant capitalism, which provided one of the preconditions for the Industrial Revolution and development of modern capitalism, the powerful force that has transformed societies and the environment around the world. Capitalism and colonialism spread together hand in glove across the African continent. Foreign rule drew new populations into the service of business and led to the structural exploitation of African labour for the benefit of European powers, helping them to become some of the richest nations on earth. With independence the cotton sector in some countries has shown both stagnation and improvements. Economic development has been hampered by the long-term decline in terms of trade, economic liberalization and unfair subsidies paid elsewhere, in the USA and now China. In tandem with the difficulties in the cotton sector, African nations have largely been unable to develop industrial bases that would enable them to produce more complex and valuable commodities, such as manufacturing finished clothes from locally produced cotton. Some clothing and textile factories were established in the last half-century after African nations began to win political independence, but they have struggled to compete with production elsewhere. Understanding the reasons behind this requires careful attention. Furthermore, it is interlinked with the emergence of China as the dominant player in world clothing production.

MADE IN CHINA AND AFRICA

CHINESE ECONOMIC EXPANSION

The Zambia–China Mulungushi Textiles factory stands semi-derelict on the northern outskirts of Kabwe, a city in the centre of Zambia. Set back from the main North–South National Highway, the 1970s factory is a large and imposing modern industrial plant. Bored-looking security guards can occasionally be seen patrolling the grounds and a reclusive Chinese caretaker is rumoured to live on the site. Paint peels from the buildings, plants grow up through the yard, and a couple of delivery trucks are gradually rusting away near the loading bay. It has been a long time since the power looms and sewing machines last produced a pair of trousers or a length of fabric. In recent years the Zambian government and its Chinese partners have tried to revive this factory, which for four decades was promoted as a focus for Zambian industrial development and an icon of Chinese-African friendship. Dreams have been shattered and blood occasionally spilt during the factory's troubled and violent past. The venture was a failed attempt at industrial modernization, proving uncompetitive in the global clothing marketplace.

Sadly, Zambia-China Mulungushi Textiles is one of many failed African industrial projects and, as such, indicative of the broader malaise which has beset African efforts at economic and social modernization. Historically, Africa's role in clothing production and consumption has received little popular or critical attention. On a global scale sub-Saharan Africa manufactures a small proportion of finished clothes, and accounts for a tiny slice of new clothing consumption. Beijing's rapid rise towards the pinnacle of global power is evident throughout Africa and influences clothing production and consumption from Algeria to Zimbabwe. In addition to China being the largest market for African cotton, clothes from China sell in virtually every street market, and Chinese management approaches have been introduced in African textile factories. In recent years Africa has begun to provide a spatial fix for the overaccumulation of Chinese capital and a new place for investment. Capital is invested via huge sovereign wealth funds; annual trade between China and Africa is around US$160 billion.[1] Meanwhile, the imprint on African economies of the era of European colonialism remains, contributing to the absence of development in the garment sectors. Africa's experiences in the textile and clothing trade illustrate some of the reasons for the dire economic performance and the absence of development across the continent as a whole. The downward spiral of clothing industry performance is illustrative of the trajectories of other African industrial sectors and can help explain the causes and consequences of poverty.

In contrast to the experience of African nations, China has successfully established the world's largest clothing and textile sectors, which has helped drive national development. The emergence of China, not just in the apparel sector but across the whole spectrum of global trade, is without question the most significant economic transformation of the last four decades. China's influence over the global economy is huge and increasing due to three factors: a dramatic growth rate, a huge labour force and an increasing openness – on its own terms – to trade. The strategic integration of China into the worldwide capitalist economy is causing a global shift in circuits of capital and commodities. Global influence is being exerted not just through the export of cheap goods, but also via the ways in which Chinese firms and investors are determining the relative value of labour, flows of investment and prices of financial assets. Most significantly, though, China has become the workshop of the world. The global cost of manufactured products, including clothes, has been reduced by Chinese expansion, affecting industrial development everywhere. China is competitive because it can produce labour-intensive products on a massive scale, drawing upon a huge population and the systematic exploitation of labour. However, very particular circumstances have enabled China to put a low-wage mass labour force to work in export-orientated factories.

China was an attractive destination for surplus capital investment in the 1980s and 1990s, as it had huge reserves of labour which would work for low salaries. But why China? Similar potential workforces could be found throughout the global South, not least in Africa. So what was it that made China particularly attractive for international investors seeking a new 'spatial fix'? At a time when much of Africa as well as South America were straddled with SAPs and therefore experiencing social crises, the main draw of the Far East was the high quality of Chinese labour. Workers were comparatively well educated, healthy and had a capacity for self-management. Society had been shaped by the hierarchical and disciplined forms of social control, as well as the welfare advances established by the Communist Party of China (CPC) between 1949 and the late 1970s. The rise of China is not a simple story of an isolated communist regime suddenly opening up to international trade, resulting in free-market development. Instead the particular preconditions for growth in China depended on the existing political economy, the earlier progress in social development, and a managed integration within the global market. Economic success was not down to unbridled neoliberalism and a 'rolling back' of the state, but rather built on what is characterized by the sociologist Giovanni Arrighi as the 'extraordinary' social achievements of the Mao-era government before the 1980s. Foreign capital intervened later, on China's own terms, and took advantage of pre-existing social progress. This fact was even acknowledged by the World Bank in 1981, which recognized how the Chinese were much better off than the poor elsewhere in the global South, having employment, food supplies, school enrolment, basic health care, family planning and 'outstanding' life expectancy.[2]

China's economic development accelerated under the guidance of Deng Xiaoping, the reformist chairman of the CPC, who came to power in 1982. Famously in 1961, Deng had said 'it doesn't matter whether a cat is black or white; if it catches mice it is a good cat'. This enigmatic phrase was later perceived as a metaphor for adopting a pragmatic approach to modernizing the Chinese economy. He led a strategic opening up and liberalization of the economy, which included the 'one country, two systems' approach that would later see the reintegration of Hong Kong and Macau into China and the coexistence of capitalist and communist modes of production. Chinese reforms nurtured and protected the domestic economy, unlike the shock therapies externally imposed on Africa through the structural adjustment programmes, which suddenly and viciously cracked opened markets. Gradualism marked the transition to capitalism. China slowly allowed foreign capital to invest in the economy, enabling labour-intensive export manufacturing across different sectors, such as electronics, hardware and furniture-making, as well as clothing and textiles, to grow.

In addition to the high quality of Chinese labour, two further factors were important in catalysing the boom in the garment sector. First, in the early 1980s the state sector played the dominant role in clothing and textile exports and helped establish the industry in the first instance, and then private firms gradually took over. Second, important 'matchmakers' linked overseas investment to a huge disciplined population that would provide a workforce. Diaspora Chinese communities in neighbouring East Asia and the global North used their cultural ties to help open up new territory for investors, enabling new clothing factories to be built. Here timing was also crucial. China's export surge came just after the East Asian newly industrialized economies' (Hong Kong, Singapore, South Korea and Taiwan) collective share of world clothing and textile production peaked in the mid-1980s. Entrepreneurs from these countries with cultural links to China and experience in manufacturing clothing for America and Europe were able to invest their profits and develop business relationships. They acted as a bridge between the relatively isolated People's Republic of China and consumer demand in the global North. China provided the perfect spatial fix for capital in the clothing sector.

Textile and clothing industries were concentrated in the accessible coastal regions of Fujian, Guangdong, Jiangsu, Shandong and Shanghai provinces, close to Hong Kong, Taiwan and South Korea. The state established Special Economic Zones (SEZs) along the eastern seaboard to provide tax inducements to attract foreign investment. Factories were built, like China Galaxy, established in the Pearl River Delta (Guangdong, near Hong Kong), which belonged to a Hong Kong company and had Hong Kong directors and managers, and produced for European and American brand-name sportswear companies.[3] Another example is Fortune Sports (FS) a subsidiary of a large Taiwanese sports shoe maker, which, after establishing a profitable business in Taiwan in the early 1970s, switched production across the Taiwanese Straits to Fujian province in the late 1980s due to the lower costs of labour, land and energy in mainland China. Through the 1990s FS grew to become the second largest supplier for Reebok in China, employing over 10,000 workers and producing 10 million pairs of shoes per year by 2002. Senior management roles were filled by Taiwanese men, whereas the domestic labour force was 90 per cent female, largely 18- to 30-year-old unmarried women from poor rural provinces, employed on insecure annual contracts. The manufacturing process at FS was labour-intensive; employees undertook dull, specific, repetitive work on production lines to maximize profits.[4]

In the early 1990s it was not uncommon for female textile workers to spend seven days and 70 hours a week in factories. Furthermore casual labour systems were widely used, which provided little employment security and paid low wages. Pay averaged just 10–15 yuan ($1.20–1.80) per day or $30–54 per month, from which 100 yuan could be deducted for food and dormitory accommodation.[5] Between 1980 and 1994 China's exports of clothing and textiles increased eightfold.[6] Following rapid growth in employment in the coastal provinces, shortages of labour developed. As China is so large, with varying labour costs between regions, textile and clothing exports were able to remain competitive as production could expand and migrate to low-cost areas, or, as happened more often, low-wage labour moved to the coastal factories. Unskilled migrant labour from inland provinces such as Sichuan was drawn into the service of foreign business, allowing the continued expansion of profit. Work for migrant employees was hard, conditions were difficult, tasks were boring and often physically demanding. Industrial accidents were commonplace. The young women were separated from their families and lived in dormitories, with six, eight or more to a room, often sharing one toilet.

Labour exploitation in China was not just driven by foreign management. Initial investors from East Asia led the way; then privately owned Chinese companies grew. Chinese factories came to manufacture most Western-branded clothing goods and serve the fast-fashion markets in Europe and North America. Despite the constraints of the MFA, China managed to continue to increase exports through the late 1990s and 2000s, as steady trade liberalization in the global North provided improved access to markets in Europe and North America. Production was further boosted by the opportunities provided by the end of the MFA in 2005, and after the bra wars most protectionist measures were removed.

The labour system in the Chinese garment sector was cruel and depended on mass labour exploitation, but it also led to industrial growth; furthermore, remittances from urban areas helped support rural development. Parallel to the economic development of China there has been a limited degree of social and political change. Protests calling for political freedoms and the massacre in Tiananmen Square in 1989 drew attention to human rights in China and have been influential in framing how the CPC is viewed overseas. The social impacts of China's rapid expansion in clothing production began to be reported on in the West. In 1992 the *Washington Post* ran a watershed article on Levi's jeans being manufactured by Chinese prison labour. Public concern in the global North about labour conditions in Chinese clothing factories spread. Levi Strauss reacted immediately by drawing up a code of conduct. Media exposés led to the word 'sweatshop' becoming a ubiquitous phrase synonymous with poor labour standards in Chinese clothing factories. Following further outcry from NGOs, churches and student groups, Western clothing companies began to introduce codes of conduct and apply some ethical standards to the factories of their suppliers. Codes usually specify that forced, bonded or child labour must not be used and that adequate wages and benefits are paid without discrimination, that overtime is not excessive, and that health and safety measures are followed. Despite the existence of codes of conduct, research on clothing workers at China Galaxy and another firm, China Miracle, found that employees in 2003 were earning 600–700 yuan a month ($75–90), which did not meet the legal minimum wage.[7] In 2005 wages at FS were 470 yuan ($60) – too low to support workers' basic needs or provide for their families. The FS factory had followed Reebok codes of conduct, but the improved labour standards still failed to meet minimal criteria. Harsh labour exploitation continues in China. While the codes of conduct have produced some minor improvements to work practices, evidence indicates that transnational clothing companies have no genuine concern for labour rights.[8]

Developing a labour-intensive and exploitative clothing industry fuelled China's rapid growth and at the same time drew millions of workers into oppressive employment. The Chinese experience is in no way unique; labour exploitation has been at the heart of many boom periods in both clothing production and national economic development. South Korean economist Ha-Joon Chang recalls how in the 1970s teenage males and females in Seoul worked in conditions reminiscent of nineteenth-century English textile mills, 'spending 12 hours or more in very hazardous conditions for low pay. Some factories refused to serve soup in the canteen, lest the workers should require an extra toilet break that might wipe out their wafer-thin profit margins.'[9] China today, South Korea in the 1970s, and nineteenth-century England have all exploited labour to establish mass clothing production, which contributed to economic growth and aided economic diversification and development. Many African countries also attempted to use clothing industries and other labour-intensive manufacturing activities to spur economic expansion in the last half century, but usually they tried to follow a different path, which has not led to industrial development. The reasons behind this failure, as well as some of the local-scale impacts of Chinese engagement in African clothing industries, are explored in the rest of this chapter.

AFRICAN ATTEMPTS AT INDUSTRIAL MODERNIZATION

Newly independent states across Africa in the 1960s and 1970s anticipated that once free from colonialism they would be able to develop and modernize their economies. Foremost among their independence strategies was the development of basic industries such as agricultural processing plants, furniture manufacturing and clothing factories. Following economic theories drawing upon the experiences of Europe and America, and both the Industrial Revolution and Fordism, modern clothing production was believed to offer an engine for economic growth and social transformation. Across Africa, small and fragile infant clothing sectors were nurtured and new factories established to produce clothing for national markets as well as exports. Kenya built a large clothing sector in the 1960s under an import substitution industrial strategy; Nigerian clothing manufacturing employed 200,000 workers at its peak;[10] Zambia had over 25,000 workers in the 1980s, including in the important factory Zambia–China Mulungushi Textiles (ZCMT).

In the 1960s, China also began to establish links with Africa, at a time when, under Chairman Mao, Beijing was committed to spreading communist ideology. The zenith of this early era of cooperation was the massive Tanzania–Zambia railway (TAZARA) linking the Zambian copperbelt to Dar es Salaam in Tanzania, built with Chinese aid.[11] China also supported the development of integrated cotton and clothing production programmes in eight countries, each of which employed thousands of workers.[12] One of these was the Mulungushi textile factory, constructed between 1977 and 1981. The project included support for small-holder farmers and involved a fully integrated chain of clothing production, from cotton growing to ginning, spinning, weaving, sewing and design. Although associated with China since its inception, ZCMT originally operated from 1982 until 1996 as a Zambian state-owned enterprise. It was the largest textile factory in Zambia and, alongside nationalized copper mines, was an icon of modern industrial development.

In the post-independence era, Zambia was a model for African development, moving towards economic and political independence through industrialization and attempting to track the pathway and approaches employed by the global North. Zambian state-owned corporations reflected the government's developmental philosophy. Workers principally in the mining sector, but also those at Mulungushi Textiles, received relatively high wages, and there was a 'cradle to grave' welfare policy which supported employees and dependants with housing, education and health care.[13] The pattern of production was similar to the Fordist model of industrial development found in European and North American clothing factories in the 1950s and 1960s. This institutional pattern brought economic growth to the advanced capitalist countries in the post-war boom, in the period before the rise of competition from East Asia and China, and provided a model for labour regimes in Zambian state-owned industries.[14] From 1982 to the early 1990s the 'Fordist' jobs at Mulungushi provided secure employment, company housing and medical care. Social benefits were as much a part of the factory's industrial landscape as the clatter of weaving machines and the rolls of colourful African fabrics which emerged from the production lines. Industrial work at ZCMT conferred respect and even prestige. The predominately male industrial workers anticipated progressing towards a 'modern' life.

Zambia, alongside other African countries such as Kenya and Ghana, attempted to follow a different development model to that of China's low wage levels and exploitation of labour. So why did Zambia try to introduce a 'high' wage regime? There are two possible explanations. The first is that Zambians were altruistic. Unlike English Victorian textile mill owners, or 1970s South Korean industrialists, or today's Chinese factory managers Zambian bosses do not want to have an inherently exploitative and cruel relationship with labour. This theory provides an intuitive explanation: evil managers treat workers badly. However, this answer vilifies culture and does not explain the structural role of capitalism in reducing labour to an exploitable commodity. Bad Korean, Chinese or English managers have treated their workers poorly, but so have Zambians at other times. Management is only the immediate conduit for oppression; it is capitalist social relations which enable labour exploitation. Ultimately it is unbridled market forces and not innate human cruelty that treats people like machines and drives the value of labour power down to a minimum.

The second explanation is to consider the advantages for capital of *not* exploiting labour. First, high wages in Fordist production systems have to be put into perspective: they are relative and not solely altruistic. The perceived 'high' level of wages rests on socially constructed expectations; workers may feel they enjoy a good standard of living, but this is a standard of living the management thinks is most appropriate at that particular moment.[15] Among Ford's key management principles were ensuring a stable family life for workers and fostering a consumer class. Second, 'high' wages and social welfare are instruments used to select and maintain the skilled labour suited to a particular system. Workers who are compliant in industrial practices are content and efficient. High wage and welfare benefits ensure the workers are healthy, well fed and turn up to work on time. However, on a global scale the use of Fordist production approaches in clothing industries was becoming increasingly uncompetitive by the 1980s and 1990s. High production costs in Europe, North America and Africa were undercut by cheap manufacturing in China and elsewhere. At the same time Zambia and other African economies underwent economic liberalization, which transformed their labour practices and exposed their industries to increased domestic competition and reduced the local market for clothing.

In Zambia the experiment with Fordist-style modernization broke down during a period of national economic crisis in the late 1980s and early 1990s.

Mines and other state enterprises were privatized. Casualization became a feature of employment. Salaries decreased under casual conditions and other costs such as health care were avoided when economic liberalization was promoted under SAPs.[16] The Mulungushi clothing factory was beset by financial difficulties, including increased competition, and began to decline from the early 1990s; it was first forced to close in 1996. The failure of clothing factories was not a specifically Zambian problem, but was a process sadly repeated across Africa textile industries in the 1980s and 1990s. The decline of clothing industries across Africa was shaped by the continent's neoliberal transformation. As African countries accumulated debts in the 1980s and were forced to implement SAPs, a new political economy orthodoxy spread across the continent. Governments had to adopt a model based on laissez-faire free-market economics. Within this neoliberal model industrial development was only presumed to be possible by reducing state control and liberalizing markets. In reality these structural changes actually disadvantaged most African clothing manufacturers as governments were no longer able to protect textile factories and thus local markets contracted. For example, in South Africa the clothing industry declined as local retailers took advantage of market liberalization under the ANC government after 1994 and sourced clothing from Chinese and other Asian producers.[17] In Kenya, clothing manufacturers faced weak markets in towns and cities due to declining urban incomes.[18] Across Africa reduced demand for locally manufactured new clothing in the 1990s was combined with competition from more affordable new, but also importantly used, clothing (explored in the next chapter). Since the implementation of economic liberalization policies in the 1980s and 1990s, the predominant trend has been decline within the African clothing industry. In Ghana textile and clothing employment fell by 80 per cent from 1975 to 2000; in Zambia it went down from 25,000 to below 10,000 in 2002; and Nigeria's 200,000-person workforce all but disappeared.[19]

CHINA'S NEW INVESTMENTS IN AFRICA

Economic liberalization transformed African economies and opened them up to new investment opportunities for foreign capital. In the late 1990s and early 2000s Chinese engagement in Africa began to grow and has rapidly become a major area of interest for policymakers, journalists and scholars. Investment from China has led to new exploitation of natural resources, such as Zambian copper and Sudanese oil, and Chinese aid has built Mozambique's new national football stadium and Malawi's parliament building. Foreign direct investment and trade between Africa and China have grown tremendously; however, many have questioned Chinese methods in this new era of engagement in Africa.[20] Research has focused on the continental level; many authors have rushed to make bold statements about the impacts of Chinese investment in Africa, as if 'China' and 'Africa' could be reduced to single homogeneous cultural entities. African populations have diverse perceptions of Chinese investment, but many populist media and NGO reports, in both the global North and Africa, contain negative portrayals of Chinese people in Africa, which often appear to be unsophisticated or even xenophobic 'China bashing'.[21] Western critiques of Chinese corporations, over issues such as human rights, may conceal anger at the comparative economic advantage they frequently enjoy over their Western counterparts.[22] Attention has also focused on controversies surrounding natural resource extraction and workers' safety. In Zambia, two major incidents at the Chinese-owned Chambishi Copper Mines stand out: an accident in 2005 that led to 52 workers losing their lives; and a wildcat strike the following year, during which two protestors were shot dead.[23]

As part of the opening up of African economies Chinese and other Asian investors began to enter the clothing sector. Incentives were provided by the Chinese state, which encouraged clothing firms to expand overseas as part of a 'going global' initiative.[24] Furthermore, trade rules were evolving that provided new catalysts for expanding export-orientated clothing manufacturing in Africa. The MFA had been developed in response to competition from Asian manufacturers and quotas, but prior to 2005 special trade preferences were given to Africa through the EU Lomé arrangement and the USA's African Growth and Opportunity Act (AGOA), which gave African clothing products tariff-free access to the global North.[25] Chinese companies invested in at least 58 clothing manufacturers between 1979 and 2000, including four of the major programmes established in the previous era of Chinese engagement in Africa. In Guinea, Uganda, Mali, Mauritius and Niger, and elsewhere across Africa, Chinese firms formed new ventures and invested in privatized factories and textile mills.[26] Alongside Chinese companies other new East Asian investors arrived, including ethnic Chinese from Taiwan and Hong Kong, in Madagascar, Mauritius, Lesotho, Swaziland and South Africa, to take advantage of Africa's special access to European and

American markets. One area of Chinese investment
was the resurrection of ZCMT. The following in-depth
case study illuminates how Chinese engagement in
ZCMT between 1997 and 2006 both exemplifies the
challenges of establishing clothing production in
Africa and demonstrates the might of Chinese economic power. It also highlights the impact of labour
casualization in global clothing industries.

CASUALIZATION AND LABOUR ABUSES AT
MULUNGUSHI TEXTILES

In 1997 an agreement was reached between the Chinese
and Zambian governments with the Qingdao Textiles
Corporation – a Chinese state-owned enterprise –
providing new investment to rehabilitate the
Mulungushi factory, forming the Zambia–China Mulungushi Textiles Joint Venture Ltd as a company
owned by Qingdao Textiles (66 per cent) and the
Zambian Ministry of Defence (34 per cent). Qingdao
also took complete ownership of a nearby cotton ginnery. Qingdao Textiles hails from Qingdao
city, a centre of intensive clothing manufacturing in
Shandong province on China's eastern seaboard.
For the Zambian government, China's unparalleled
rise in the global economy and leading role in clothing manufacturing gave it credence as a model and

partner for development. Moreover, Chinese investment in Mulungushi had come at a time when other
international investors were reluctant to commit to
the Zambian economy. With Chinese assistance the
Mulungushi factory's machinery began to spin and
weave once again, producing 17 million metres of fabric, and sewing 100,000 items of clothing a year for
domestic consumption and export.[27] However, struggles between workers and the Chinese management,
along with competition from international clothing
and textile sources, rendered the business unsustainable and the plant closed again in 2006.

Qingdao's investment in Mulungushi was wel-
comed in 1997. The arrival of Qingdao offered a fresh
opportunity for development. Thomas Muwowo, secretary of the Kabwe Chamber of Commerce (KCC),
commented: 'We are very impressed with the Chinese
investment. We need it. We have no option if this town
is to survive.'[28] There was optimism among employees at Mulungushi, who were 'excited', 'grateful' and
'very happy'.[29] People were desperate for gainful
modern formal employment, including salaries and
working conditions similar to those experienced in
the previous era of Zambian management. However,
the Chinese investors did not live up to expectations:
as a weaving machine operator observed, 'the way

we were seeing there'd be a future, but what happened is a hell'.

In industrial societies the workers in clothing factories are split into two social groups: managers and the managed. At Mulungushi the division was not based merely on this dimension of the organizational structure, but also on race and culture, as Chinese people constituted a specialist management class. The management regime adopted by differing cultural groups can be influenced by the wider institutional patterns prevalent in the given society.[30] Chinese managers organized work in a radically different way to their Zambian predecessors and were influenced by the evolution of the Chinese economy and society. In her case study of clothing factories in Tanzania, C.K. Lee discusses how Chinese managers had been influenced by reforms to socialist models in China, which saw changes to the labour regime, including the casualization and strict disciplining of workplaces in centres like Qingdao. These labour reforms, rather than welfare policies combined with a high-wage model, are subsequently seen as the key to running an efficient capitalist enterprise and a prerequisite for the development of profitable clothing businesses. Lee also records how the Chinese managers to whom she spoke believe workers must make sacrifices for the sake of national economic take-off and industrial development.[31]

Qingdao Textiles transformed the social organization of the Mulungushi factory, which involved implementing new work patterns, casualizing and disciplining the workforce, and allowing safety standards to decline. Chinese management changed the way long-serving labour experienced the factory environment, and introduced a new group of industrial workers to oppressive and exploitative employment conditions. The workforce expanded from approximately 600 (pre-1997 under Zambian management) to between 1,200 and 1,800 employees and workers were divided into 'permanent' and 'casual' categories. In 1997, 600–700 mainly long-serving, skilled former Mulungushi Textiles employees were rehired on permanent terms; alongside them approximately 1,000 new workers were employed on a casual basis. There was a large difference between the monthly pay of casual (K60,000–120,000 ($16–33)) and permanent (K180,000–350,000 ($50–97)) workers. Furthermore, most permanent employees also had housing provided.

Casual conditions of employment are common throughout clothing industries in the global South. Employers pay low wages and do not provide social welfare benefits in recognition of workers' basic rights. Casual workers at ZCMT lost money for days taken off for illness and could be fired without notice for not reporting for work, or indeed for getting pregnant. Similar conditions of employment are prevalent in factories in China.[32] ZCMT employees spent up to ten years working on casual terms, even though, legally, after six months they should have been granted permanent status.[33] Casual workers found their wages were not enough to maintain a livelihood: 'the salary, it was too low for us to sustain our working ... It was like slavery. It was just survival of the fittest ... In Zambia there is unemployment. If you left this job you would not get work elsewhere, that's why you would keep doing this work.'

Complaints about low wage levels were not confined to casual workers; permanent employees were also very unhappy, as an office secretary commented: 'No, it [the pay] was very little compared to the work I was doing.' The wages paid to both casual and permanent employees were well below those required to support basic needs in Zambia. Employees could not properly provide for their families; the wages were therefore just part of a household's livelihood survival strategy. The capitalist mode drives wages down to, and even below, the subsistence level.

Work in clothing factories in the global South thus often does not provide sufficient income for people to support dependants.[34] Employees at ZCMT would seek alternative means to supplement their wages, such as taking on other paid work outside of the factory or selling goods.

Companies form and tailor a labour force according to their own requirements.[35] For the Qingdao Textile Corporation, new to Zambia, the Mulungushi factory was an opportunity for expansion, a spatial fix and further capital accumulation. Qingdao's managers would have been influenced by their experiences of employing casual labour in China and knew the advantages of a large low-skilled and low-paid workforce in the labour-intensive textile industry, and therefore did not subscribe to the Zambian vision of a modern Fordist industrial society. The workforce at ZCMT became increasing casualized between 1997 and 2006 as the Chinese managers gradually retrenched permanent employees, putting great pressure on workers' and their dependants' livelihoods. Working in the clothing factory in the 1980s had been something to be proud of, but it was now a cause of shame, as a young worker recalls: 'I would even hide it [the job at Mulungushi] from my friends.'

DISCIPLINE AND PROFIT

Changes to the work patterns at Mulungushi involved more than lower wages and casualization; they included increased discipline and surveillance, new shift patterns, a greater degree of target setting and reduced safety standards. Chinese managers changed behaviour to increase profits at ZCMT. Employees were closely supervised and movement severely restricted. Most workers were casual machine operators toiling on ranks of weaving and spinning machinery, performing low-skilled and highly repetitive jobs to produce rolls of textiles. They were not allowed to talk or stand up and had to get permission to visit the toilet. Some felt they were treated as 'schoolchildren' or even 'slaves'. Strict workplace disciplining enforces respect for regulations and increases speed and output, generating greater profit. The automation of machinery was used to dictate work patterns: 'The work was very hard'; 'It was difficult to cope with the machines'; employees worked 'under pressure' and often 'the [targets] margins were too wide'. A production supervisor discussed how automation acted on workers' minds and bodies, as control over them became inscribed in the mechanics of the productive process itself: 'When you work for the Chinese you become like a machine.

You can't take a rest. Only when the machine has [a] fault can you take a break.' The Chinese management ran the factory 24 hours a day, with three consecutive eight-hour shifts. At the end of each six-day working week, machine-operating employees would swap shifts, which was very unpopular. Keeping the machines running constantly dictated the rhythm of workers' lives. The company would lose money when the machines were not working; therefore the shift system increased the rate at which clothing products were manufactured as well as putting greater strain on impoverished workers.

Workers were further exploited through an unsafe working environment, operating machines without adequate safety equipment and training. Industrial accidents caused injury and disability, and ruined future livelihoods. A casual machine operator who lost his lower right forearm in a machinery accident was interviewed:

I was involved in an industrial accident. [After the accident] the Chinese visited the hospital and made some promises to ensure my wellbeing … Unfortunately after I was discharged it was a different story … The management at the company contrived with the hospital to destroy or hide the

file ... Without this information it is very difficult ... for me to be compensated in the future ...
maybe the company wanted to run away from its
responsibilities.

After the accident this worker was re-employed and
continued to receive casual wages and have his medical
treatment paid, but he never received any compensa-
tion payment. Horrific injuries were common and
other ex-employees have also been left maimed.

Global competition in the clothing sector leads to a
continuous downward spiral in conditions of work.[36]
Chinese managers, having introduced labour reform
in their own textile and clothing industries, spread
the ideas of neoliberal globalization and introduced
the new harsh working regime to Africa.[37] Labour
exploitation enabled them to extract more surplus
value from the workforce. In the Chinese production
system the maintenance of a productive workforce
at ZCMT did not hinge on the physical condition of
individual labourers, and in a context of high unemployment and weak legal protection incapacitated
or unproductive workers could readily be replaced.
To expand production and suppress costs, Chinese
management drew upon prior experiences with
Qingdao Textiles in eastern China. Hence a Chinese

manager in a textile factory in Tanzania thought African workers had a 'backward' work ethic and believed they were unwilling to make sacrifices to break out of poverty – suggesting the racial stereo-typing of Africans.[38]

Qingdao's investment failed to lift Zambians out of poverty; the Chinese employees, who lived in an isolated compound in Kabwe, became categorized as 'bad' and 'racist'. Workers complained that the Chinese management were 'not proper investors' and that 'they should go back to their own land'. Zambians were used to a less disciplined organization of labour and became discontented; they articulated this as a dislike of Chinese people. The anger felt by ZCMT workers may have been greater than equiva-lent groups of workers in China who grew up under the CPC. Differing social experiences can influence whether cultural groups are satisfied or dissatisfied with a particular work process and organizational structure.[39]

The negative views of Zambian workers towards the Chinese were produced as a consequence of ZCMT's organizational structure. The tense Chinese–Zambian racial division at Mulungushi may appear superficially to be an entrenched difference, but the racial schism was socially produced. As fabrics were woven and cloth sewn together, understandings of racial and cultural difference were also manufactured at Mulungushi. It was a function of the social and economic relations that marked the work experience. Similar patterns have been found with Chinese and Taiwanese managers in South Africa and in Tanzania.[40] As C.K. Lee explains,

> [Chinese managers] have come to Africa with life long experience in state owned enterprises, and have now basically rejected the socialist firm as a viable form for economic development. They often attribute China's lift from backwardness and poverty to its abandonment of the iron rice bowl mentality and practice [a social safety net]. They demand of their African workers the same work ethics and sacrifice they believed have allowed the Chinese to develop, and have yet to be found among the African workforce.[41]

China has followed a model of rampant capitalist development dependent on the exploitation of labour. This world-view is not confined to the Chinese of course; it has become the globally dominant ideology and is found throughout the clothing manufacturing sector in the global South today.

LABOUR DISCONTENT AND THE CLOSURE OF
MULUNGUSHI TEXTILES

Workers organized collectively to struggle against their ill-treatment by the Chinese management at Mulungushi. Although permanent employees were formally represented by the Zambia–China Mulungushi Textiles Union, it failed to negotiate improvements in pay and conditions. Casual workers attempted to negotiate directly with Chinese managers. Workers complained that labour leaders were intimidated during negotiations and ineffective, so the workforce took part in strikes 'every year'. Up until 2006, these sporadic labour disputes had little impact, as one disillusioned ex-union member explains: 'There was a strike; we really fought hard to rectify the problems. Nothing happened.' Employees were unable to challenge the management regime forcibly and the pressure to maintain a livelihood compelled them to resume work. This type of dispute is not unique to Zambia; in Lesotho and South Africa workers have struck over wages and working conditions in Taiwanese-managed textile factories.[42] Serious labour disputes erupted at ZCMT when the state introduced a national minimum wage in June 2006, requiring all employers to pay at least K268,000 ($74) a month,[43] which ZCMT refused to pay. Workers now had a new incentive to strike aggressively against labour practices legally recognized as exploitative. Violent disputes broke out and strikers blocked the main highway outside the factory, throwing petrol bombs from the barricade. There were pitched battles with police, as a former casual worker explains: 'We had made [a larger strike]. It was broken up by the police. They came with tear gas when we organized that strike.' Protests extended beyond complaining about the Chinese management to directing anger towards the perceived failings of the Zambian state and politicians. The factory became increasingly crisis-ridden. Mulungushi ceased production in December 2006.

The closure of Mulungushi was likely due to a combination of factors: market forces, financial difficulties, the pressure for a higher level of wages and the violent discontent of workers. Trade agreements such as AGOA also began to expire in 2005 as the MFA drew to a close, exposing African production to competition from cheaper imported, particularly Chinese, clothing in both home and foreign markets. This had a disastrous effect on textile production across Africa, spreading further crises.[44] The macroeconomic climate made ZCMT uncompetitive, although the ex-workers believed the factory 'made a lot of profit' and that it was '[t]he strike [that] led to it shutting down'.

In contrast Che Ming, the Chinese managing director, is reported to have said that ZCMT had problems paying the minimum wage of K268,000 and that it was this that led to the closure in January 2007.[45] Many ex-employees have since struggled to find formal employment, and hence to sustain their livelihoods; yet others have managed to secure alternative means of subsistence and even found that life is better, feeling a sense of liberation from exploitation, with one remarking that 'It is very different. I'm free now. I was suffering too much.'

Zambians' experiences of working for Chinese managers at ZCMT left them deeply dissatisfied with their encounters with an exploitative employer. In simple terms Mulungushi may not have been able to compete in the global clothing sector and pay workers adequate wages in a liberal free-market economy. The production costs for ZCMT are not accessible, but evidence from Lesotho compares the costs of manufacturing jeans in sub-Saharan Africa and in China. For jeans that would retail in the USA for $20–40, the cost for fabric, buttons, zippers, denim wash and finishing, overheads and labour, and excluding any duties and freight, has been calculated as $7.49 for Lesotho compared to $6.51 for China; however, when current duties (at 16.08 per cent for China) and freight costs (similar for both countries) are factored in, the bottom line is that the 'total landed cost' is very similar for Lesothan ($7.78) and Chinese ($7.84) jeans.[46] These figures are only a rough approximation, and costs in Zambia may be very different, but they at least illustrate that African production may be competitive, although throughout the fast-fashion supply chain firms do relentlessly squeeze margins to maximize profit. Firms in the clothing sector continue to seek out the lowest cost locations for production possible.

Peter Gibbon, who has written extensively on the African clothing sector, has posed the question, 'Does it make sense to demand wage levels whose implementation, given local capabilities and distance to market, would probably lead to a shift of orders to lower-cost locations?'[47] From the perspective of businesses and policymakers operating within the rules of contemporary capitalism, the only logical response would appear to be 'no', but really the answer is immaterial. Gibbon's question recognizes that businesses will take advantage of a spatial fix when faced by the challenge of increased salaries. Instead of debating the consequences of wage suppression for one set of clothing workers (such as those from Mulungushi) compared to those in another location (be it eastern China or elsewhere) in a temporary stalling of a race to the bottom for labour standards, the problem of the uneven development of capitalism needs to be confronted. The immensity of this challenge and the alternatives to labour exploitation are discussed in the Conclusion. Before reaching that point, the other side to Africa's engagement with the clothing sector, one of the most hidden aspects of the global garment trade, which also affects the competitiveness of clothing industries, is opened up and explored, as the focus shifts from clothing production to the impacts of second-hand clothing consumption in Africa.

SECOND-HAND AFRICA

SUPER BOWL'S OTHER WINNERS

On 2 February 2014 the Denver Broncos and Seattle Seahawks met in New York to contest Super Bowl XLVIII, America's annual football spectacular. This Super Bowl was special. It was a long-awaited appearance at the Big Apple, and as the first ever played in an outdoor, cold-weather location the game was being called the 'Ice Bowl' ahead of the biggest weekend in the US sporting calendar. In the end temperatures were not as freezing as expected, yet more surprisingly the Seahawks, against all expectations, defeated the Broncos 43–8 in the largest margin of victory in a Super Bowl for 21 years. Millions were glued to the most watched programme in US television history. Jubilant quarterback Russell Wilson lifted the Vince Lombardi Trophy up high to the crowd as confetti fell all around him, wearing a 'Seattle Seahawks Super

Bowl Champions' T-shirt. Banners, caps, sweatshirts and other merchandise were ready and waiting for Wilson's teammates and the Seattle fans.[1] Tens of thousands of souvenirs were sold in the following days. But what would have happened if the Broncos had lived up to the expectations of millions and won Super Bowl XLVIII? Surely there were celebratory T-shirts awaiting them too? So, what became of all that unwanted gear?

Every year a large surplus of unwanted championship merchandise is produced. National Football League (NFL) rules bar the sale of losing Super Bowl apparel in the United States. Rather than destroying the merchandise, the evangelical Christian charity World Vision, which has operated in partnership with the NFL for 17 years, accepts all the losers' championship clothing, which it freely distributes overseas. In 2013 over 100,000 items from losing finalists the San Francisco 49ers were donated, for which the NFL got a hefty tax deduction. Similar arrangements exist with Major League Baseball, the NBA (basketball) and the NHL (ice hockey). For example, in 2010 defeated Indianapolis Colts shirts were supplied to Haiti; in 2008 Pittsburgh Steelers jerseys went to Armenia, Nicaragua, Romania and Zambia; and in 2007 Chicago Bears caps went to Chad and Romania.

Alongside other companies, NFL gifts in kind distributed by World Vision have apparently been worth in excess of a scarcely believable $1.1 billion.[2] Promotional images show grateful Africans and other poor people proudly wearing counter-factual champions' clothing. Stories periodically appear in the mainstream media such as Bloomberg, CNN, ESPN, the Huffington Post and *Time* magazine; indeed the Super Bowl donations receive more publicity than any other story relating to unwanted or second-hand clothes in the USA. In the post-Super Bowl hubris they make for a diverting human interest feature and generally provide positive publicity for the NFL and World Vision.[3] Sometimes commentators engage with the subject critically, questioning if the donations are really 'bad aid', as these clothing items are all readily available in the countries that receive donations. The argument follows that gifts undermine local clothing markets and contribute to forging relationships of dependence, depriving poor people of work and dignity. Alternatively these overvalued donations are viewed as a curious public relations sidebar and tax dodge, which accompanies the carnival of excess consumption (clothing, drink, food, multimillion-dollar commercials, etc.) that Super Bowl represents. The donation of unwanted sporting goods is really just the barely visible tip of the iceberg of a much more widespread commercial trade of unwanted clothing sold from the global North to the global South. World Vision intends to donate all the sporting goods, but inevitably some is resold by recipients who would rather have cash than clothing. Most receiving countries already have established second-hand clothing marketplaces and the donation of unwanted championship sports apparel is not normal. The Super Bowl story provides a diverting curiosity which belies the much larger hidden for-profit second-hand clothing trade. The NFL/World Vision system of provision is comparatively small scale; yet it does play an important role in legitimizing the broader culture of donating second-hand clothing. In the main Americans as well as Europeans unquestioningly accept that it can only bring benefits to poor people in the global South, which reinforces the popular idea that clothing donations must be doing good. The reality, though, is not so straightforward.

SECOND-HAND CLOTHES IN AFRICA

Sub-Saharan Africa became one of the major marketplaces for second-hand clothing imports in the 1980s. As the previous chapters have demonstrated, weak domestic clothing industries lost protection as economic liberalization was introduced via IMF- and World Bank-sponsored structural adjustment programmes. As incomes declined, the availability of cheap used clothing provided relief from price inflation for the poor. Imported used clothing, as well as cheaper new garments and textiles from East Asia, outcompeted locally produced goods while factories closed across the continent. Money previously spent on domestically produced goods was diverted to purchases of imported clothing, and profits flowed out of African economies to the commercial exporters and charities operating in the global North as well as Chinese and other Asian manufacturers. Used clothing provides the major source of garments in many African nations, for example accounting for 81 per cent of clothing purchases in Uganda.[4] The trade is important in most of Africa, including Kenya, Malawi, Mozambique, Nigeria, Rwanda, Senegal, Swaziland, Tanzania, Zambia and Zimbabwe.[5] However, it is a much smaller proportion of the market in South Africa, Africa's most industrialized economy, where imports have been restricted.[6]

From thriving West African coastal cities like Accra (Ghana) which capitalize on the transatlantic trade, to depressed rural areas such as the inflation-hit highlands of Zimbabwe, the economic and social impacts of second-hand clothing imports have been felt across the continent. Different groups of Africans, including second-hand clothing traders, textile workers and impoverished consumers, have had varied experiences, but their individual interests should not be considered in isolation. Some people have gained, others have lost. The argument is frequently made by charities and trading companies that second-hand imports provide jobs and are promoted as a positive activity. Some people do work selling second-hand clothes but separating the winners and losers among the poor gives a fragmented view of society and can embed the view that inequality and uneven development are somehow inevitable. For instance, while African market traders may gain, at the same time clothing factories have closed and factory workers have lost their jobs. Analysis of the second-hand trade must be linked to a discussion of industrial decline and clothing culture in Africa.

Vast container ships ply the Atlantic and Indian Oceans filled with mixed cargos, including thousands of tonnes of used clothes bound for African ports such as Abidjan, Cotonou, Dakar, Dar es Salaam and Maputo. Export destinations are influenced by the cheapest shipping routes to available markets and depend on existing trade geographies (see Table 3,

p. 187, for examples from around the world). Used clothing is often exported as return cargo in otherwise empty vessels, which have brought valuable primary products such as coffee or hardwood timber from Africa to the global North; as part of triangular trade patterns; and as mark-up cargo (additional cargo added to fill excess capacity and charged at a lower cost). Containers heading for Africa can transit via global hubs such as Dubai or export-processing zones in India, which conceal their final destination from exporters, as well as their origin from consumers.[7]

Transport geographies are influential in forming trade patterns, but markets are also determined by economic and political factors. Charities and companies in the used-clothing trade need to be constantly adapting, as African markets are very volatile. For instance, in the 1990s in Rwanda and Zaire (Democratic Republic of Congo, DRC) civil unrest and warfare disrupted business, impacting on the second-hand clothing trade.[8] The degree of protection or other import restrictions can also change rapidly. For example, due to market instability and changing regulations, Oxfam switched exports of used clothing from East to West Africa. Fluctuating geographies are difficult to map, especially as official trade statistics have many missing records or inaccuracies. The used-clothing system of provision is a shifting *process*, rather than a *structure*. Firms and charities respond to changing conditions. The importance of African markets shifts, and they become more or less profitable. However, across Africa demand usually exceeds supply. American and European exporters look for the best market and switch trade routes to make more money. As the British exporter Intercontinental Clothing explains: 'it is certainly not competitive as far as selling is concerned because you always have (if you are any good) more customers than you can supply.'[9]

Evidence from different African markets shows that people often do not know the origin of second-hand clothes. Used-clothing vendors in Soweto market, Lusaka, Zambia were confused as to where old clothes came from. They believed the garments were German when the clothes were recognizably – through the names of brands and logos – items from Britain.[10] In Maputo several vendors at Xipamanine market thought used clothing came directly from China, because of the 'made in China' labelling. Market traders knew the clothes had been previously worn, but were unaware that they came from Canada or the United States. Throughout Africa used clothes are given different labels and names in various languages, which pertain to their ambiguous identity.

In Zambia used clothing is *salaula*, a Bemba word meaning 'selecting from a pile in the manner of rummaging'.[11] In Lagos, Nigeria second-hand clothing is named *okirika* after a colonial port as well as 'London clothes' and 'bend down boutique';[12] in Congo-Brazzaville it is *sola*, 'to choose';[13] in Zimbabwe the term used is *mupedzanhamo*, 'where all problems end'; in Kenya *mitumba*,[14] a Swahili term meaning 'bundles' is widely used and in Tanzania they are *kafa ulaya*, 'the clothes of the dead whites'. All these names conceal or obscure the true heritage of the clothes. It is not surprising that vendors do not know clothes' origins, given the difficulty in accurately mapping trade patterns. Tracing where clothing comes from and how it gets to market is methodologically challenging for any researcher.

In 2004 the journey of a single blouse was followed from the UK to Zambia; although this example is anecdotal and the tracing of the journey of one item difficult to replicate, this case study is illustrative of international trade routes. The blouse was first donated at a Scope (the organization for people with cerebral palsy) clothing bank in a supermarket car park in Ashby-de-la-Zouch, Leicestershire. The bank was owned by Ragtex UK, which collects about 95 tonnes of clothes a week from around 200 recycling banks in the Leicester area. Ragtex donates £100 ($167) a year per licensed bank to Scope for the use of their name. It also collects for other charities (including Rainbow Hospice, mentioned in Chapter 3). Scope likewise works with other companies.[15] The blouse went to Ragtex's textile recycling plant in Leicester and was packed into a 45 kg bale containing similar blouses; it was then loaded onto a Maersk shipping container and exported aboard the *Sealand Michigan* to Beira, Mozambique. In Beira port the container spent a week in customs before being taken by road to Chipata in Zambia. The bale was then acquired by Khalid, an Indian clothing wholesaler who is one of around a hundred merchants in Chipata who come from the same part of Gujarat. Khalid buys 20 container-loads of clothing a year and then sells the bales of clothing on to small traders. The bale containing the blouse was finally purchased by Mary, a Zambian market vendor, and sold in the open-air Kapata market in Chipata.

This example illustrates the multiple actors involved in this system of provision, with different cultural heritages, trading specialisms and financial resources including: Scope (a UK disability charity), Ragtex (a long-established British rag merchant), Khalid (an Indian expatriate wholesaler), Mary (a Zambian market trader), along with the transport operators (including the American-owned Maersk container and *Sealand Michigan*, a vessel from the same fleet as the MV *Maersk Alabama*, the hijacked ship famous for the heroics of Captain Phillips). Auditing the economic and social impact of the donation of this blouse or other clothing items is incredibly challenging. This donated blouse was likely combined with both other charity donations and non-charitable collections. The blouse could even have been mixed in with illegally acquired clothing, as Ragtex has been prosecuted by North West Leicestershire District Council after carrying out house-to-house collections without a licence.[16] A clothing item donated at another time to a different Scope bank could have followed a completely different route to its final market. A multitude of different counter-factual pathways can be imagined. This type of network has little coordination, and frequently retailers – like Mary in Zambia – have little information about where the bale of second-hand clothing comes from or what quality of clothing it contains, which creates problems for those at the end of the supply chain.[17]

USED-CLOTHING ASSIGNMENTS

Clothes which sell well in Africa include women's light short-sleeved cotton tops, men's rugged cargo shorts and colourful children's T-shirts – apparel that suits the predominantly tropical climate and a youthful population, garments that are hard-wearing and well made, but also have some appeal to local fashion. Such desirable goods are not always in ready supply. One factor which determines profit is the make-up of cargo assignments. African clients have to accept a mixed packing list of different categories of 45 kg clothing bales in container shipments.[18] They are not permitted to select the items they would prefer. For instance, a batch might contain, say, desirable warm-weather items such as T-shirts and shorts, as well as less popular heavy coats and suits. Notably, undesirable used curtains, overcoats and nightgowns sell for low prices in Mozambique, Kenya, Malawi and Zambia. The market conditions, where demand normally exceeds supply, are taken advantage of by organizations like Oxfam, the Salvation Army and Ragtex, enabling them to profit from less desirable bulky cold weather and unfashionable items and accumulate a greater total income. Controlling the packing list allows suppliers to maximize profitability and demonstrates how exporters in the global North have power over their customers in the global South. Additional money is made from passing on inferior stock, which includes unpopular items as well as lower-quality, torn and soiled clothing. As Simone Field, who carried out research in Britain, found, because 'of the high returns from quality clothing and the limited availability of high quality donations in the UK, it is common for textile merchants to include a small proportion of low-grade clothing into a higher-grade category in order to maximize profit'.[19] Furthermore, the exporter Intercontinental Clothing stated that 'If you do the grading properly (like we do) then there is not vast profits. Whereas if you put things in that people will just about accept without complaint then there is more money to be made and obviously you get a lot more for it.'[20] Business strategies in the global North increase the profitability of exports, but reduce the opportunities for African companies to accumulate capital from the import and sale of second-hand clothing.

Olumide Abimbola has extensively researched the second-hand clothing trade between the UK and West Africa. He argues that, in general, there is 'information asymmetry' between exporters and final retailers, but some systems of provision are more coordinated. Igbo apprentices from West Africa who serve importers based in Benin work in many British second-hand clothing firms to assist the sorting of second-hand clothing. They create 'standardized goods' for export:

Large-scale importers of second-hand clothing send an apprentice to the British exporting company, where the apprentice would act as a quality assurance person. He makes sure that what is sent to the West African market is what the people would buy. At the same time, he also helps his boss overcome the information asymmetry problem that is stacked against him by inspecting what is actually exported to him.[21]

This arrangement is mutually beneficial. Exporters utilize the free expert labour of a worker who is aware of the styles and preferences in the African marketplace. Importers maintain a degree of influence over the grading process; the apprentices have the experience of living in the UK and acquire skills and money, which enables some of them to start their own businesses when they later return to West Africa.

The role of Igbo apprentices illustrates how some used-clothing trade networks are highly coordinated and export processing is undertaken for a specific retail market and client. However, this pattern of trade is unusual. Abimbola argues that these relationships are connected to a deeper Igbo culture of apprenticeships. Furthermore, it is not just consumer demand that shapes this system of provision, as the styles of clothing from which the Igbo apprentice select are unwanted donated British clothes. West Africans' influence over provision and their ability to (re)produce desirable second-hand clothing goods is completely dependent on these donations.

Firms require expertise and money to succeed in the competitive world of used-clothes trading. One of the largest private companies in Tanzania, Mohammed Enterprises Tanzania Ltd (MeTL) was an early entrant. MeTL was already established as a manufacturing company producing textiles, clothing, soap and bicycles. The company supplies printed African fabrics to neighbouring parts of East Africa and is the largest textile manufacturer in sub-Saharan Africa.[22] In 1985, following Tanzanian trade liberalization, MeTL met with American used-clothing exporters. Ten years later it had grown to import 4,000 tons (4,064 tonnes) of used clothing per month via Dar es Salaam. MeTL was one of the first businesses in the trade, because it had sufficient funds as well as an existing warehouse and distribution network. There were few barriers to entry for Tanzanians at that time, especially as many had diasporic connections in the United States and Europe who could link MeTL to supplies of used-clothing bales. These cultural networks built trust between suppliers and markets and helped reduce exports of low-quality stock.[23] MeTL is a further example of how second-hand and new-clothing sectors are linked.

The importance of immigrant communities and long-established networks of trust demonstrates how used-clothing systems of provision cannot be explained by a strictly classical economic model of market forces, or the so-called 'invisible hand' of the market. Firms and individuals invest in building relationships and may depend on family or kinship ties rather than just minimizing costs. Neither is there clear correspondence between supply and demand, as sourcing used clothing depends on the uncontrolled donation of unwanted clothing (albeit stimulated, for example by leaflet drops and the positioning of clothing banks). The importance of cultural history, especially the role of charity in encouraging donations, is key to these trade patterns. Trading relationships are built on shared heritage and international relationships, such as the legacy of British–West African colonialism, Igbo traditions of apprenticeship, networks of Tanzanians in America and long-standing Indian trading families in southern Africa. Connections and personal ties can help ensure profitability. Established and embedded networks are difficult to compete with, even for well-funded organizations. This is a challenge that Oxfam found in Senegal.[24] Equally, it is the African market traders who find it hardest to make a living from used clothing. The business environment is competitive, but there is a further issue which impacts profits and trade patterns: the widespread smuggling of second-hand clothing. Nigeria, Africa's most populous and pivotal country, is the epicentre of illegal imports.

NIGERIA: ECONOMIC TURMOIL

It is a cliché of travel writing to call a country 'a land of contrasts'. Everywhere has diversity: people who are richer or poorer as well as cultural differences and social inequalities. Inequality within individual cities can be as great as the divide between rich and poor across the global North and South. In Lagos, Nigeria, there is huge gap between the affluent and the impoverished, who live separate lives in different parts of the city. Victoria Island and Lekki are elite enclaves accessible by bridge from other parts of Lagos; they are frequently guarded by paramilitary checkpoints. Amid the embassies and five-star hotels the mega-rich enjoy luxury hyper-consumption, driving top-of-the-line SUVs with darkened windows, wearing designer labels from Europe and heavy gold jewellery. Many have countless millions hidden away in foreign bank accounts. Across the lagoon in mainland

Lagos poverty is everywhere. Shacks and slums are built alongside the water; people are packed in tightly together and diseases like cholera can spread easily. The iconic image of Lagos is of lines of yellow buses queuing in never-ending tailbacks. Among the disorderly and chaotic streets are hundreds of informal marketplaces selling contraband 'London clothes', second-hand garments coming from the UK and elsewhere in Europe and America. Traders make a living selling to the poor, and hawkers take advantage of the long traffic queues, carrying loads atop their heads and trying to tempt passengers with their wares. Walking past a luxury Jeep or Range Rover in a traffic jam is as close as they are ever likely to get to the super-rich lifestyle.[25]

Wealth in Nigeria comes directly or indirectly from the vast oil reserves, which have been pumped out of the Niger Delta for five decades and account for 90 per cent of export earnings.[26] Oil wealth has brought little meaningful development to most Nigerians. They are mainly poor consumers who live in poverty and often wear second-hand clothes. Despite economic growth in the last ten years, fuelled by increasing oil prices, the quality of life of the average Nigerian is extremely low. The persistence of underdevelopment in resource-abundant nations, particularly Nigeria and Africa's other 'petro-states', such as Angola, Equatorial Guinea and Gabon, has led to much debate as experts attempt to explain the apparent paradox of the coexistence of fossil fuel wealth and persistent poverty. Evidence suggests that in states with weak institutions and poor financial management the inflow of money from natural resource exports can weaken the state in a number of ways. Oil revenues reduce the impetus for generating domestic taxes, discourage discussion over how revenues are managed, and weaken the 'social contract' – the reciprocal responsibility shared by state and citizens. Government institutions and bureaucracies lack authority, and the absence of reciprocity undermines the rationale for democracy. Control of state power guarantees access to oil wealth; hence Nigeria and other resource-abundant states have moved towards authoritarianism. Budgets are not managed transparently, which enables frivolous spending and the diversion of significant sums into the pockets of members of the political elite.[27] The extent of corruption and of the pilfering of Nigeria's oil wealth is quite staggering, with an estimated \$400 billion 'disappearing' since Nigeria began producing oil in the 1960s.[28]

Oil shapes all economic activity in Nigeria. The state attempted to protect domestic clothing industries by restricting the import of used clothes, but the policies failed; this failure needs to be considered in the context of the oil-dominated economy. In 1989, nearly 96 per cent of tariff lines for textiles and clothing were subject to import-prohibition regimes.[29] These import restrictions were part of a broader effort to promote domestic manufacturing and wean the economy off oil dependency, by following an import substitution approach to industrialization (ISI). Import controls were never implemented effectively due to the weakness of state institutions and the fact that Nigeria is one of the largest markets for second-hand clothing in the world. Imports are partially accounted for in official import statistics: Nigeria ranked number 15 out of 50 African nations in terms of reported used-clothing exports sent from the global North in the 1980s and 1990s, despite the market being officially closed to used-clothing imports during this period.[30] This does not give the full picture, however. A far greater quantity of used clothes are imported than register in official statistics, as the large differences in import policies in neighbouring countries provides an impetus for smuggling. Aloysius Ihezie from Choice Textiles explained that although used clothing has been 'contraband for the last forty years' Nigerian borders are 'porous'; he estimates that '75 to 80 per cent' of the used clothing imported to West Africa is finally retailed in Nigeria.[31]

Several key West African countries import a disproportionately high volume of used clothing relative to the size of their populations. Between 1980 and 2010 the levels of official imports to Nigeria were very low in comparison to Togo and Benin, two much smaller neighbouring countries. Cotonou (Benin) and Lomé (Togo) have no restrictions on used-clothing imports; smuggling across the land borders to Nigeria of second-hand clothing alongside other goods formally banned or heavily taxed is rife. The Beninois economy is dependent on Cotonou acting as an entrepôt for banned and restricted goods entering Nigeria. Trans-border trading communities of Igbo and Abiriban merchants control import routes and their activities oscillate with the strength of Nigerian restrictions.[32] Firms in the global North are complicit in this illegal system of provision as they are fully aware that the mass exports sent elsewhere in West Africa filter through to Nigeria with its huge population of 197 million.

The relative poverty of most Nigerians means they choose to buy illegally imported second-hand clothing rather than locally made clothes. It was the logical response for impoverished people. During the 1980s and 1990s, the Nigerian clothing and textile industry declined dramatically, and Nigerian textile firms continue to fail.[33] For Nigerians, used clothes represented a cheaper alternative to expensive domestically produced garments, even with all the inflated transaction costs associated with smuggling and the bypassing of import tariffs. The Nigerian example shows how an attempt to implement ISI to facilitate economic growth was undermined by widespread illegal trade practices, which illustrates how the second-hand clothing trade has had negative impacts on African development. Fault does not lie just with second-hand clothing traders, as the bans on used-clothing imports were not supported by robust customs controls. Institutions have been weakened and corruption has proliferated in the oil-dominated economy. Former Nigerian president Olusegun Obasanjo even accused the customs service of 'making nonsense of government's import prohibition policy'.[34]

Nigeria is not unique. South Africa, the other major economy in sub-Saharan Africa, has also tried to restrict the import of second-hand clothing to protect domestic industries. South Africa has been more successful than Nigeria, but used-clothing markets can be found in Johannesburg as well as Durban and Nelspruit close to the Mozambican border. South Africans visit market traders in Maputo to buy up used clothes, despite imports being severely restricted by government legislation. Clothing industries have declined in South Africa, although it is also important to note that South African firms have fared poorly primarily due to competition from imported new Asian-produced clothing. Elsewhere, punitive tariffs were imposed in Zimbabwe in 1995 restricting second-hand clothing imports after local textile and clothing manufacturers had lobbied the government. However, widespread illegal informal sourcing processes continued.[35] So-called 'suitcase traders' skip across the border daily between Mozambique and Zimbabwe carrying stock, either masquerading as their own clothes or to which the customs officials turn a blind eye for a few cents. In Kenya Moses Ikiara, executive director of the Kenya Institute for Public Policy Research and Analysis, complained that 'New imported clothing comes in disguised as *mitumba* [used clothing] and it gets into the market, and of course without paying taxes, which makes it a big challenge for domestic textile producers to be able to find a market.'[36]

Customs officials are frequently complicit in smuggling and extract bribes from importers. Corruption is a reality of the socio-political context of many states in Africa, but is also an outcome of opportunities presented by the weakening of African governments in response to structural adjustment and destabilization caused by neo-colonialism. Economic liberalization throughout Africa has tended to accelerate both pilfering of existing state resources and the diversification of the state bureaucrats into private activity, as formerly 'grey' areas of economic life have become seemingly legitimate.[37] There are external costs for others outside such privileged networks. The majority of Africans experience the detrimental impact of circumvented import costs and forgone government revenues, which reduces social expenditure and impacts upon economic policy, such as Nigeria's failure to protect domestic clothing industries. Economic liberalization has not provided opportunities for poor Africans to become entrepreneurs and rise out of poverty; it has instead served the interests of a narrow elite, such as the residents of Victoria Island in Lagos. Most Africans can only dream of economic freedom. The smuggling and corruption further demonstrates how the used-clothing trade is associated with deviant economic activity and continues the long-term connection with criminality. Due to widespread illegal trade, accurate economic modelling of the undocumented trade is very problematic, which contributes to the difficulty of assessing the full impact of second-hand clothing imports on the decline of clothing industries in Africa.

USED-CLOTHING IMPORTS AND THE DECLINE OF AFRICAN CLOTHING INDUSTRIES

Used clothing has outcompeted and displaced African clothing manufacturing in Kenya, Malawi, Mozambique, Tanzania, Zambia and other countries which permitted imports of second-hand clothing, as well as in countries like Nigeria where they are traded illegally. Various African policymakers have accused second-hand clothing importers of 'killing' local textile and garment sectors. A report published by the World Trade Organization assesses the impact:

With the liberalization of the second-hand clothing market, the already deteriorating textiles and clothing industry was severely affected. The garments produced in Malawi have been found to be more expensive than second-hand clothing, and as a result, some of the major factories could not compete with the cheaper prices offered by the second-hand clothing industry and they were forced to close. Initially, the influx of second-hand clothing was seen as 'the best thing that ever happened to Malawi', but the consequences to the clothing industry were devastating.[38]

This argument may have been accurate for Malawi, but the decline of African clothing industries is not just due to second-hand clothing imports; this is too simple an explanation for a complex problem. The ultimate cause of crisis has been economic liberalization; the opening of weak African markets to international competition. The increased import of old clothes from the global North is a key effect of uncontrolled trade. Second-hand clothing is dominant in many African marketplaces, but the reason for the failure of clothing factories was not simply because poor consumers switched from buying more expensive locally made goods to cheap imported second-hand clothing. As the previous chapter demonstrated, African clothing factories faced multiple challenges in the 1980s, 1990s and 2000s. Other factors operated in concert, with the import of second-hand clothing exacerbating the problem. African incomes declined, reducing the poor's purchasing power, which depressed demand. Factories failed when state-owned firms were privatized and suffered from profiteering and poor management.[39]

Weak border controls meant clothes flowed between African countries, increasing competitive pressure for local producers in regional markets. For example, colourful African printed fabric featuring geometric and floral designs is manufactured in Congo (DRC) and Tanzania and exported to neighbouring markets in Mozambique and Zambia. East African printed cloth now competes with cheap textiles from China and India, as well as second-hand clothing. In these instances, imported new clothing may be displacing textiles produced in neighbouring African countries.

Africa's economic liberalization and open borders are part of globalization. Throughout Africa the process of economic and cultural globalization had unpredictable effects. In Mozambique and Zambia shoe-sellers combine imported new counterfeit Adidas, Nike and Reebok sneakers and cheap dress shoes with imported second-hand shoes. The new products can even be deliberately scuffed and tarnished to look like authentic original Nikes imported from North America. Robust shoes in good condition originating from the global North that match international fashions are highly prized and can sell for up to $20, much more than low-quality new imports. Traders mix up the stock to try to conceal the new shoes' heritage and deceive the consumer. The last example shows how individual traders are finding new ways to deal with the challenges of selling used items. More in-depth evidence is needed to illuminate how vendors make a living from this hidden trade network as well as revealing the interconnections with new clothing manufacturing. Research from Mozambique in the next chapter provides insights into how people struggle to survive in the second-hand clothing trade.

PERSISTENT POVERTY

GROWTH WITHOUT DEVELOPMENT IN MOZAMBIQUE

The former Secretary General of the United Nations, Kofi Annan, was one of Africa's most celebrated statesmen. The Ghanaian led the UN between 1997 and 2006, during which time he was a co-recipient of the 2001 Noble Peace Prize. Respected for his even-handed decision-making, Annan was someone who knew African politics; his judgements were carefully considered and rarely controversial. His was one of many voices to have highlighted Mozambique as a shining example for Africa. On a trip to Maputo in 2002 he said that 'Mozambique's continuing success story and the climate of trust it has generated is the best possible antidote to the sceptics and cynics about Africa', celebrating what he saw as development gains made in the decade following the end of the civil war.[1] Since Annan's visit this southern African country has consistently been held up by the main Western donors as one of the continent's major success stories. In 2013, Annan's successor as UN Secretary General, Ban Ki-moon, visited Mozambique and hailed the country as an 'important success story for the global community'.[2] Mozambique was widely championed as an example of a nation that has moved from warfare to peace and stability, as well as from economic stagnation to rapid growth, and is said to have achieved both these goals by following the dual Western policy prescriptions of democracy and pro-market liberal economic reforms.

This all sounds like good news, but if we look more closely at the experiences of most Mozambicans the harsh reality is much more painful; indeed evidence indicates that Annan, Ki-moon and the donors may well be wrong. It is true that the country has been largely peaceful for over 25 years, although there have been recent troubles, and has experienced economic growth, but rather than an ongoing success story Mozambique is a place of persistent poverty where levels of impoverishment rival those of war-torn states. Mozambique has experienced a growing economy without a sustained and meaningful reduction in poverty. What is of further concern is how

Mozambique's recent history is being twisted to support political positions. Annan's argument that this example can counteract cynics and Ki-moon's statement that it represents an 'important success story for the global community' are insightful. These platitudes are for an international audience. Mozambique is held up as a success story to show to other nations because it embraced globalization, adopted the neoliberal development model and is one example that could – it is mistakenly believed – support the market-friendly policies long championed by the global North.[3]

Mozambique has been ruled exclusively by the Frelimo party since gaining independence from Portugal in 1975. Under the charismatic Samora Machel and his comrades, Frelimo led the freedom struggle and later fervently supported Mandela's ANC through the final years of apartheid. Like many of Africa's independence movements, Frelimo was once dedicated to Marxism, a legacy evident in the names of Maputo's avenues: Avenída Vladimir Lenine, Avenída Mao Tse Tung and Avenída Karl Marx. Over four decades Frelimo has faced many challenges, which have made it difficult to steer the nation away from impoverishment and have led many of the party members to abandon their socialist ideology. Throughout the twentieth century

Mozambique's industrial development was aggressively constrained, first by Portuguese colonialism and later by a devastating civil war fuelled by support for insurgents from the white minority regimes in neighbouring Rhodesia (present-day Zimbabwe) and South Africa. Insecurity restricted the emergence of industry, including clothes manufacturing. Mozambique was left desperately poor and severely indebted. Under pressure from the West a World Bank and IMF-inspired structural adjustment programme was implemented in 1987. The country was left as poor as anywhere in the world.

Following the fall of apartheid in South Africa and the subsequent ceasefire in Mozambique, peace was made in 1992, after which Frelimo embraced further free-market reforms under the guidance of donors. Multiple elections have been held since 1994, which Frelimo has dominated. The hard-won peace is something that should be rightly celebrated. However, the country has not been successful in combating poverty. The peace dividend led to growth in the late 1990s and the establishment of an important aluminium processing industry, albeit one which employs few people. Recently, discoveries of coal and gas reserves have fuelled economic expansion, although financial gains are unevenly distributed. Nigeria's experience with oil offers a prescient and cautionary lesson for policymakers. Despite widespread optimism among the international community as well as Frelimo politicians, Mozambique remains one of the poorest countries on earth, as the African Development Bank notes: 'growth has as yet created limited jobs and has had a less-than-desirable impact on poverty reduction.'[4] In the Human Development Index, calculated by the United Nations, Mozambique ranked 180th out of 189 countries in 2019, below barely functioning conflict-ravaged societies such as Afghanistan and Congo. Figures from the World Bank illustrate that since 2003 GDP growth has averaged over 7 per cent per year; meanwhile the percentage of people living below the poverty line was stable at 54 per cent between 2003 and the last survey in 2009. Life expectancy is only 42 years and gross national income per capita is just $501 per year.[5]

In Maputo, the names of left-wing icons such as Lenin and Marx may still be found on the capital's streets, but Frelimo has moved in a dramatically different direction and fully embraced economic liberalization. Since the end of the civil war the state has not intervened to establish planned industry, as happened in China in the 1980s and 1990s, and South Korea in the 1960s and 1970s; it has instead followed a laissez-faire approach towards national development.

New policies have not fostered the type of economic growth that is based on the establishment of large-scale labour-intensive industry, but instead have promoted the extraction of natural resources, providing GDP growth but few jobs. Sectors like the small clothes- and textile-making industries have fared poorly since the 1990s and the few state-owned factories were privatized with catastrophic effect. Private owners lacked capital, management capacity and competence. Unscrupulous bosses stripped clothing factories of assets to enrich themselves, buying BMWs and Mercedes and furnishing their houses. There are even examples, including in Nampula, where once the resources of clothing factories were used up the buildings had been transformed into warehouses for selling second-hand clothing. The pattern of deindustrialization was repeated in other economic sectors, including cashew-nut processing, flour mills and furniture manufacturing.[6] Industry stagnated or declined; at the same time second-hand clothing and other consumer goods were allowed into the reformed market. The small clothing sector faced myriad problems because of the wider socio-economic impacts of SAPs in Mozambique. Urban incomes fell for many formal wage-earners and declining basic services affected businesses. In 1993 Texmoque, a privately owned textile factory, was forced to close due to a lack of materials and electrical power.[7] Challenges for the garment industry continued in the early 2000s, when clothing factories were left idle and 'mothballed'.[8] The failure of local manufacturing provided further opportunity for cheap imports of new and used clothing, as detailed in a report by USAID:

Substantial imports of used clothing underscored the limited means of most Mozambican consumers. Thus, local demand for new clothing and the productivity and size of the apparel industry could not sustain the capital investments that a competitive spinning, weaving, and finishing industry required simply to survive. Saddled with debt, rising labour costs attributable to new regulations and laws, and a centralized industrial strategy that put wealthy consumers in export markets beyond their reach, Mozambique's textiles and apparel industries dwindled to a few small suppliers of local niche markets.[9]

On a very modest scale, Mozambique has experienced growth in the clothing sector since the mid-2000s, but total employment is only around 2,000 workers.[10] The Texmoque factory reopened in 2008 following investment from MeTL (the Tanzanian firm discussed in the previous chapter), and the Moxtex factory launched in 2009, and has since expanded from producing garments for South Africa to also exporting to the United States.[11] One of the reasons for the small growth in manufacturing is that export-orientated factories have relocated from South Africa to southern Mozambique due to lower wage levels.[12] This is another small-scale regional example of capital seeking a spatial fix. In South Africa, 'unrealistically progressive' labour market policies are making it difficult for clothing factories to grow profits, so entrepreneurs have tried relocating to lower-wage Mozambique.[13] While employment in clothing factories may bring work for a few Mozambicans, this is another example of a race to the bottom for labour standards in the garment sector. Under current economic policies most Mozambicans are unlikely to ever get jobs in industries like clothes-making, and many more have to engage in unsecure, poorly-paid, informal ways of making a living, such as selling imported second-hand clothes.

SECOND-HAND CLOTHING IMPORTS AND WHOLESALE

Second-hand clothing is found everywhere in Mozambique. In many instances, used clothes are the only garments available for the impoverished population, and are widespread even in remote rural areas. Maputo in the south, along with the port of Beira in the centre, are regionally important Indian Ocean trading hubs. Second-hand clothes come from Australia, Europe and North America, and are sold in Mozambique and exported to Malawi, South Africa, Swaziland, Zambia, Zimbabwe and elsewhere. Despite the liberal market reforms, arranging the import of second-hand clothing requires the right contacts. Imports get held up by the *alfândegas* (customs officials), who negotiate both *impostos* (import taxes) and additional *taxa* (informal charges). Corruption is commonplace in Mozambique. A continuing process of 'state capture' – the control of national assets and political posts for personal gain – by a narrow elite within Frelimo means that importers often have to make backhanded and under-the-table payments to ensure their goods are allowed into the country.[14] The misuse of state office has contributed to the rising inequality and helps explain why economic growth is not reaching the poorest Mozambicans. Used clothes are imported primarily by Indian traders with transnational links to the global North and connections to local politicians. Anne Pitcher believes that 'many African consumers as well as industrialists view Indians as parasites who undermine productive activities and charge high prices. Some argue that the government protects Indians because of their electoral support for Frelimo.'[15]

Used clothes are imported from the global North by firms such as AHP Commercial, Armazém Nguesse Commercial, Fatah Trading, Sabah Enterprises and UMUT World Connection.[16] UMUT has a warehouse close to the large Xipamanine market in Maputo where many importers are based. Twenty-foot shipping containers holding 250–300 45 kg bales are unloaded at the side of the street and carried into storage. Consignments of bales are determined by a packing list; as with Oxfam's clients, UMUT does not control what types of clothing are sent from the global North. UMUT is typical of the importers working across East and West Africa, importing on average two or three shipping containers per month. A supervisor at UMUT believed that most of their clothing originates from Spain and Germany, but his company procures it from Nigeria. Evidently someone associated with UMUT works in Nigeria and purchases the clothing from Europe.[17] AHP Commercial sources clothing from Australia: Australian Salvation Army-branded bales can be seen inside the warehouse. Sabah Enterprises and Armazém Nguesse Commercial both import used clothing from Canada. Bales of second-hand clothing are usually labelled with a description of the contents, such as 'LTS–LS–MIX' (ladies T-shirt, light/summer mix), as well as the origin. One label common in Maputo is from Canam International. Canam first exports clothing from North America to grading facilities in India and then re-exports processed second-hand clothing to East Africa. It employs 700 people in India, taking advantage of low labour costs and incentives in a special economic zone in Kandla. This west Indian port is a hub for the labour-intensive processing activity 'between' the collection nodes in North America and retail in Africa, even though it is thousands of miles from both continents.[18] The geographies of international shipping routes, including the access provided by the Suez Canal and shipping lanes which avoid Somalian piracy, make Kandla a strategic location. Similar hubs in the Arabian Gulf are used by firms exporting second-hand clothes from Europe to East Africa.[19] UN data show that $40.5 million worth of used clothing was exported to Mozambique in 2017, equal to 34 million kilograms of garments, or the equivalent of 65 million pairs of jeans or 276 million T-shirts, equivalent to ten per Mozambican. This is likely to be an underestimate of the total size of the market.[20]

Import firms in Maputo have specialist warehouses (*armazéns*) where second-hand clothing bales are stored and sold. Local market traders buy intact bales and sell individual clothing items to consumers. Shipments of second-hand clothing are irregular and the inconsistency of supply creates problems. For instance, Paulo, a market vender who sells second-hand shirts, found that there had been a serious shortage of bales around the general elections in November 2009 when few boats delivered shipments into Maputo. At other times there can be a surge of imports and the cost of bales can decrease. *Armazéns* then send text messages to traders advertising new and discounted second-hand clothing bales. Across all clothing supply chains the rate of sales is important for maintaining profits: selling goods quickly generates more money.[21] As with fast-fashion firms in new-clothing systems of provision, *armazéns* attempt to accelerate their rate of transactions to gain a quick return on their investment. They are helped in this process by local speculators known as *mamães grandes* (literally 'big mothers'), who try to control the sale of clothing bales and manipulate the market. *Mamães grandes* are favoured clients of *armazéns* who purchase large numbers (50–100) of bales of desirable clothing, which allows *armazéns* to quickly complete sales. *Mamães grandes* attempt to monopolize supply and are especially active when there is a shortage of

Table 1 Types of 45 kg used-clothing bales advertised for sale by an
importer in Maputo

Type of clothing bale	Price (MZN)	Price (US$)
Children's clothing (0 to 7 years)	3,000	103.44
Mixed shorts	1,500	51.72
Pants (women's)	1,400	48.28
Pants (men's)	1,700	58.62
Skirts (denim)	1,800	62.07
Skirts (cloth)	2,500	86.21
Shirts (with collar)	1,500	51.72
Shirts (without collar)	1,300	44.83
Khaki pants (men's)	1,500	51.72
Khaki pants (women's)	1,800	62.07
Jeans (for men and women)	2,000	68.97
Underwear (men's)	3,500	120.69

Note: Prices recorded 8 June 2010.

clothing bales. When they have control of the trade
mamães grandes then charge market vendors a premium of around 300 Mozambican meticals (MZN)
(approximately $10) for a bale

The two main risks in second-hand clothing trading
are currency fluctuations and poor-quality clothing.
Risks to profits are passed from wholesalers to market traders, reflecting the power relationships in this

system of provision. Importers' contracts with suppliers in America and Europe are agreed in US dollars. When the Mozambican metical weakens, importers increase prices. However, when the dollar falls against the metical, prices are not reduced by the *armazéns*. Market traders complain, but have been unable to end this practice. Sergio, who sells boys' T-shirts, argued that market traders are treated *sem seriedade* (without seriousness) by importers and local authorities, which may reflect the close ties between *armazéns* and Frelimo politicians. Price inflation is a common cause for complaint, but the greatest challenge is bad-quality stock. Used clothing is inherently variable; some items are clean and like new, others are dirty rags that are falling apart. Stock quality is the major factor determining profits, and there is an unequal relationship between importers and the market traders who retail clothes. Bales are sold 'blind': as intact, unopened packages. Market traders only know what category of clothing – such as men's jeans, socks or floral dresses (see Table 1) – they are buying from *armazéns* and cannot examine the contents in advance. If they are lucky they can get many good items in nearly new condition, which are stylish and the right sizes, or they may be unfortunate and open a bale to find items that are ripped or rotten, unfashionable or too large.

Maria sells used fabric and curtains in Xipamanine market. Visiting the *armazéns* takes her half a day. When she brings a bale back to Xipamanine she is always anxious and excited. Her stall is located towards the rear of the market. She makes sure her regular customers know when she is going to open up a new bale, as the first rummage through the stock always attracts a large number of clients keen for a prize purchase. A sharp knife is used to slice through the thick, tight plastic strapping, then the bale sacking springs open to reveal the packed stock. Everyone bends down to pick through the textiles. She recorded her contrasting experiences on two consecutive days. The first day was 'not a good day because I opened a bale of curtains without there being one piece sold'; this failure meant she had to return and try a different importer the next day. This time she was luckier: 'I opened a bale of cloth. I sold 1,200 meticals' worth ($37.50). It was a good day.'[22]

Soiled or wet articles included in bales can damage a whole package, as mould, dirt and soiling permeate through the fabrics in the tropical heat. Hygiene issues are both a practical concern and a matter of dignity. In Ghana the government has banned imports of second-hand underwear for this reason, to mixed reactions from consumers, who find used underwear cheaper and often of a higher quality than new goods.[23] This issue stands out as it exemplifies the inequalities in the global clothing trade: should anyone have to wear second-hand underwear? In Maputo all the traders consider each bale bought to be a real game of chance, which is known as a *totobola* or lottery. A winning bale can be very profitable and can double or triple their income, whereas poor-quality stock will make it difficult even to recover the cost of the bale from retail sales. *Armazéns* do not offer refunds on bad-quality clothing. However, individual African traders are not completely powerless in the face of the larger international importers. For instance, Judite, who sells skirts, sometimes pays a bribe of a couple of dollars to a worker at the warehouse so they select a good bale for her, without the knowledge of the *armazém* manager.

Another problem encountered by traders in Mozambique is the size of clothing. North American clothing, especially, is often too large for Mozambicans. Mario and other jeans traders discussed how this creates a major problem for them. The diet and lifestyle of many Americans, which have led to mass obesity and a national health crisis, have resulted in jeans with a 42-inch waist or larger becoming commonplace in used-clothing imports. Few Mozambicans are so big. If a trader opens a bale and finds many pairs of very large jeans, they are faced with two problems: first, the jeans are too large to sell; second, there will be fewer pairs of big jeans in a single bale (which are sold at set weights of 45 kg) so they end up with less stock. Super-size clothes sell for a low price, as they are less useful. Large jeans alongside other undesirable clothing, like ripped and dirty garments, are bought by specialist vendors who sell them at a very low price outside of the main market area to people in extreme poverty.

Every garment sold in the second-hand clothing markets is unique; each has its own biography and shows marks of its former lives. Market traders check and empty pockets, occasionally finding US or Australian dollar bills. Sales tags are sometimes left on items, including those of the Australian Salvation Army and Value Village used-clothing retail shops – indicating garments that had previously been marketed in these shops but were not purchased and instead ended up being exported. Used clothes also display names indicating where they were first consumed: these may be sports teams, government institutions or businesses – for example, 'Andalucía Volebol', 'New South Wales Police Service', 'Walmart USA'. National brands are sometimes identified: for instance, George at Asda and Marks & Spencer from the UK, and Billabong, a popular and distinctly Australian brand. Other labels, such as Fruit of the Loom, H&M and Nike are multi-national brands, retailed around the world, reflecting the internationalization of the clothing industry. New-clothing 'seconds' (substandard products) are very occasionally found – an example being tens of pairs of identical new Crocs sandals.[24] And there have been reports of the unwanted championship clothing from the NFL, discussed in Chapter 6, finding its way to market in some African countries.

WORK IN THE SECOND-HAND CLOTHING SECTOR

Few researchers have tried to understand the livelihoods of second-hand clothes traders in Africa. The work that has emerged has tended to paint a positive picture on account of the employment created.[25] For example, Simone Field, who undertook research in Zimbabwe in the 1990s and Kenya in the 2000s, considers that the business provided very valuable self-employment opportunities for informal traders, as well as advantages for consumers and the economy as a whole. She describes the local economic benefits, indicating the advantages for importers, wholesalers, market traders, consumers and the state, as well as pointing to other spin-off benefits. Field asserts that in Kenya the second-hand clothing 'trade directly or indirectly affects 5 million people through employment and income generation', a claim that is repeated by the UK-based Textile Recycling Association as evidence of the 'crucial contributions this industry makes to the world economy'.[26] But researchers have to be careful when making such bold claims. The total population of Kenya is around 37 million people; therefore 5 million people represents 13.5 per cent – a very high proportion. Field does not state how she produced this figure. There is, however, another source to consider: a national survey by the Central Bureau of Statistics of Kenya, which recorded that second-hand retailing accounted for 8 per cent of the total number of small and medium-sized enterprises and employed only 103,961 people in 2001.[27] Even if each person supported five dependants or indirect beneficiaries, this would give a total of approximately 500,000 people, one-tenth of Field's figure, indicating that her estimate is excessively high. Nevertheless, a similar very large claim is made by the Salvation Army: 'in Ghana it has been estimated that up to 20% of the working population is employed in the used clothing chain'. The source for this data is not referenced.[28] Again, when contrasted with the 8 per cent of small and medium-sized enterprises (not total working population) in

Kenya, this figure seems unlikely. To conclusively disprove these figures cited by Field and the Salvation Army is difficult, given the weakness of employment statistics in many African states. With regard to Mozambique, a conservative estimate would be that the people employed in this sector number only in the tens of thousands, and proportionally far fewer than claimed by Field and the Salvation Army.[29]

In Maputo there are over 1,000 vendors selling second-hand clothes in Xipamanine market and thousands of others at smaller markets around the city. In Xipamanine traders mostly work alone, selling clothes from small stalls a couple of yards square. Stalls are built from odd lengths of wood, corrugated iron and packaging from used-clothing bales. The market is a former soccer field; the remains of the goals can be found in the dark alleyways. The stalls are owned or rented and vendors pay a small daily fee to the municipal council. Most vendors have been selling for many years; indeed it is not unusual to find sellers who have been trading in used clothing for over a decade. People have drawn on friends and family for loans or obtained credit from moneylenders to start selling second-hand clothes. Others have taken to selling clothing using money earned from other types of trading, such as selling food, mobile-phone credit or soap. In a further example of the impacts of economic liberalization, some use redundancy payments from formal-sector jobs, such as at the train station or university, after the loss of employment due to structural adjustment programmes. Retailing used clothing is not an occupation people choose because they are interested in fashion or style; rather, it is a livelihood born of necessity.

Earnings in the market are very variable. Due to the low quality of stock it is not unusual for people to make daily or weekly losses as overheads exceed sales. Vendors risk capital on the lottery of new bale purchases. They have to work hard in the market to retail second-hand clothes to poor customers, attempting to maximize prices while maintaining turnover. Traders specialize, selling only certain types of clothes. They are risk-averse: once they know local preferences and prices they tend to stick with, say, jeans or T-shirts. Successful vendors may record short-term losses, but are able to take a long-term perspective on trading, constantly building-up, renewing and depleting stock and money. Market traders have different strategies when pricing clothes. Sergio sells boys' T-shirts at fixed prices between 45 and 70 MZN ($1.40–$2.20). Others price items individually, like Maria, who sells curtains. Maria sometimes changes the quoted price of pieces of fabric over time as potential customers make repeat visits to her stall to negotiate a purchase. She will try to haggle for a higher price if she thinks a potential client is relatively well off. Customers with more money to spend pick out appealing items, especially young women and men who want to emulate international styles, like those associated with American hip hop and R&B cultures. Young men favour clean and immaculate striped polo shirts and high-quality, loose-fitting cargo shorts, which traders market at high prices. By contrast, if a trader is in need of money and desperate for a sale – maybe if they are short of food at home or unable to pay the rent – they can price items artificially low (i.e. below market price). For a week Mario had to drop the price of jeans down to 85 MZN ($2.70), below his usual retail prices of over 100 MZN ($3.10), because he was short of cash to support his young family. These examples of variation in price show there is interplay between local fashions, clothing trends and the business models and livelihoods of second-hand clothing vendors.

To understand how much money different charities, companies and traders in second-hand supply chains make it is important to consider the rate of transactions, as the tempo of sales is a fundamental feature of profitability in trade. In Maputo, market traders can sell used shirts for twice the wholesale cost, a higher percentage mark-up than the *armazéns* gain from selling complete 45 kg bales. But the rate at which they sell clothes is much lower: this is slow rather than fast fashion. Market traders frequently remain with the same stock for a long time and can go days without making a sale; thus they are losing money. The *armazéns*, for their part, experience the rapid sale of stock. In any trade system, sellers need their capital to be active and must have turnover, which enables them to make money. Traders consistently reported how it is the day's relative *movimento* (the movement of goods) which determines their profit levels. Slow sales and variable quality limit their ability to profit from the trade and escape poverty. In order to fully map how much money different groups make from the entire second-hand system of provision, the accounts of all the businesses involved across the global North and South would need to be opened up and studied, but this is unrealistic.

The average income of second-hand traders in Xipamanine is around 172 MZN ($5.40) a day.[30] In the context of one of the poorest countries in the world, selling used clothing can be the basis for a relatively good income for a single young individual, but it is harder for someone who is a household head to support a family on this amount. If $5.40 is shared between a typical family, including a partner and three or four children it is around a dollar a day per person. There are always tensions between reinvesting profits and using revenue to support dependants. Second-hand clothing vendors are poor, but they are not among the most impoverished of people in Maputo. They tend to own mobile phones, which are useful for contacting *armazéns* and regular customers, and often spend money on remittance payments or school fees to support their parents and children. Trading second-hand clothing represents a step up compared to other types of market work, such as selling vegetables or soap, but traders are still very poor and experience hardships and difficulties. For instance, they frequently go without meals and people have gone out of business after a succession of bad bales of unsellable clothing.[31]

For all traders it is very difficult to expand their second-hand clothing businesses, because the inherent variability of items makes saving money hard. A bad bale can wipe out profits earmarked for expanding a business. Selling used clothing in Xipamanine market is, as Francis Wegulo found while conducting research among second-hand shoe vendors in Kenya, a way to escape 'sheer destitution' but not for traders to get beyond 'keeping their heads above the water'.[32] Vendors interviewed were not content with their livelihoods; they looked to the future hoping for better formal work outside the second-hand clothing market. Working in the market is a reaction to the absence of development and other opportunities in Mozambique, rather than a livelihood which should be celebrated as a successful entrepreneurial way to make a living. Older vendors, who had previously been formally employed in modern professions, were especially sad that they were left selling used clothes and working on the margins of the global economy.

THE UNUSUAL CASE OF HUMANA-ADPP

Most of the second-hand clothes in Mozambique are sold in markets, either large organized urban markets like Xipamanine or small informal stalls at the side of the road. However, one significant importer has a different business model and sells used clothing in its own shops. Humana–ADPP is an international organization that imports used clothes to Mozambique as well as to neighbouring countries such as Malawi and Zambia. ADPP (Ajuda de Desenvolvimento de Povo para Povo – Development Aid from People to People) is a Mozambican Association and member of the International Federation 'Humana People to People'.[33]

In 2009, two Humana retail second-hand clothing shops were opened, in Maputo and Matola; in total there are 12 such shops in Mozambique, including four in Beira and others in Cabo Delgado, Nampula and Quelimane. An employee from West Africa, who had previous experience working for Humana elsewhere in Africa, emphasized in an interview that the Humana shop in Maputo, which sells approximately 300 items per day, provides poor people with the opportunity to purchase low-cost clothing:

> We do it because we need to help people and we also did it because people need work … It really is not a business, because business means that you buy and sell and have a lot of money. We are helping people as the clothes are cheap.

Profits are said to go to fund education and HIV/AIDS projects, and clothes are sometimes distributed directly to children or people impoverished by the disease.

Clothing sold by Humana in Mozambique comes from countries that include Australia, Italy, the UK and the USA. Humana or its affiliates collect the clothing themselves in the global North. They have been involved in some controversy. In the UK, for instance,

the organization TRAID, which currently has 11
stores selling second-hand clothing across London,
'worked with the Charity Commission to close down
Humana UK due to concerns over how the organization was managed and funded. The remaining
assets were used to establish TRAID in July 1999, [as]
a brand new charity.'[34] Media reports have covered
the controversies. The charismatic leader of Humana
is Mogens Amdi Petersen, who created 'the many-
tentacled Humana People to People NGO, operating
under a baffling variety of names and spheres of
interest'.[35] In different parts of the world it operates
under the names 'Gaia', 'Planet Aid' and 'Tvind'. The
management of the organization has been associated
with illegal activities in Africa, Europe, the USA and
Mexico. In the USA, Planet Aid is a controversial collection agency linked to poor practices (discussed in
Chapter 3). Another commercial operator related to
Tvind, USAgain, works in states including Illinois
and Washington. A former manager reported that
USAgain 'never explained the for-profit nature of
the company to owners of sites where boxes were
placed'.[36] Controversies have also been reported
in the African press; for example, 'Employees at
Development Aid from People to People in Malawi
(DAPP) have turned against their employers, accusing

them of secretly swindling money for unknown activities.'[37] Unethical practices extend much further; indeed Tvind has been likened to a manipulative cult. A group of investigative journalists have set up a website, Tvind Alert, which makes allegations that this 'charity business' runs scams, embezzles cash and its leaders enjoy luxurious lifestyles.[38] These claims cannot all be substantiated. Nevertheless other reporting suggests that Tvind/Humana may be connected to illegal activity elsewhere. What is clear is that Mogens Amdi Petersen is a wanted man, a warrant for whose arrest has been circulated around the world by Interpol. The suspected cult leader went underground in 2006 and is believed to be on the run in Mexico. He was sentenced *in absentia* to a year in prison in 2013 by the Danish authorities for embezzling millions of kroner from a Tvind fund in the 1990s.[39] The network of organizations which make up Humana clearly require further investigation, but full explanations as to the origins, history and practices may have to await the apprehension of Petersen. The malpractices with which Tvind, Planet Aid and other linked operations have been associated once again highlight the concealed trade practices and criminality that are prevalent in the international second-hand clothing trade.

SHOPPING FOR SECOND-HAND CLOTHES
IN MOZAMBIQUE

The poor in Africa cannot dwell on the controversies associated with used-clothing systems of provision. Poverty determines what clothes they buy. Second-hand clothing is frequently preferred by consumers not just on account of the lower price, but also as it is of a higher quality and will last longer than new garments. Used and new clothing are both on sale in Xipamanine market, but tend to serve discrete market niches. New clothes are more aspirational in style, including for instance counterfeit English Premier League soccer shirts and versions of the tight-fitting ladies' tops retailed in more expensive stores in central Maputo, such as Logas das Dames. The new items are often of low quality as they are made to narrow cost margins to be sold at affordable prices to poor people. In contrast used clothes are locally less fashionable as they are typically clothes that were popular several years ago in the global North. However, the quality of the material of used clothing – notwithstanding that many items are worn or soiled – is often greater than affordable new clothing, as the items were first produced for a more affluent class of consumers in Australia, Europe or North America. Used-clothing items are on average 35–40 per cent of the cost of new clothes sold in Maputo. Table 2 gives examples of the different prices of new and used clothes sold in Xipamanine based on a survey of 2,789 sales. Monthly household expenditure on clothing in Mozambique averages 303 MZN ($10.50) in urban areas and 167 MZN ($5.80) in rural areas.[40] In Maputo a household would be able to afford only the equivalent of one average pair of men's new trousers each month. Consumption decisions are therefore crucial and people take care in deciding what to buy.

Table 2 Average prices of second-hand and new clothes sold in Xipamanine market

	Average price (MZN)	Average price (US$)
SECOND-HAND CLOTHES Men's shirts	104.7	3.61
Men's trousers, including jeans	128.1	4.42
Men's tracksuit bottoms	127.3	4.39
Men's tracksuit tops	207.0	7.14
Women's tops and blouses	53.0	1.83
Skirts	80.1	2.76
Women's night gowns	24.0	0.83
Women's shorts	83.4	2.88
Boys' and unisex T-shirts	66.0	2.28

Boys' shirts	60.3	2.08
Boys' trousers	72.4	2.50
Girls' dresses	53.4	1.84
Girls' tops and blouses	57.2	1.97
NEW CLOTHES Men's shirts	219.2	7.56
Men's T-shirts	179.7	6.20
Men's trousers	304.9	10.51
Men's shorts	286.4	9.88
Tracksuit trousers	250.0	8.62
Coats	770.0	26.55
Skirts	246.0	8.48
Women's tops and blouses	215.4	7.43
Women's trousers	217.0	7.48
Dresses	325.0	11.20

Note: Reported sales prices recorded between July 2009 and June 2010.

Despite the widespread poverty in Mozambique there is a degree of differentiation in consumption. Specialist traders search around the markets collecting the best items to sell in the centre of Maputo. Along the wide tree-lined avenues in the centre of town, high-quality second-hand shoes suitable for clerical workers are sold close to offices at Jardim dos Madjersumai, handbags are on sale outside boutique shops on Avenída 25 de Setembro, and rucksacks and satchels are hawked at the gates of schools such as Escola Josina Machel. Sometimes new items are sold alongside them and traders conceal the origins – both used sold as new and new sold as used. Intriguingly, some unscrupulous traders position cheap, poorly made shoes from China within supplies of used shoes, in order to trick customers, as second-hand items sell for more due to their higher quality. Second-hand clothes can also be physically transformed. Tailoring activities, though not common in Maputo, do occur; for instance, delicate bra straps are often repaired as they get damaged through processing and packing, and in the scurry of activity when potential customers rummage through a newly opened bale. Sometimes used clothes are tailored to meet local styles. Eduardo is one of the more entrepreneurial traders in the market. He records higher profits as he buys bales of long-sleeve ladies' tops, which sell at a relatively low price. He takes the tops to a tailor, who removes the sleeves. Short-sleeved tops are a local fashion among young women and are worth more. His stall is normally busy and he has a rapid stock turnover. Tailoring second-hand clothing is not common in Maputo, though. Elsewhere in Africa, there are examples of clothes being remade in Kenya and Zambia.[41]

People do things in Africa to *revalue* used clothing. Karen Tranberg Hansen argues that in Zambia this redefines used clothing as 'new' garments. A physical transformation or a change in the meaning and symbolic value facilitates, in her opinion, a second 'life'. Second-hand clothes can be altered to give them greater value, yet new clothes are not being produced. Tailors and traders who modify and select used clothes are performing a similar role to the Igbo apprentices who select items in the UK and send clothes directly to colleagues in West Africa.[42] They are influencing the provision of certain types of clothes. Second-hand clothing is not 'produced' as a commodity at any single moment; processes which make used clothes more or less valuable continue up to the point of final sale. Throughout the used-clothing trade all the sorting, repairing, altering and retailing activities depend on the manufacturing process that initially produced new-clothing goods for the global North, as detailed in the biography of jeans.

There is other evidence of used clothing being transformed in Africa. Oxfam reported that ladies' denim jeans are frequently retailored to fit male physiques, as African women tend not to wear jeans.[43] Such generalizations are problematic; this may be reported information Oxfam receives from West African clients, where body shapes and cultural values are different from those in Mozambique. In Maputo, it is common for men to purchase and wear ladies' trousers; however, tight-fitting jeans and trousers are also very popular among girls and women, especially in younger age groups. Field research in Mozambique showed that the availability of imported ladies' jeans stimulates demand. Furthermore, cultural diffusion affects their value. As discussed in the earlier biography of jeans, the international media, particularly film, television and online, present aspirational imagery, which is reinforced by return migration and diaspora connections as well as local advertising and domestic fashion icons. International fashions are influenced by the *leakiness* of trends which spread through globalized society. Fashion tastes in the global South are shaped by the Northern-dominated new fast-fashion systems, which affects the symbolic value of second-hand clothing.

While culture is important, ultimately what is consumed is a response to the goods available on the market. Placing an overemphasis on consumption as purely about individual choice – where people freely decide their own outfits – ignores the fact that decision-making is primarily framed by the affordability and material use-value of garments. The majority of Mozambicans cannot realistically aspire either to enjoy 'fast fashion' or to buy the clothes they really want. The first priority of the poor is to meet basic needs. Mozambicans and other Africans do respond to advertisers and media imagery, although postcolonial desires are aspirational, distant and overwhelmingly unachievable when measured against a Western model of (over) consumption. There is a rich and diverse history of African clothing culture and a continual development and flourishing of contemporary trends, but the global clothing industry is dominated by a First World marketplace shaped by producers manipulating demand for (unnecessary) goods. Consumption in the global North is restricting the vibrancy of clothing culture in impoverished communities. Elsewhere, in societies which are not as poor as Mozambique, second-hand garments perform a different function. In the global North retro old clothes can be very desirable, and the used garment trade has diverse socio-economic impacts across different cultural groups. The next chapter explores some contrasting and vibrant examples of vintage fashion and used-clothing consumption from around the world.

8

OLD CLOTHES AND NEW
LOOKS

THE M65 US MILITARY FIELD JACKET

Clothing helps narrate our identity. It tells us about
people's role in society, presenting a visual story to
read. Film-makers and other artists capitalize upon
and amplify the cultural values associated with
clothes. Hollywood contributes to shaping how we
perceive different garments and what qualities we
attribute to the people who wear them. In the 1976
movie *Taxi Driver*, Travis Bickle, played by Robert
De Niro, wears an olive drab ex-military M65 field
jacket. Square-cut and hip-length, made of functional
hard-wearing cotton and nylon fabric, with four large
pockets for ammunition, maps and snacks, and a zip
hood in the collar, the M65 produced by Alpha industries was first developed for US servicemen in 1965
and became a design classic. Millions were produced

in black, grey, khaki, navy, olive green and jungle camouflage, providing a Cold War uniform for all branches of the American military and seeing service from Vietnam to the Gulf War. Demobilized soldiers kept hold of their old M65s, which took on new and unforeseen meanings beyond the theatres of war. As disillusionment with the American war in Vietnam grew, M65s were worn by angry veterans and fellow protesters. Surplus M65s became reappropriated symbols, part of an authentic visual message, along with beards, long hair, peace badges and floral prints; a subversive uniform which demonstrated opposition to US military policy. Not all M65s represented this single narrative. In *Taxi Driver* Bickle's M65 is an essential part of the framing of his aggressive persona. Director Martin Scorsese paints a picture of De Niro's character as a flawed, violent drifter forced to the margins of society; his M65 represents violent prowess and his status as a former Marine. Subsequently the M65 field jacket became an iconic part of the uniform of Hollywood hard men and renegades. Another rogue veteran, John Rambo, played by Sylvester Stallone, wears one in *First Blood*, as does the maverick Sergeant Martin Riggs (Mel Gibson) in *Lethal Weapon*. Arnold Schwarzenegger has a redesigned one in *The Terminator*. M65s became popular across different social groups, including hippies, hunters, artists and photographers; and came to have resonance with diverse values – anti-establishment, heroism, masculinity – as well as being an essentially functional jacket with a high use value. Osama bin Laden even wore an M65 in his video addresses, perhaps a remnant of CIA supplies to mujahideen fighters in the 1980s, but surely also a careful choreographed part of his violent message.

The symbolic values and the different signs an M65 represents, along with the abundant used supply and the jacket's practicality, have made it a consistently popular second-hand buy in the USA, as well as being an item that has long been exported across the global North. An extensive system of provision has evolved, spawning many reproductions and influencing the design of other new militarized fashion apparel. In London, expensive boutique stores such as Rokit vintage clothing and the Vintage Store in Covent Garden specialize in mid-twentieth-century Americana, selling authentic examples which have been careful selected and repositioned to appeal to an affluent and savvy clientele. Neighbouring shops like H&M and Zara stock new fast-fashion styles, including some ever-evolving collections inspired by military uniform. M65 design cues and other army styles have crossed over to influence female blouses, blazers and trench coats. Cheaper M65s can be found in flea markets around Camden Lock in North London, although these also come with a high price tag, as the consumer is not so much buying an old army jacket as paying the price for the specialist work which has gone into picking out, supplying and then curating the right type of jacket. Vintage clothing is *curated*, as, like an ancient museum artefact or an artwork on display, it has to be carefully situated and presented to the consumer so as to maximize its symbolic value. An M65 has come to fill a specific and sought-after market niche. Reproductions sell for around $50, whereas authentic vintage originals are likely to reach $100 on eBay. The M65 demonstrates how second-hand clothes form an important part of everyday cultural landscapes in the global North.

Old clothes influence new looks. This chapter explores further hidden sides to the second-hand clothing systems trade. A mosaic of different mini case studies shows how old and vintage clothing plays a role in communities around the world. Used clothes are not just exported from the global North to the South; the real economic geography is multi-layered (see Table 3). Second-hand apparel passes between different groups both within the same societies and internationally.[1] The ways in which different values are attributed to 'vintage' second-hand clothes and how symbolism is shaped and enhanced merit critical attention. Vintage clothing is both praised as an environmental alternative to the excesses of fast fashion and celebrated as a way to produce distinctive looks.[2] The true story is somewhat different as retro garments also play an important role in inspiring new clothing collections and fuelling fast-fashion trends. The two sectors can, and do, operate in tandem.

Vintage fashion is a much smaller sector than the global North–South trade, but attracts greater popular attention. This chapter begins to redress the balance: examples from around the world are discussed, complementing the patterns and trends identified in Africa. Poor people may have little say in what types of second-hand clothes are sold in developing countries, but they respond in creative and unanticipated ways. Imports of used garments have diverse affects within different societies. Norms of dress are transmitted by the prevalence of Western clothing. Yet, rather than everyone being passive receivers of second-hand clothing and foreign fashions, some individuals give textiles a new lease of life and re-create their own trends. Table 3 gives examples of how second-hand clothing circulates around

Table 3 Examples of second-hand clothing export and recipient countries

EXAMPLES DISCUSSED IN THIS BOOK
Australia to Mozambique, Papua New Guinea
Benin and Togo to Nigeria (re-export of used clothing)
Canada to Mozambique, Zambia
India to UK (remade fashions)
Japan to the Philippines
Mozambique to South Africa, Swaziland and Zimbabwe (re-export of used clothing)
Mozambique to Germany (trade in designer fashions)
New Zealand to Papua New Guinea
Poland to Afghanistan, Uzbekistan (re-export of used clothing)
Spain to Mozambique
UK to Benin, Ghana, India, Kenya, Lithuania, Malawi, Mozambique, Pakistan, Poland, Senegal, Tanzania, Togo
US to Bolivia, Chile, Japan, Mozambique, Tanzania, UK, Zambia
OTHER NOTABLE EXAMPLES
Germany to Kurdistan (Northern Iraq)
Italy to Algeria
Senegal to France (trade in designer fashions)
USA to Costa Rica, Hong Kong, Tonga

Note: The list provided in the table is not an exhaustive account but illustrates the diverse geographies of the used-clothing trade.

the world. There are even instances of used clothing being traded from the global South to the North, including 'upcycled' fashion. The final section of this chapter explores examples of the reproduction of valuable new garments from used clothes.

VINTAGE FASHION IN COOL CITIES

Wearing vintage or retro second-hand clothing emerged as a countercultural practice when people began to browse markets, charity shops and thrift stores out of curiosity rather than necessity. Affordable second-hand clothing could be used to produce individual and unique looks. Early research conducted by Jacqueline Wiseman from California in the 1970s found that 'women go because they can pick up items that would be too frivolous for them to consider buying retail, such as sequined blouses and gold-threaded leisure jump-suits'; other customers included 'Hippies hunting exotic clothes of by-gone eras'.[3] Cheap used clothing offered American and British urban youth the opportunity to produce affordable yet distinctive new looks and play with narrating their identity. Second-hand shopping was a social experience: consumers were more likely to discuss purchases with one another and to participate in putting together outfits which differentiated them from the mainstream at a time when rigidly prescribed patterns of modern behaviour were breaking down. Identities such as punk saw teenagers play creatively with the language of fashion, introducing a new grammar to the way in which outfits were constructed, and drawing upon and amending affordable used clothes to make powerful visual postmodern statements.

Second-hand clothes stores and markets are still searched for different types of authentic goods. Consumers attempt to attach themselves to the latest style or re-create a retro theme. Indeed the trend appears to be growing in popularity. Looks which have been *in* among young people in London include fads for American cowboy boots in small female sizes; 1930s and 1940s men's tailoring; and David Bowie-inspired costumes. Vintage fashion allows people to form an authentic style, but is not just about subscribing to a specific group identity. This is documented by Janna Michael, who interviewed Fred from Hamburg:

> Fred describes his passion for classic, English tweed looks and other specific traditional clothing. In these cases, where an expressive yet consistent style is chosen, the intention is not to indicate membership of a subculture, but rather a unique style that had to be found individually.[4]

Hipster sensibilities and uniqueness cannot persevere in isolation for long, hence interest in vintage clothing has crossed over and steadily become co-opted into the mainstream as retro trends are remade by fast-fashion brands. Clothing designers constantly borrow from fashion's past. This symbiotic relationship means that certain used-clothing articles become invested with enhanced symbolic value, as fads for flares or trends for 1920s revival emerge. For instance, jeans designs from the 1950s influence Levi's new collections, and Nike has produced an M65 jacket from new synthetic materials which has the same shape and design features as the 1965 original. Distinctive vintage-inspired ideas are relayed through the fast-fashion system, leading to new cycles of production. Cool and quirky second-hand clothing shops have spread across cities and towns of America and Europe and have even made it to Italy, where there are now some 3,500 vintage stores. Retro style is becoming a new way to form identity, in an increasingly post-industrial society, at the heart of Europe's fashion sector.[5]

The emergence of vintage boutiques has been part of gentrification in the North's global cities; examples include Castor & Pollux in New York's Meatpacking District, Razzo in Berlin's Prenzlauer Berg, and another branch of Rokit vintage clothing in Brick Lane in London's East End. All these shops are in cool areas, which progressed from being disadvantaged inner-city neighbourhoods to in-demand localities for retail and leisure. Gentrification alters the social mix of cities. Long-standing blue-collar communities are displaced and former areas of industry transformed. Apartment blocks, factories and warehouses are remade in a seemingly beneficial process. According to urban geographer Tom Slater this is 'the popular, and increasingly scholarly, image of gentrification. The perception is no longer about rent increases, landlord harassment and working-class displacement, but rather street-level spectacles, trendy bars and cafés, i-Pods, social diversity and funky clothing outlets.'[6] Retro clothing shops fit within this broader landscape of renewal, although as trends shift i-Pods are themselves becoming retro technology! Used clothes and industrial architecture are reappropriated by urbane trend-setters and are emblematic of many American and European cities' changing social relationship with their past histories as industrial centres. This type of cultural 'progress' and urban change often results in displacements and makes large parts of cities unaffordable for the working classes.

Elsewhere in London, high-end stores specializing in vintage wedding dresses and retro couture in the West End compete on price with contemporary designer goods. On Oxford Street in one of Europe's most iconic retail locations, Topshop's flagship store has an internal vintage boutique. Topshop, a mass fast-fashion retail outlet, has attached itself to the perceived authenticity and originality of second-hand clothing. Associations like this can have a halo effect, reflecting positively on the broader brand. Worn items like aged vintage Levi's 501s sold in Topshop's boutique or a Rokit retro store are a prized second-hand purchase. Aged denim encapsulates the symbolic values of authenticity and robustness, which new designers try to re-create through the 'lived-in' manufacturing processes.

It is not just 'any' pair of jeans that end up as an expensive vintage good. Before second-hand jeans become valuable a highly specific type work is required. Skilled buyers search for the right garments and recognize which jeans represent the cultural zeitgeist and can be positioned in a new marketplace for a high price. This type of work can create new value and wealth. It is not simply factory work and manufacturing that creates wealth,[7] other types of work can be very profitable in the world of fashion. Making clothes has become less important and specialist skills concentrated in small groups of people make money. The vintage fashion sector is a great example. Particular work processes go into internationally sourcing supplies of retro clothes, identifying and promoting trends, window-dressing and curating second-hand fashions. Vintage fashions are sourced from sorting plants and local marketplaces. Choice garments are identified by expert pickers working on the conveyer belts at sorting plants, which can lead to great profits. For example, a pair of Christian Louboutin shoes were found at Oxfam Wastesaver and priced for second-hand sale at £340 ($566); and clothes such as 'vintage wedding dresses, cashmere and "Gatsby-style" items all sell well'.[8] These trendy clothes are purchased by used fashion retailers or sold directly by Oxfam Vintage, an online store sorted by 50s, 60s, 70s and 80s or at eight specialist boutique shops. On a local scale buyers search through markets, thrift stores and charity shops seeking bargains and fashionable items which can be repositioned and expensively retailed in retro stores. Profits are made through this skilled work and the cost of vintage goods is inflated as the consumer is captivated by the fetish of market relations. Vintage clothing is re-*made* into a new commodity not through sewing, tailoring or dyeing, but by being repositioned in the market to appear more alluring. Consumers are not so much paying for the cost of a item, but supporting a system of provision. As rock star Steve Tyler of Aerosmith once sardonically observed: 'You have no idea how much it costs to look this cheap.'[9]

For some people pre-owned garments have romantic associations, and used clothes can even embody an imagined persona which is both nostalgic and individualistic.[10] The new owner may reflect upon their distinctive history – perhaps thinking about the last person who wore a pair of jeans. Nostalgia and heritage can be influential in shaping fashion. The promotion of heritage is a powerful cultural force. Museums and galleries, such as the Metropolitan Museum of Art in New York, Paris's Musée Galliera and the V&A in London, are devoted to the preservation and popularization of past clothing styles and thereby contribute to the commercialization of certain artistic second-hand clothing styles. The cultural economy which surrounds consumption – exhibitions, blogs, themed parties, commercialized nostalgia – is all part of the social landscape that enables vintage clothing systems of provision.

The exchange of used clothing is as old as clothes themselves, but vintage fashion is relatively new, something which is distinctly postmodern, coming after the breakdown of Fordism and the flourishing of increasingly diverse clothing collections. Symbolism is the lifeblood of vintage fashion. Clothes have two types of value: a first-order function, such as covering your body and keeping you warm or being well-made and hard-wearing, which is their use value; and a second-order symbolic value, such as their style, appearance and fashionableness.[11] The vintage fashion sector brings items with use value back to the market and amplifies their symbolic value. It draws upon wider cultural trends to make old clothes more alluring. Vintage fashion trends are shaped by a whole suite of factors including nostalgia, class and gender relations, advertising, politics and media. For instance, film history and anti-war protests both affected the value of M65 jackets. Material culture can give rise to and erode the values of old clothes. Most of the time cultural trends make old clothes worth less as styles go out of fashion, but this process has also enabled the emergence of vintage fashions which have symbolic values that appeal to particular cultural needs. The following case study of the jeans sector in Japan provides a further example of how unique clothing systems of provision can develop.

JAPANESE JEANS

In Tokyo and Osaka some of the most exclusive and sought-after pairs of jeans in the world can be found. Specialist and artisanal producers such as Eternal,

Fullcount, Strike Gold and Sugar Cane manufacture expensive and carefully detailed denim.[12] High-quality, expertly tailored jeans are made in Japan, although at first glance the styles look like they come straight from 1950s America. Dark blue denims with tight and fine weaves are produced to exacting standards, and hand-finishing techniques are used for stitching jean patterns. Japan's denim industry provides a good example of how the new and used-clothing trades influence one another. This system of provision depended upon particular political and cultural events, which shaped production and consumption.

Following the Second World War, US forces occupied Japan. After the ravages of mass bombing campaigns, including the atomic devastation wrought on Hiroshima and Nagasaki, Japan was left broken. Large US Marine and Naval bases were established at Okinawa, Yokota and elsewhere. Both sides had suffered deeply. Among the Japanese, anti-American feelings were steadily replaced by a yearning for American culture; the US lifestyle became a model for the Japanese. Occupying Americans provided aspirational figures, and many servicemen wore denim jeans when off-duty.[13] Jeans were part of an American man's modern identity and were the trousers of choice for relaxed casual wear. The Japanese dubbed jeans

'G-pans' and the style crossed over and became popular among local youths, although getting hold of them was tough, as Rachel Snyder explains in her history of jeans: 'Because they were rare, jeans in Japan could cost upwards of half a month's salary in the immediate postwar period. Around Tokyo, secondhand markets for soldier's cast-off jeans thrived.'[14] From the 1960s onwards a domestic denim manufacturing sector emerged. In Japan, jeans did not have a local history as workwear; the industry specialized in replicating the look of the post-war American blue jeans worn by off-duty Marines, which became highly desirable leisure clothing. Meanwhile, the Japanese continued to source second-hand American jeans, which remained some of the most sought-after styles. A commercial trade developed, which extended to Japanese 'pickers' working in second-hand clothing sorting plants in the USA identifying classic styles, like Levi's 501s, which were popular back home. However, by the 1980s there was an insufficient second-hand supply of the 1950s raw unwashed styles popular in Japan, as these had been phased out of the US market in the 1960s. Denim aficionado Mikiharu Tsujita recalls how desirable styles were in short supply: 'At the time, many Japanese bought vintage jeans from the US ... It was becoming more and more difficult to find them, and they were becoming expensive. So Yamane and I suggested that we'd make vintage jeans ourselves.'[15] Despite the existence of a local denim industry, enthusiasts wanted a 'perfect' pair of jeans closer to the iconic US styles from the 1950s. In response Tsujita started his own brand, Fullcount. This was just one of several premium Japanese denim brands which emerged in the 1980s and 1990s as a fashion sector centred on Osaka grew up specializing in producing vintage style jeans. New techniques for treating, finishing and washing emerged, on account of which Japanese denim gradually established a reputation for innovation and quality.

Today, Japanese firms are some of the finest producers and their denims are exported to premium markets around the world, including North America. Japanese weaving mills have become expert in producing denim textile that encapsulates values associated with vintage wear. Technical processes give denim a lived-in aesthetic, but not the appearance of workwear. As a Canadian denim importer explains:

Japanese fabrics are known to be some of the best in the world. The attention to detail, texture and colour makes the fabric stand out from the rest … Over time, these indigo layers break away and you are left with an exposed white core, which will give your jeans a personalized, vintage look.[16]

Japanese jeans makers work hard on the detailing of their trousers, including features such as hidden rivets and chain-stitched hems, which are in demand among denim devotees. Manufacturing is often done using old machinery and specialist labour processes, approaches which are difficult to replicate and contribute to raising the cost.[17] Labour in Japan is also expensive, even compared to the EU countries and the USA. In Japan there is only a small immigrant population, which frequently fills repetitive production-line roles in the remaining fashion industries elsewhere in the global North. The Japanese workforce for blue-collar manual labour is shrinking and denim weaving is an ageing profession. These factors make for a sought-after and expensive product. Japanese jeans brands now sell for over $300 in North America. Simultaneously there also continues to be buoyant demand in Japan for authentic used items from the USA, which have great symbolic value, as Snyder notes: 'they still covet the post-World War II-era vintage look; more than two thousand tons of vintage and contemporary American jeans are shipped annually to Japan.'[18]

The story of Japanese jeans shows how society and culture can shape the trade in new and used goods. US servicemen first provided an aspirational image in Japan and the post-Second World War second-hand markets duly supplied jeans. Both the contemporary second-hand imported US jeans and the premium new Japanese manufactured denim trade are systems of provision which emerged because of the particular cultural values inscribed within jeans. As demand grew, a specialist domestic manufacturing sector inspired by mid-twentieth-century styles developed. However, this was not a piecemeal re-creation of American manufacturing. Jeans did not start out as *just* utilitarian wear in Japan, as they did in the USA; they were an expensive and indulgent fashion. And so a high-quality denim sector developed. The co-dependence and linkages with 'vintage' second-hand clothing persist and a parallel system of provision specializing in importing retro American jeans flourishes. This case study shows that it was not Levi Strauss, Lee or Wrangler that brought jeans to Japan; nor is there a mere imitation of vintage Americana, or a pattern which can be explained in narrow economic terms. Instead creolized patterns of production and consumption dependent on specific socio-historic circumstances are thriving.

USED-CLOTHING MARKETS IN THE
GLOBAL SOUTH

Due south from Japan, across the Pacific Ocean, and as far away as can be in terms of economic development, Papua New Guinea's clothing systems of provision were shaped by isolation and poverty. Across the economy there are few indigenous Papua New Guinean businesses and no history of industrial clothing manufacturing. Australians, Filipinos and Indians run most companies, but Christian organizations including American evangelicals, Catholics and Lutherans are also powerful economic and political actors. Missionaries are active, trying to convert communities and translate tribal languages to enable the Bible to be written in every native tongue. Used clothes are brought to Papua New Guinea predominately by Christian organizations such as the Salvation Army. They are able to source clothing from their congregations and collection activities in the global North. Many of the clothes come from Melbourne and Sydney, a trading relationship that mirrors Papua New Guinea's broader dependency on Australia, which governed it as a colony until 1975. Through the strong role of churches, which can readily access supplies, and the absence of local factories, second-hand clothing has become an entrenched system of provision. Used clothes make up the lion's share of the apparel market. Elsewhere in the Pacific used clothing is important in Tonga and Vanuatu as well.[19] The limited quantity of new garments sold in Papua New Guinea come from Asian producers and are sold in the stores run by Filipinos and Indians.[20]

In major towns like Madang, Mount Hagen and Port Moresby large warehouse-like stores have numerous rails of second-hand garments. Kalibobo Haus Colos (Kalibobo Clothing House) is one of the largest retailers in Madang; it claims to sell (an implausible) 10,000 items every day. Profits are rumoured to be high. Donations are regularly made to support local church activities.

Security guards patrol the entrance and often turn away customers who they do not like the look of. Retail is carefully managed; for instance coloured labels are stapled securely to shirts and jeans to prevent customers tampering with prices, or picking up garments and pretending they are their own. Nevertheless crime is rife. Theft has long been a challenge for both second-hand and new clothing retailers around the world. In the case of Papua New Guinea, the problem is exacerbated by a traumatic relationship with modernization and social change. Many Papua New Guineans do not fully understand the connections between production, retail and the market due to their late and partial integration into the global economy. As manufacturing is not understood, there is less social recognition of the work and transactions that bring products to market, and thus less obligation to exchange clothes for money.

During the Second World War many Papua New Guineans were first exposed to Western manufactured goods such as canned food, clothing, radios and vehicles, as well as money, but these supplies disappeared after the foreign troops left. Cargo cults materialized as an attempt to explain the origins and circulation of these things, as communities had no experience of capitalism and market relations. Some people believed that this 'cargo' was coming from their ancestors 'but that Europeans have schemed to hijack these shipments so that they fail to arrive'.[21] Prophets prescribed ritualistic behaviour to entice new supplies and cults emerged promising that new cargo would be delivered by Americans or other powerful outsiders. The term 'cargo cult' has grown to become a powerful label for internal cultural dynamism and to explain the enchantment with modernity, but it also signifies a lack of understanding of how factories and businesses work. Some Papua New Guineans may feel entitled to steal used clothing and other imported goods, as they deem them to be their rightful inheritance from ancestors. Cargo cults and other millennial thinking illustrates how used clothing has confusing origins that are not easily explained to local people. Second-hand clothes also get used in unusual ways. In one Highlands village men took to wearing flowing ladies' floral dressing gowns, garments that became a way to show off; it was a statement associated with masculinity that was completely divorced from the gowns' previous symbolic values. Second-hand clothing dominates the garment sector; as with many developing nations, Papua New Guinea has grown to become dependent on used-clothing imports. In this society the opportunities for establishing factories and making local clothes are constrained by a lack of money and business know how.

Second-hand clothing markets are found throughout the global South. Contrasting examples from Bolivia, India, Pakistan and the Philippines show how systems of provision are shaped by interactions between politics, culture and economics. Clothing was highly politicized in Bolivia. Imports of second-hand clothing were made illegal in 2006, but continued to flourish. Research by feminist geographer Kate Maclean explored the cultural and economic impacts. An estimated 8,000 tonnes of used clothing, worth more than $40,000,000, were imported each year from the USA via Chile.[22] The trade was banned after a contested government report estimated that the cost of imports was 'some $513,000,000 US in terms of jobs, tax and sales tax, on the assumption Bolivian production of clothing would have more of the market'.[23] Prohibition came about as President Evo Morales rejected neoliberalism and sought to protect national production. The ban led to protests, and then counter-protests. In the Bolivian cities of La Paz and nearby El Alto, however, markets dominated by female traders still sold *ropa american* (American clothes). Affluent urban women and poor rural migrants searched for designer bargains; identities were re-created and negotiated as people found styles from Gap to Gucci inside clothing bales. The politics of the second-hand clothing trade were associated with national identity and a reassertion of gender roles. Informal second-hand clothing markets provided an opportunity for female economic empowerment, but were in tension with state-led policies which valued the female citizen only 'for her role in the reproduction of population and culture'.[24]

In India a long-standing ban on the import of second-hand clothing was much more successful at protecting domestic production, as it is a legacy of the opposition to imports of new British clothing that formed part of the independence struggle. India has partially resisted economic globalization and has strategically integrated into the world economy. India has not simply opened its borders to imports and instead has taken control of its economic destiny and experienced rapid economic growth, although the country has many inequalities and widespread poverty. In contrast, neighbouring Pakistan is more economically liberal and as a consequence it is one of the largest importers of used clothing from Europe. For instance, Choice Textiles, the commercial partner of Help the Aged, sends a large volume of white dress-shirts to Pakistan, where there is great demand among lawyers, as this style is expected in the law courts, yet another legacy of British colonialism.

India does not import second-hand clothing for local consumption, but facilities such as Canam's plant in Kandla take advantage of India's strategic integration into the world economy to import second-hand clothing from North America, then sort, grade and re-export clothes to Africa. In addition to re-exporting used clothes, India is also a destination for recycling rags and clothing waste. This includes the garments collected in the global North that are of too low a quality to be re-worn. Western waste garments are imported and deliberately torn, to prevent the possibility of them being illegally resold. Sweaters and coats are remade into Indian blankets in Panipat, Haryana, as Lucy Norris found: 'old woollens are sorted into colour families and stripped of their fastenings, linings and labels before being industrially shredded and pulped. Then the fibres are teased out, carded and spun into brightly colored new yarn, ready for reuse.'[25]

There is also a vibrant domestic trade in second-hand clothes that pass from the rich to the poor, which represents a microcosm of the global system. In a single wholesale market north-west of Delhi 2,000 dealers buy and sell used clothing, in a scene that is replicated across India.[26] Some clothes are obtained in a manner similar to that of the roving traders and rag-and-bone men that operated in America and Europe in the nineteenth and early twentieth centuries. Indian housewives and servants barter away unwanted clothes in exchange for new cooking pots and other hardware. Used garments clothe the poorest in society, but they are valued differently across India's diverse social and cultural landscape. For instance, in the southern state of Kerala, where there is a high level of social development, occasionally people wear second-hand clothes, but it is not something they would openly talk about. Surplus supplies of used clothing are traded from Kerala to northern India, where there is less stigma attached.[27] Used Indian clothes are also recycled in various ways. Elaborate old saris which are too shabby to be worn again are burned to release and reclaim their gold thread. Saris and other patterned Indian fabrics are also transformed into new consumer products for foreign tourists. Out of piles of torn old clothing come new 'cushions, bedspreads and wall hangings … halter-neck tops, skirts and trousers', which are produced as 'Western consumer goods'.[28] This is an example of the upcycling of old clothing, which is discussed further below.

Inequalities in the global clothing trade are particularly acute in the Philippines where used and fast fashion collide. On the one hand there is a flourishing Filipino clothing industry which produces for both the domestic market and the global North, but on the other there is a burgeoning second-hand clothing trade. There are two main routes for imports: clothing comes from North America, Western Europe, Australia and Japan under the model described in Chapter 3, and through a different pathway from Hong Kong. In the 1970s rapid economic growth in Hong Kong accompanied by increasing consumer participation in fashion, with accelerated cycles of buying and discarding, provided a ready supply of used clothing. At the same time, many working couples in Hong Kong began to hire Filipino maids, which enabled them to access used clothes. Filipinos in Hong Kong provided the opportunity for used-clothing entrepreneurs to link the supply to markets back in the Philippines. Clothes from Hong Kong come in standard boxes priced according to quality. Clothing from Hong Kong and Japan is preferred in the Philippines, as the fit is better than with American jeans and T-shirts, which are often too large. The problem of low-quality stock is less than in the African case studies. Indeed some entrepreneurial individuals have accumulated profits and made the progression from market vendor to importer. Filipino business people have access to money and transnational connections and the traders work in a well-developed market. In the street markets of Baguio City competitive operators position branded goods like Gap, Nike, Lacoste and Levi's to attract consumers, and new stock arrivals are promoted. Some select stores specialize in selling the highest quality and cherry-pick items from market vendors, including hats and briefs. Filipino customers often prefer second-hand clothing because it may be higher quality than locally produced goods. As B. Lynne Milgram observes, 'Baguio City shoppers explain, for example, that the colour in my T-shirts will last longer because these garments are "from your place", regardless of the fact that my T-shirt was most likely produced outside Canada.'[29] Indeed Milgram's T-shirt could even have been made in the Philippines. Nevertheless, the important elements of the fashion industry found in Canada or elsewhere in the global North, including design, marketing and retail as well as affluent consumer demand, ensures the provision of high-quality goods in Canada. The second-hand clothing trade has affected the balance of trade, as imports have undermined sales of locally produced garments and market traders have shifted from selling *new local* to *used foreign* clothes, because these goods have higher profit margins.[30] This example shows some of the real inequalities of globalization. The Philippines 'closes the circle', making new and importing old garments. The same people who manufacture clothing for export may end up purchasing those same items years later as imported second-hand clothes. Filipino wage levels do not permit factory workers to wear the garments they make; they are the losers in globalization. The uneven development of the clothing sector plays a part in keeping locations of new clothing consumption rich and areas of production and second-hand consumption poor.

UPCYCLING

In Japan, Papua New Guinea, Bolivia, India, the Philippines and around the world, people use old clothes in new ways. Worn jeans, old ladies' dressing gowns and torn saris take on different lives in secondary markets. In some cases used clothes are physically transformed into new garments or other items. A vibrant 'upcycling' movement can be found in California, Paris, Stockholm and elsewhere. Upcycling uses old clothes as the basis for fresh fashions, reflecting both an environmental concern with the overconsumption of new clothing and a longing to invent unique garments that draw inspiration from past patterns of dress. Some people alter clothes themselves as an affordable way to change their look, or just for fun, whereas others have built up boutique businesses. Tired fabric and hard work are combined to cut and tear away the old, and weave new life into dresses, skirts and shirts. Upcycling approaches replicate the handcraft practices of the pre-modern era. Energy and motivation are required for prospective upcyclers to sort through rails of used clothes in thrift stores and charity shops to find appealing items worthy of a second life. Old clothes take on new looks as dress hems are altered, blouses are adorned with buttons, and trouser pockets and zip fastenings are removed or refashioned to reflect new trends.

One Swedish upcycling designer is Amanda Ericsson, who has her own fashion brand dreamandawake and an accompanying arts project The Life of a Dress. The two currents represent both a successful small business and an artistic initiative. In the latter, dresses are presented together with powerful images to provide an abstract story of a woman and her dress's journey around the world to give audiences a hint as to how clothes travel, both as new garments and as second-hand goods.[31] Ericsson's projects have travelled to Mozambique and there provided the inspiration for Mima-te, a developing Mozambican upcycling fashion brand which takes dresses from Xipamanine market and remakes the garments into unique and original fashion pieces. Mima-te is run by sisters Nelly and Nelsa Guambe, who describe the business thus:

Our intention is to upcycle and renew these textiles, bringing those forgotten clothes back to life and turn them into fashionable, modern clothing … Upcycling these clothes therefore becomes an innovative way of creating a new image of Mozambican clothing and at the same time serves to harness environmental awareness, both in Mozambique and in the origin countries of these clothes. It also allows Mozambican people – from the seller to the sewer at the market – to be involved in creating something beautiful and new instead of just reselling things that were not wanted in rich countries anymore.[32]

The Guambes' creativity has attracted interest from international media and their redesigned second-hand clothes have even been exported to and sold in Germany. One of their aims has been to take the clothes back to their original markets as a way to forge a successful and profitable business, and to highlight both some of the ethical and environmental issues raised by the overconsumption of fast fashion and the large scale of the trade in second-hand cloth-ing from the global North to Africa. Businesses such as dreamandawake and Mima-te use second-hand clothes as a starting point to produce new clothing fashions. These small-scale activities have complex relationships with the vintage and international used-clothing trades. They generate buzz and excitement around second-hand clothing, but also operate on the fuzzy boundaries between business, art and activ-ism, and in so doing act as a critique of fast fashion and global inequalities. In the global North, vintage fashion and upcycling are much more visible than the export trade in second-hand clothing, but, as previous chapters have demonstrated, larger and hidden exports of second-hand clothes forge deep connections and relationships of dependency between the global North and South. The patchwork of diverse case studies throughout this chapter show how second-hand and new clothes affect different societies; yet it is not actually the clothes themselves that change people. Rather, it is the social relationships – such as those between film-makers and audiences, retro stores and hipsters, 1950s American Marines and Japanese youths, American churches and Papua New Guineans, Bolivian women and state authority, vintage fashion designers and affluent consumers – that shape and produce different modes of clothing provision. The particular cultural connections that are enabled by the trade of second-hand clothing provide new opportunities for making money through globalization. Vintage clothing shops in the rich cities of the global North enhance the symbolic value of old clothes and provide inspiration for new patterns of fast-fashion production and consumption, whereas the largely hidden activities in second-hand markets in Asia, Africa and Latin America provide a lens through which to view the uneven development of the global economy. Second-hand clothing is very important, but it is only an undercurrent to the main flow of fast fashion from the global South to the North. To critically analyse some of the proposed solutions to the structural inequalities of the globalized clothing industry we first have to explore the myths and realities behind new ethical approaches to production and consumption. This is the subject of the next chapter.

ETHICAL CLOTHING MYTHS AND REALITIES

TOMS SHOES

A trend in footwear is steadily spreading across the USA. Throughout malls and college campuses it is easy to spot the distinctive slip-on espadrilles, flat unisex canvas shoes with a neat blue and white striped Toms flag sewn across the backstay of the heel. Toms shoes are popular, comfortable and different – fashionable and affordable while embodying distinctive values associated with care and compassion. The Toms success story is an important new chapter in the annals of so-called responsible capitalism. From the brand's humble origins in 2006, this example of social entrepreneurship has become one of the most talked about instances of the contradictions of ethical consumption. The Toms model is simplicity itself: buy one, give one. For every purchase of Toms footwear a child in a developing country is given a pair of shoes. As the company's marketing material proclaims: 'When you buy a pair of Toms Shoes, you're also helping improve the health, education and well-being of a child.'[1] Blake Mycoskie, the driving force behind the Toms project, is the epitome of a twenty-first-century socially responsible entrepreneur. In his early forties, with scruffy hair and a beard, Mycoskie has met the Clintons and has featured in *Time* magazine's 'How to Fix Capitalism' feature authored by Bill Gates.[2] He came up with the 'one for one' business idea when travelling in Argentina, where he found himself near Buenos Aires after Googling 'polo lessons cheap'. While hanging out with wealthy Argentines he saw that they donated their unwanted shoes to local villages. This provided him with the inspiration: 'It just hit me,' he says. 'Instead of a charity with handouts why not create a company where that's the whole purpose? I thought, you buy one pair of shoes today so we can give one tomorrow. We'll call them Tomorrow Shoes. No we'll call them Toms Shoes for Tomorrow.'[3] Blake's business has been a runaway success, and especially effective at encouraging young consumers not just to buy shoes, but to buy into an idea. People like the shoes and the ethical benefits. The simple 'classics' design that is the mainstay of Toms product lines is modelled after the Argentine *alpargata* (aka espadrille) shoe, a basic timeless shape which both signals personal authenticity and has powerful social resonance. After going shopping and slipping their bare feet into a pair of canvas Toms, wearers can feel content with themselves, maybe even a little smug, as they imagine their poorer counterpart also happily pushing their toes inside a new pair of shoes.

What is special about Toms is that the brand has gone beyond being an ethical business and has become a minor cultural movement, particularly in colleges and among teens. A sense of community is fostered through the online presence: toms.com is half online fashion store, half social advocacy website. As well as shoes, the marketplace features sunglasses, scarves, laptop sleeves and clothes; and shoppers can choose to sort ethical products by cause, region of impact or brand. In a biographical section Blake Mycoskie is pictured tanned and smiling, fitting red and white striped espadrilles on a young Hispanic girl. Stories and videos from the global South look like materials from an up-market Peace Corps campaign rather than corporate advertising. In a crowded market, these images help differentiate the brand and are particularly in tune with the cultural moment. Toms provides information and direction for young people, introducing devotees to development issues associated with education, health and well-being, just like an advocacy NGO. Foremost is the annual 'one day without shoes' event, which is when the Toms community goes barefoot to raise awareness for children around the world who do not have shoes. Images show groups of students walking around college campuses barefoot carrying large Toms flags as if supporting a political party or radical protest movement, rather than endorsing a shoe manufacturing company. The appealing and simple message has inspired other interventions, and indeed Mycoskie has carried the idea further. Toms are sold in Canada, France, Germany, the Netherlands and the UK. Mycoskie has written a bestselling book, *Start Something that Matters*, and has made many media appearances. Somewhat inevitably there has been a backlash involving important criticisms of the 'one for one' model. These require close analysis to separate the myths from the reality.[4]

The issue of the appropriateness of the donation is the first factor to consider. Do shoes actually satisfy a real need? Buying shoes in America leads to someone deserving getting shoes, but why shoes? Maybe something else, another item of clothing or cash, would be more useful. The poor are not consulted in the process and are cast as helpless, passive recipients of aid. Would it not be better to find target communities and identify what their greatest need is, such as access to clean water, or skills training, or debt relief, rather than arriving with a set 'solution' to a specific problem? A lack of footwear does not stand out as the most pressing development issue facing the poor in the global South.[5] Next, the economics of the project must be explored. Toms adult shoes sell for between $48 and $140 in the USA, far beyond the cost of manufacturing the *alpargata*-style shoes, which retail for around $5 in Argentina (which includes the local seller's profit). Without knowing the detail of private company accounts, there would appear to be plenty of opportunity for Blake Mycoskie to make money from these sales, while maintaining the donation system. At best a $48 purchase of shoes represents a $5 donation. Additionally, the cost of distributing shoes in the global South is partly borne by the Toms 'community'. Espadrilles are handed out in recipient countries through 'shoe drops' by Toms' volunteers.[6] Toms shoe drops are very popular, oversubscribed volunteer experiences. The young people who take part pay their own air fares and when they return provide testimonials, becoming brand ambassadors. The cost of intercontinental flights would be more effective 'aid' if the ticket price were instead donated and directed towards employing local people to distribute the donations, but then that would not help foster the sense of community which has become such an essential part of the Toms brand. The whole system of provision is self-financing and provides more good news stories for the Toms website.

The Toms programme has given away more than 10 million pairs of shoes across 60 countries, a not insubstantial number.[7] The impact of this programme on global footwear production and markets is minimal, though, when we remember that there are billions of poor people in the world. Nevertheless, the potential economic relationships of the 'buy one, give one' approach are worth debating. As with the cheap imports of second-hand clothing, free shoe drops can displace existing footwear manufacturing in the target countries, reducing local markets and making it harder for industries which need protection to grow and compete.[8] Research carried out in El Salvador by economists working in cooperation with Toms found 'modest evidence' that donated shoes had negative impacts on local shoe markets, but results were inconclusive.[9] It is also important to consider scale: should the small percentage of affluent people in the global North be freely choosing to buy (or not buy) ethical goods which aid only a tiny fraction of the impoverished majority of the global population in the South? Would it not be better to ask deeper questions about the inequalities of the global economy? Rather than providing products, people should be empowered to escape poverty and not become structurally dependent on handouts.

Fostering solidarity between different groups can be a powerful force for social change. Good intentions are laudable, but often there are complex motivations for participating in seemingly virtuous interventions. The 'one day without shoes' initiative can be considered an example of 'slacktivism', the type of easy politically unengaged acts which have become a marker of the digital age.[10] In the global North people are able to access information about pressing social issues around the world, but we are not inclined to disrupt our own lifestyles to take direct action to alleviate poverty or environmental degradation. Concerned people just add their email address to an e-petition, 'like' campaign posts on Instagram; stream charity music videos; or spend a day trying to walk around barefoot. Buying Toms is another *slack* attempt to change the world. Some consumers are motivated to buy ethical goods because they want to attach themselves to values of care and compassion. Young people especially compete to look cool; making distinctions is notably fuelled by particular brands which drive forward competitive consumption.[11] Toms are associated with charity and poverty alleviation; people want to link themselves to these ideals, rather than their purchases simply being a moment of pure altruism. One can envisage that most Toms shoppers already have several pairs of shoes, and so this type of consumerism is arguably as much about offsetting guilt as addressing poverty. In contrast, some Toms customers may just like the espadrilles and not even be aware of or interested in the charity aspect. Criticizing Toms for being shoes which make someone feel good about themselves may sound harsh, but this is normal, for actually all individual consumption – beyond that which is required to sustain life – satisfies a desire. Yet, it is deeply problematic that the sale of a pair of espadrilles should give someone the feeling that they are actually curing a problem or addressing a social issue when they are not. This is a particularly fetishistic characteristic of so-called ethical consumption.

Another issue that has been raised in the prominent critiques of Toms is the conditions of production. Would it not be better to think first about the shoe factory workers and make sure that there is an ethical supply chain? The 'trade not aid' argument has been one of the major lines of denunciation. To give

Toms some credit, their founder has embraced this criticism: 'If you are really serious about poverty alleviation, our critics said, then you need to create jobs. At first I took that personally, but then I realized that they were right ... using our model to create jobs is the next level.'[12] Toms currently make most of their shoes in China. They made plans in 2013 to produce one-third of their shoes in the regions where they give them away, and have manufactured shoes locally in Ethiopia, India and Kenya, but this seems like a modest goal and limited progress. Addressing the exploitative relationships which exist between workers and businesses in the fashion industry would alleviate some of the causes and consequences of uneven development.

The arguments against Toms have been raised by numerous commentators on social media as well as news outlets. A counter-reaction quickly follows, which paints critics of the brand as particularly callous individuals. Armchair detractors are labelled hateful figures by the Toms community, envious because they have never started a business, launched a brand or empowered a social movement.[13] Whether one believes Toms is 'a step in the right direction' or simply 'a cynical marketing ploy', the example opens up just one ethical dilemma associated with clothing consumption and production. The basic question boils down to this: should First World consumers of espadrilles be determining what footwear others in the global South access? Toms have harnessed a conventional fashion business to a parallel supply system directed towards the deserving poor. This does not address the embedded inequalities of the linkages between clothing consumption, production and poverty and is not the solution to uneven development. Similar criticisms can be made of many other socially responsible brands. The further contradictions of ethical consumption are explored throughout this chapter.

ETHICAL CONSUMPTION IN THEORY AND PRACTICE

Most Americans and Europeans love to consume. The great majority are largely uninterested in radical political change. Consumption means not just buying goods like clothes, but also eating out at restaurants, going on holiday, watching sports and movies, purchasing cars, carrying out home improvements and spoiling children with treats. Meanwhile, through the mass media and cultural globalization, people are more conscious than ever of global inequalities and of issues like climate change. Despite an increasing awareness of and a proclaimed concern for pressing developmental and environmental problems, widespread disenchantment with and indifference to conventional political processes are a hallmark of postmodern life. Capitalism, in partnership with liberal governments, has been effective at forestalling political dissent and inventive in bringing new forms of commodity to the market.[14] The political importance of shopping and its role in shaping life in the global North seem to be increasing to the point whereby citizens have become defined primarily as commodity-choosing consumers. In the USA a potential Democrat or Republican can be readily identified by the ways in which they spend their disposable income. Vacation destinations, transport decisions, what we eat and the clothes we wear are all potential markers of political persuasion as well as social standing.[15]

As consumption has grown and diversified, new politicized ways to exercise consumer choice have developed. Rather than engaging with formal political parties, progressive liberals are attracted to the fairly controllable and instantaneous consumption of new ethical products. Responsible capitalism has become a new means to promote environmental and social justice. Shopping for 'good' goods mediates our engagement with an ever-expanding range of economic, environmental and social topics. Wearing ethical clothes such as Fairtrade cotton T-shirts, second-hand dresses from charity shops or organic woollen sweaters is a way to demonstrate solidarity with good causes. Buying commodities like recycled paper and fish fingers from sustainable maritime sources is shopping as a guilt-free and transformative exercise, marketed as a way to prevent deforestation, resolve overfishing or alleviate other global challenges.

Some clothing companies make ethics central to their businesses. Patagonia, an American outdoor apparel company, is a prime example. It promotes fair labour practices, provides mapping of the social and environmental footprints of its products, and uses fabrics like organic cottons and recycled polyester. Environmentalism is at the heart of the brand's appeal. Images of people fly fishing and mountaineering in pristine environments in the company's adverts help build associations with authenticity and the outdoor lifestyle. This extended to a unique ad campaign which featured the prominent strapline 'Don't Buy This Jacket', where the core message was that 'customers need to think twice before they buy'.[16] A self-serving connection is evident in the Patagonia system of provision. Buying ethically helps protect the environment; the consumer can enjoy both natural landscapes and the clothes when they go hiking and adventuring in nature. This type of consumption is distinguished by ethics, morality and the politics of responsibility, which motivate actions in a complex way. While it is a growing sector, the power of ethical consumption should not be overstated. One of the most striking observations is that there is a large gap between intention and behaviour; people readily identify themselves as ethically minded consumers yet rarely purchase ethical products.[17]

A more radical approach to changing shopping habits is pursued by anti-consumption and boycott movements. Examples of anti-consumption protests in the clothing sector include the notorious PETA (People for the Ethical Treatment of Animals) 'I'd rather go naked than wear fur' photo shoots. Appearing in these anti-animal-cruelty adverts has become a near rite of passage for female celebrities. Such politicized acts are expressions of opposition to the consumption of specific types of unethical commodities resulting from 'unmet expectations', 'symbolic incongruity' or even 'ideological incompatibility'.[18] Supermodel Naomi Campbell featured prominently in the naked PETA campaigns, but later sparked outrage on social media after posting a photo of a Christmas gift that appeared to be real fur, showing how some celebrities may have limited engagement in ethical issues. Another form of activism is consumer boycotts, a temporary suspension of consumption. Boycotts are an appealing option for consumers because they are a temporary measure, explicit within a boycott is the principle that the consumer will buy the goods again once conditions improve. Boycotts are thus in line with the mainstream idea of commodity-choosing citizen consumers opting to take individual responsibility for social and environmental issues.

Capitalist social relations are fundamentally ill-suited to resolving the problems of uneven development and environmental degradation fostered by economic globalization. Ethical consumption brings together morality and the market in what seems to be a contradiction in terms. To understand this let us first revisit the idea of commodity fetishism. One of the foundations of capitalism is that goods and services are purchased with money, a special type of commodity. Money always mediates relations between producers and consumers and in doing so creates a moral vacuum. Inequalities in exchange are hidden from view by apparently open and voluntary social relationships: one can choose to give Gap $50 and get a pair of new jeans; whereas if one 'chooses' to work sewing jeans in eastern China for eight or even ten hours a day one receives $1.80 a day.[19] As the case studies throughout this book have demonstrated, different people in the fashion industry are unaware of the networks of exploitation and the various ways in which profits are made. Commodity fetishism transforms the abstract and subjective value of Gap jeans, vintage dresses, Toms shoes or any clothing item, turning them into objective things which people believe have intrinsic economic value. This is true of any commodity, including that other special type of commodity: human labour. Commodity fetishism makes it easy to assign variable wages to different types of work. Throughout the global fashion industry different subjective values are assigned to various types of workers, which are exploited to a greater or lesser extent, be they Malian cotton growers, employees of Cambodian garment factories or Walmart shop assistants.

Ethically produced goods are an attempt to defetishize the commodity. The most prominent example is Fairtrade. Food and beverages were the first Fairtrade products; premium bananas, chocolate and coffee have widespread appeal and are growing in popularity among middle-class consumers in the global North. Fairtrade has expanded and encompasses clothing products from babygrows to waterproof jackets. Buying Fairtrade may be intended by the consumer to be a kind gesture of good will, but does little to disrupt the pre-existing relationships between businesses, workers and the environment. Liberal-minded citizens in the global North can indulge in their consumption habits without calling for the large-scale structural changes that could threaten their own privileged status in global society. Fairtrade aims to modify market relations by providing a *just price* for work in the Third World, but does not aim for equality. The value assigned to Fairtrade work is a small premium above the market rate, but often covers only subsistence plus the basic cost of health care and education. Capitalist social relations are complicated; they include diverse cultural perceptions of value, but the salient point is that they are *modified* and not *transformed* by Fairtrade networks.[20]

VALUING FAIRTRADE CLOTHES

Shopping for clothes in the global North is about much more than just buying a 'thing'. It involves either passively or voluntarily choosing a fashion and a lifestyle. The material culture that surrounds the consumption of Fairtrade garments is an integral part of the Fairtrade business model. Links between the people who produce and consume Fairtrade clothes are shown through adverts, documentaries and packaging, which lead to the reworking and creation of new spectacles for consumption. Karl Marx was one of the first to argue that shopping is stimulated by narratives and aesthetics: 'The need which consumption feels for the object is created by the perception of it. The object of art – like every other product – creates a public which is sensitive to art and enjoys beauty.'[21] So much of what determines the symbolic value in clothing is the *spectacular* activities that lie beyond the realm of sewing clothes in factories. Place can be influential in establishing value. With Fairtrade and other ethical goods, locations of production are often attractive parts of the global South, with which an enlightened and progressive consumer in the global North may be familiar, such as Himalayan blouses from the mountains of Nepal. Sometimes celebrity *artists* are able to play a key role in this performance and help customers choose ethical goods. In adverts and documentaries they play a role to create ideal images – such as visiting happy workers in stereotypical tropical landscapes – which are not an objective record of the conditions of production but, rather, a new fetish. As with other processes of image making in ethical consumption, this can serve to reinforce and perpetuate economic relationships that undermine other more radical efforts to address pressing social and environmental issues.

Yet political engagement has never been the only motivation for choosing 'good' clothes, as they also serve as means of making distinctions and class positioning. The premium pricing of most ethical garments makes them unaffordable for poorer consumers in the global North as well as the global South. At worst they can be considered a petty-bourgeois indulgence. For proponents of globalization ethical businesses are an elegant solution to the challenges and criticisms raised by the alliance of trade unions, NGOs, faith groups, celebrities and others. The limited progress and change that projects like Fairtrade represent and the small number of goods involved allow business as usual to continue in other sectors of the economy. For instance a customer might buy one Fairtrade T-shirt, but what about the other 20 T-shirts they own? Ethical trade offers a partial solution, while embedding the logic of inequality. Proponents argue that they are socially progressive, even though they also foreclose radical political possibilities. By absorbing some of the opposition to, and critiques of, capitalism – centred on the lack of care and compassion for labour in the global South and environments around the world – more radical alternatives are crowded out. This is not achieved by force or fierce competition, but by a tepid *revolution in shopping* without a revolution in society.

Certain demands are addressed while at the same time international inequality between the global North and South persists.[22]

Fairtrade and other goods signify 'ethicalness'. The contradiction within Fairtrade is that, while partially acknowledging the inequity of market exchange Ethical businesses depend upon the persistence of the market, globalization and international inequalities. A voluntary premium is paid; yet, to maintain the price gap between conventional and Fairtrade products, consumption has to be further stimulated through the creation of symbolic values. This results in the production of consumable adverts and producer vignettes which create a romantic and idealized vision of landscapes and livelihoods in the global South.[23]

VIVIENNE WESTWOOD AND POLITICAL CONSUMPTION

One example of the performance of ethicalness comes from Vivienne Westwood's 'Made with Love in Nairobi' fashion line, which is ethically manufactured in Kenya. Vivienne Westwood is an influential British fashion designer. In the 1970s she established her celebrity status and credibility by popularizing punk identity while highlighting the politics of social inequality in Margaret Thatcher's Britain. Later, she became a

celebrated campaigner on gender, social and environmental issues and has been a critic of overconsumption. During the 2011–12 London Occupy protests she
proclaimed, 'We were all trained up to be consumers
… throw away the past, the future will take care of
itself, catch the latest thing and suck it up. We don't
have any art today.'[24] Previously she had famously
issued the rebellious statement 'don't buy clothes',
but this was also an inauthentic message given that
Westwood was the head of a very successful clothing
label with a turnover in 2011 of £23.8 million ($39.6
million).[25] Through participating in countless seasonal
fashion shows her brand helps inspire the fast-fashion
system of provision, as Vivienne Westwood and other
designer labels drive forward new clothing trends,
which migrate rapidly from the catwalk to shopping
malls. The conclusion to be drawn from Westwood's
grandstanding is that her commodities are not just
clothes or handbags, but are something above and
beyond that. They are commodified art and have
symbolic value among an affluent audience which is
excited by her rebellious 'political' messages as well
as the new fashionable designs.

Westwood's 'Made with Love in Nairobi' collection has been produced in collaboration with the
International Trade Centre (ITC) since 2010. The ITC

Ethical Production Model aims to reduce poverty by generating 'trade opportunities for marginalized communities and micro-producers in the developing world' and 'enables international fashion companies and distributors to source from African communities' by following 'a rigorous code of ethics and gender equality' designed to empower women and raise their incomes.[26] Like Fairtrade the model is 'not charity, just work'. ITC's 'Ethical Fashion Africa' initiative connects international fashion designers to African producers and organizes manufacturing activity, which 'enables some of the world's poorest people to enter fashion's value chain as producers, while also allowing designers, who want to source ethically, to do so'. In this scenario the emphasis is on liberal *choice* as individual designers have to 'want to source ethically'.[27]

In Kenya working conditions meet Fair Labour Association criteria, as a consequence of which craftswomen's incomes have increased from $3 to $6 dollars a day, enabling them to pay school fees and medical expenses. This evidence suggests that the value assigned to labour in the ITC programme is comparable to Fairtrade: wages include a small premium above the market rate, but do not enable much more than the physical reproduction of labour power. The women work on designs sent from London to Nairobi, which require 'community groups to be trained in the use of the specialised equipment needed to achieve them'.[28] Westwood says the ethical Fashion Africa approach 'gives people control over their lives'. Yet control over the system of provision is constrained when they are unable to design and market the goods. Africans do not have access to distant international customers who have the power to pick and choose, and thus decide whether or not they support an ethical cause.

Through the ITC a new model of development is being promoted as a way to fuel African economic growth, but this is unlikely to lead to widespread poverty alleviation. There are three main problems with the economic geography of this type of intervention. First, rather than establishing 'modern' industrial patterns – as previously existed in Kenya and elsewhere in Africa – ITC advocates a fragmented approach to organizing production and 'essentially spread[s] out the different parts of a factory over entire regions'.[29] This promotes uneven development and only helps small isolated groups to enter the global clothing economy on marginally better terms. Second, dispersed community-level production is also disadvantageous for labour as it reduces wage earners' bargaining power: it is difficult for them to negotiate for better salaries from big international firms. Third, the ITC wants to develop large-scale production, but does not promote state intervention, preferential access to overseas markets, industrial development, or production for local consumers, and only responds to 'market demand'. The WTO sponsors ITC's ethical Fashion Africa initiative. Yet it is important to note that the WTO's broad mission is to open up global trade, and encourage the economic liberalization imposed upon Africa through structural adjustment programmes. This process of globalization contributed to closing African clothing factories and eroding wage levels. Today's 'Made with Love in Nairobi' craftswomen are the daughters of a generation which had an established clothing industry that proved to be uncompetitive in a globalized free market. This type of niche production and small-scale employment cannot contribute to widespread poverty alleviation; rather than well-intentioned market 'solutions', more radical shifts in the world economy are required. The re-establishment of an industrial working class will be necessary before poverty reduction can be achieved on a large scale.

MARKETING 'MADE WITH LOVE IN NAIROBI'

'Made with Love in Nairobi' has been promoted through magazine photo shoots, videos, Westwood's personal blog and numerous interviews. Vivienne Westwood has made a big 'media splash'.[30] The images and personal vignettes represent a controlled attempt to de-fetishize the commodity. Nairobian craftswomen have identities which add symbolic value to the commodities. In Fairtrade the romantic commodification of production has been used to a similar effect. Vivienne Westwood ramps this up by using her celebrity identity to draw greater attention to the production location and shape consumers' knowledge. A stylized vision of a de-fetishized relationship is offered, which is actually a caricature of reality. The creation of a new commodity fetish begins with the name of the products, 'Made with Love in Nairobi', which instantly draws attention to the conditions of production. The use of 'Love' cynically reworks the commodity fetish to capitalize on the notion of 'caring at distance'.[31] The acts of 'love' represent a two-way interaction: on the one hand, the bags are explicitly made 'with love' and carefully manufactured; on the other hand, the implicit subtext is that the consumer is performing a reciprocal *act of love* towards a deserving African woman by buying the bag. What could be a more effective way of obscuring the unequal relationship between consumer and producer? The name 'Made with Love in Nairobi' really says more about consumers' construction of their own identity than about the producers' situation. People are choosing a fashionable bag and aspiring to buy into a compassionate image.

The primary imagery used in 'Made with Love in Nairobi' projects a powerful message of lifting impoverished African female urban workers out of poverty. Photographs are shot in a 'slum' landscape of dusty and impoverished Nairobi streets, rubbish dumps and local workshops, showing where the goods are produced and who will benefit from their sale. In most of the photos local people are in the margins of the frames; Vivienne Westwood herself takes centre stage alongside established African supermodels. The promotional material presents a 'one-way' consumption of life.[32] A new text is created by Vivienne Westwood so that the consumer can 'know' what life in Nairobi looks like, but this is in one direction as the producer does not 'know' the consumer. In some of the images Westwood re-creates a typical African scene after recognizing the commonplace practice of selling second-hand clothes and accessories in open-air markets;[33] 'We brought so many accessories with us to Africa that Juergen [the photographer] suggested we pretend we had a shop and were selling things like everybody else. I think you can see that I'm having fun selling.'[34] Westwood seems to mock the situation of the people around her. She places the $300 handbags among second-hand clothes consumed by the poor out of necessity rather than choice. The imagery in the adverts follows classical European representations of the continent, where Africans are reduced to the role of bystanders.[35] This marketing activity contrasts sharply with the livelihoods of African market traders, which are beset by risk, uncertainty and hardships.[36]

Some of the revenue from sales may help alleviate poverty in Kenya on a small scale, but meanwhile the promotional campaign creates new commodity fetishes that undermine the broader efforts to challenge the politics of global inequality. The Vivienne Westwood stylized and romantic vision of Kenya is obscuring the inequity between global North and South in a manner comparable to that of other celebrities' interventions in Africa, including Bono, Bob Geldof and Madonna.[37] In this case study a celebrity personality is attempting to allow individual consumers to make moral and economic connections to African producers in a flawed effort to de-fetishize commodity culture. Rather than eliminating the commodity fetish, the celebrity artist conjures up a new performance. The knowledge flows – newspaper and magazine features and interviews, blogs, and the ITC and Vivienne Westwood websites – formulate a new fetish and create another form of 'spectacle' for Northern consumers.

As with Fairtrade and the other ITC products, 'Made with Love in Nairobi' offers a limited acknowledgement of the inequities at the heart of capitalism, but still depends upon the market and ordinary business practices. A premium is paid to the Kenyans who make the handbags, but to sustain the consumption of this product the commodity-choosing consumers have to be stimulated to buy the goods through Vivienne Westwood's celebrity appearances, which grab their attention and so her goods command high prices. The proclaimed aim to move away from a charity is contradicted by the images of Kenyans which fall into the category of deserving poor rather than equal partners. Westwood wants the consumer to help poor Africans: 'It's quite incredible to think that we might be able to save the world through fashion.'[38] Instead of providing something different to charity, the result of 'Made with Love in Nairobi' is itself a contradiction which undermines efforts to give greater recognition to workers in the global South.

ETHICAL RECYCLING AND NEW CYCLES OF CONSUMPTION

Consumer ethics also play a role in how people in the global North dispose of clothes. Getting rid of old clothes and making rubbish are firmly entrenched as part of the broader practice of everyday consumption and use.[39] People are increasingly being directed towards ways to dispose of the masses of old, unwanted clothes that result from the global North's overconsumption, especially the same middle-class consumers who enjoy buying ethical products. This includes the growth in doorstep and clothing bank collections already discussed, but also new ethical commercial solutions are emerging. The link between shopping and disposal is something that retailers are beginning to exploit as they mix fast fashion and sustainability. Foremost is H&M, the world's second largest apparel retailer. H&M has initiated a garment collection scheme across thousands of stores worldwide: 'customers are encouraged to bring in unwanted garments of any brand and in any condition to H&M stores in all 53 markets to be given a new life.'[40] Cecilia Brannsten, project manager in the UK Sustainability Team, outlines H&M's aim: 'Basically, we want to change the mindset of the customer [so they] see their old clothes as a resource rather than throwing them into the garbage or letting them pile up at the back of their closet.'[41] When customers visit H&M they can hand over their old clothes, for which they get a voucher in return to encourage more shopping.

In the USA, H&M offers a 15 per cent discount voucher for every bag of used clothing, with a limit of two vouchers a day. This is an incentive to bring in old clothes, but is not very generous when one considers that the company routinely posts a gross profit margin of around 60 per cent and a net profit margin of 15 per cent.[42] Clothes are sold on to I:CO, a Swiss headquartered textile recycler, which processes used clothing for second-hand markets in the global South, vintage retail in the global North, and recycling – just like the international used-clothing trade which has already been discussed at length. The claim is that it is a non-profit-making venture, with revenues covering H&M's running costs.[43] Donations are also made to charities: 'for each kilogram of clothes that H&M collects 0.02 Euro will be donated to a local charity organization chosen by H&M'.[44] This represents a small contribution when compared to the market price of used clothes.

Accepting donations of old clothes is not unique to H&M. Other retailers are establishing similar programmes, some of which involve closer integration with charities. In the UK 'JJB Sports has launched a new in-store trainer-recycling scheme to raise funds for [children's disability charity] Whizz-Kidz' with each donor receiving a £5 [$8] JJB voucher in exchange for every pair of trainers they donate'.[45] The used shoes are sold by JJB: 'All profits that JJB makes from the sale of the unwanted shoes for re-use or recycling will support many more young disabled people.' A similar scheme has been operated between Oxfam and Marks & Spencer since 2008: 'Oxfam and M&S have teamed up to help shoppers support the world's poorest people. Just bring your old M&S clothes or soft furnishings to an Oxfam shop and we'll exchange them for a £5 [$8] voucher to use at M&S.'[46] Donations then go on to be sold in Oxfam shops or processed at Wastesaver.

Getting rid of clothes makes more room for new consumption. Commercial recycling by stores like H&M explicitly links discarding unwanted clothes to a new cycle of consumption, demonstrating a direct connection between the new and used-clothing systems of provision. Clothing retailers want to provide a virtuous outlet for unwanted clothing in the global North, without interrupting the sale of fast fashion. They have begun to develop their own solution to the problem of clothing overconsumption. As with other collection schemes, the marketing materials downplay the broader social and economic impacts of the second-hand clothing trade in the global South. H&M and I:CO place a special emphasis on textile recycling, stating that it is possible to recycle up to 30 per cent of textiles and highlighting how these can be 'down-cycled' in to materials such as cushioning, flooring or packaging, or alternatively 'upcycled' into new clothes of equal or higher value.[47] Despite these narratives, profitability in clothing recycling is driven by the value of re-wearable garments rather than by remaking old clothes into new apparel or other goods. Closed-loop recycling, where textile fibres could be reused and woven into new fabrics, is an appealing idea, but techniques and technologies are currently underdeveloped and not economically viable on a commercial scale. The problems with this vision for the future of fast fashion are discussed in the conclusion alongside the expanding environmental impacts of overconsumption.

Ethical recycling provides an appealing and intuitive solution to the issues of fast fashion, yet this does not address the myriad development and environmental problems that are formed through the interconnected new and second-hand clothing systems of provision. As has been shown in earlier chapters, second-hand clothing donations have diverse effects upon the economies and cultures of the global South. From an environmental perspective, the 'clothes miles' associated with the circulation of millions of tons of new and used textiles are a further issue that should be considered within any ethical audit of the global clothing trade. Local rather than international commodity chains may offer greener solutions. Furthermore, the environmental impacts of new clothing production, as well as use, need to be more extensively explored. Solutions are likely to require radical action. The challenges of making green garments have become the preoccupation of a sustainable fashion movement.

SUSTAINABLE FASHION

Sustainable, green or eco fashion is a design philosophy and part of a wider trend towards sustainable forms of consumption. From origins among alternative and counter-culture groups, sustainable fashion has spread towards the mainstream, finding favour mainly among the middle classes in the global North. The language, if not always the reality, of sustainability has been leapt upon by the mainstream fashion press, most notably *Vogue,* and collections have found their way into malls and department stores. The overall concept of sustainability rests upon three pillars: society, economy and environment. Within fashion it is fair to say that the greatest attention has been drawn to the environmental pillar. The politics of the environment are malleable and business can shape the eco agenda to dictate new ways of bringing profitable clothing goods to the market. In theory, through sustainable design, consideration is given to the lifespan of products, including the broad ecological footprint of clothes. However, there are many layers of engagement in greening fashion. While the more committed proponents seek to dramatically rethink the relationships between design, consumption, use and reuse, and end of life, at the other limit of the spectrum some eco interventions resemble little more than token gestures, as business has capitalized upon the popularity of environmental movements to bathe their products in the appealing aura of greenness.

Corporations have grown concerned about their brand image; in consequence, major fast-fashion companies have made limited efforts to think progressively about material selection, resource flows and supply chain efficiencies.[48] Some of these interventions have the collateral benefit of making manufacturing and distribution more profitable, or enabling products to be attractively marketed. It can pay to consider the environment; however, reforms rarely extend to changes that will significantly disrupt the profitability of production. The crux of the matter is the inherent contradiction of sustainable fashion. Importantly, 'normal' or 'fast' fashion is driven by the logic of the market.

Fashion in the broadest sense means the prevailing or conventional – that is, the socially acceptable – way of dressing. New clothes are framed as being *the latest fashion*, implying that there is change afoot and soon current fashions will become outmoded and obsolete. Fashions are the accelerating metronome for consumption, producing advancing beats, pulsing ever faster to draw more commodities through the world of fast fashion. Zara's model of continually changing fashion lines and other strategies of ongoing replenishment compel the committed shopper to buy, and keep on buying, fast fashion. Ownership becomes transient as affordable garments are made of inferior materials and are constructed speedily in ways which mean they will fray, thin, unravel and fall apart.

Fashion is a practice that directly underpins the rapid despoiling of the earth's environmental systems. Under capitalism the necessity to continually increase profits brings more and more products to the market. Varied styles and makes of clothes all have different and baffling biographies that involve a near infinite array of ecological impacts. Difficulties in auditing and accounting for the effects of consuming particular items of clothing stymie effective collective action, even though it is evident that clothes-making harms environments around the world. On a global scale

evidence abounds of the varied ways in which everyday life is exceeding planetary boundaries; usage of
fresh water, food and minerals has grown exponen-
tially since the onset of the Industrial Revolution.[49] To
go further back, ever since humans began to change
the environment around themselves, they set in
motion an irreversible destruction of what was natural. The size of the challenge is immense. How can
consuming clothes be reconciled with preserving the
environment through ecologically limited and careful
practices that necessitate living within the boundaries
of ecological systems? How can fashion become sustainable? These are big questions. The focus of this
book has been on humans and poverty, directing
knowledge towards the social and economic (non)sus-
tainability of systems of provision. The work of others,
with a greater sensibility for design and knowledge
of materials, is both advancing the understanding of
the environmental impacts of clothing consumption
and challenging how we think about the very idea of
fashion. Foremost here is the work of Kate Fletcher,
who recognizes the need for a holistic approach that
looks across systems of provision. Viable alternatives
must be located, studied and popularized to unlock
creativity and challenge contemporary relationships
between people and the garment sector:

Ideas and expectations of fashion are 'locked in' to conventions, habits, social norms and industry structures that reflect a vision of our fashionable selves as individuals consuming new clothes, but … other forms of fashion expression and provision exist and reflect resourceful, fulfilling and empowering engagement with garments. Tentatively, this points to a situation where ideas of progress are no longer tied to a societal narrative of economic growth through market transactions.[50]

PERSPECTIVES ON ETHICAL CONSUMPTION

When debating the impacts of ethical consumption one of the fundamental issues to consider is whether the success of businesses is consistent with social advancement and human development. If capitalist progress is inherently good, then most enterprise will have ethical benefits. The reality, however, indicates otherwise. The global market economy has led to uneven development and environmental degradation. Ethical consumption is both compatible with and supportive of liberal free-market approaches to governance of the global economy and environment. As such, the ways in which ethical consumption is popularized dismantle a sense of praxis. This means that more radical alliances and voices of dissent can get crowded out as partial and deeply flawed ethical solutions grab attention. Critical work which has been undertaken on Fairtrade and similar products has illuminated many of the problems of ethical consumption and exposed how this type of activity sustains the smooth functioning of global capitalism rather than being a brake on an exploitative mode of production. To reiterate, ethical production systems alter rather than eliminate the exploitation of workers, especially in the global South. 'Made with Love in Nairobi' provides a signal case of particular interest as it uses advertising imagery which mimics African second-hand clothing markets, reinforcing the links between new and used clothes, but also embedding the logic of an uneven world in which different people have and do not have access to new clothes.

Ethical consumption satisfies a longing for 'action' on environmental and social issues by producing commodities with highly specific use values which meet people's real (or imagined) needs. Yet, as the radical philosopher Slavoj Žižek argues, 'from the absolute standpoint of the system as a totality, the satisfaction of individuals' needs is just a necessary means to keep the machinery of capitalist (re)production going'.[51] Buying ethical clothes like Toms shoes is an individualized form of 'political' consumption which represents a limited force for social change that focuses attention only on convenient ethical topics. The maintenance of individual consumer sovereignty fits perfectly with extreme notions of liberalism whereby social relations are becoming 'purely atomic' and civic responsibility is rejected in favour of the 'apotheosis of the individual'.[52] This type of positional ethical consumption as class differentiation feeds into the reproduction of inequalities. Clothing is one of the most important types of consumer commodity, as it stands in for identity. People want to wear clothes that represent their personality, and so garments which are associated with values such as compassion and care are popular among certain consumers. 'Going green' or supporting other topical issues can even be fashionable. From an environmental perspective the individually responsible decision is to choose to shop less often, wear clothes until they are worn out, and then repair or recycle them within the household or replace them with locally produced goods. Slowing the rate of clothing consumption by buying fewer higher-quality clothes is a far more environmentally friendly approach than continuing to buy fast fashion and donating excess clothes. However, these solutions are an 'opt in' approach to a massive problem and are unlikely to be taken up by more than a small section of society in the global North who have the opportunity to make the decision. Fundamentally, more radical social change is required, to which business as usual does not provide the answer.

FAST FASHION

FAST FASHION AND THE ENVIRONMENT

An estimated 100 billion garments are manufactured every year.[1] Styles change rapidly, clothes are often replaced and cheap items are poorly made from low-quality materials. The production and consumption of fast fashion has far-reaching environmental consequences. Some are visible, others hidden from view. Unwanted clothes are an abundant source of waste, yet a less obvious, but far-reaching and ecologically damaging impact of fashion has escaped attention. This issue is linked to the pressing problem of ocean plastics pollution, but is more obscure. Single-use plastics pollution has become a hot topic in environmental politics. Celebrities including the respected naturalist David Attenborough and yachtswoman Ellen MacArthur have highlighted how bottles, crisp packets, polystyrene fast-food wrappers and other forms of trash are

accumulating in marine environments. Masses of discarded plastic materials are blown into streams and
rivers, then flow into lakes and oceans, and other items
of rubbish are dumped directly into the sea. Swirling
flotsams of plastics are accumulating in the oceans
and disrupting ecosystems. Debris in the north central
Pacific Ocean have become caught in a vortex of circu-
lating currents halfway between Hawaii and California.
The Great Pacific Garbage Patch extends almost across
the width of the Pacific and has become a cause célè-
bre featuring in documentary films and news reports
that focus attention on the environmental impacts of
consumer society. Pollution from packaging and other
single-use plastics has gone from being a hidden phenomenon to a visible relic of global environmental
change.[2] Ocean currents and society's insatiable consumption of plastics have co-produced an exceptional
example of marine pollution that has spurred political
action. The European Parliament voted to ban a range
of single-use plastics by 2021 including plastic cutlery,
plates and straws, and there is political pressure for
much-needed further reductions, yet there is another
source of marine pollution that requires urgent attention as it is potentially even more fearsome.

Fast fashion is doing untold, hidden damage to
ecological systems. Invisible micro-scale pollution

is transforming rivers and oceans. Fish and other aquatic species are ingesting tiny fragments of synthetic thread when they feed. A major source is artificial micro-fibres released when polyester garments are laundered.[3] Single strands of polyester and other synthetic fibres can hardly be seen by the naked eye as they are smaller in diameter than a human hair. Cumulatively these tiny fragments have a substantial impact on sea life. Organisms of all sizes consume fibres and other microplastics. Plastics may be toxic or inert, but all synthetic fibres can become lodged in the bodies of fish, shellfish and crustaceans. Micro-pollutants take up space in the digestive system and are often unpassable, reducing both survival and reproduction, as well as increasing the uptake of chemical pollutants that bind to fibres and other materials.[4] Impacts start with organisms that feed by filtering large volumes of water, then bioaccumulate through the food chain from small sea creatures to their larger predators. Worryingly for the millions of people who depend upon seafood in their diet, humans sit at the top of these food chains and consume marine organisms, including farmed and coastal fish that have micro-pollutants in their bodies. These plastics are accumulating in people's guts with as yet unknown long-term health implications.

The widespread production, use and laundering of synthetic fibres is leading to an environmental crisis. Polyester, nylon, acrylic and other synthetics account for around 60 per cent of clothing material.[5] Cheap fast-fashion garments increasingly use low-quality fibres that break down when laundered. Laundry involves a physical process that agitates as well as cleans fabrics. As heat, movement, detergents and water dissolve stains, they also weaken textiles. Surface fibres are abraded, break off and are released into the waste water and enter the sewerage network.[6] Treatment plants discharge micro-pollutants into waterways. All garments shed fibres yet plant- and animal-derived natural fibres like cotton, linen and wool are broken down by micro-organisms, light, air or water and do not have the same negative effects on marine life. Biodegradable natural fibres pose few problems in comparison with artificial fibres. Tiny strands and coils of polyester and acrylic flushed into aquatic and marine systems, contribute to the escalating problem of plastic pollution in rivers and oceans.

The problem of artificial micro-fibre pollution is a signature example of the challenges of what environmental scientists are starting to call the 'Anthropocene'. The Anthropocene is a name for a new geological era that has arisen as a concept for contextualizing both the extent and severity of contemporary environmental change. It is a way to help us conceive of the ecological predicament of the twenty-first century and understand major global environmental challenges including climate change.[7] Since the onset of the Industrial Revolution, spearheaded by clothing production in northern England, the global environment has undergone tremendous change. Landscapes, ecosystems and species distributions are being transformed by human-made or 'anthropogenic' forces, sometimes irrevocably.[8] The extent of human-led change varies between places, but few, if any, environmental systems have escaped the impacts of modernity. Arguments that popularize the notion of the Anthropocene coalesce around emerging and unpredictable patterns of climate change, fuelled largely by carbon emissions. The chemistry of the global atmosphere in which life is encompassed has been reformulated by human hands. Yet the Anthropocene concept envelops more than a new cocktail of climatic gases. Rather, it is the full spectrum of environmental changes led by human action. Agriculture and industries are disrupting environmental systems and crossing thresholds of dramatic and irreversible planetary harm.[9] Synthetic fertilizers have altered the nitrogen cycle, nuclear energy and weapons have produced radionucleotides changing the radioactivity of soils, and species extinction rates are around a thousand times greater than they would be without human activity.[10] The fashion industry is at the forefront of these environmental transformations. It is one of the largest manufacturing sectors and accounts for around 2 per cent of the world's gross domestic product. Textile production contributes 1.2 billion tonnes of annual greenhouse gas emissions, greater than the combined amount of all international flights and maritime shipping. Fast fashion has fuelled this huge environmental impact as global clothing production has doubled in the last 15 years.[11] Emissions continue throughout the life of garments as laundry is an energy intensive process as well as a polluting activity. Seventy per cent of the greenhouse gas emissions associated with cotton clothing come from washing at home, rather than agriculture and manufacture.[12]

The challenges of climate change, single-use plastic and micro-fibre pollution typify the Anthropocene. Their histories are embedded within the co-development of capitalism, industrial manufacturing and the global dependency on oil. Modern life is underpinned by unsustainable patterns of resource use and consumption that are dictated by norms and values, such as the social desire for new and fashionable garments and the cultural necessity to dress in fresh-smelling and unstained garments. Furthermore, the effects are irreversibly changing marine environments. Cumulatively the use of plastics is so great that it will imprint an indelible signature on the fossil record. Deposits of artificial micro-fibres, plastics and other pollutants in sea- and river-beds are leaving an impression within sediments that will be present in the earth's geological record alongside other markers of past and future epochs. Leading scientists argued that humans have become a powerful and permanent geologic force significant in the history of the earth. This was recognized by the International Geological Congress in 2016, which officially designated the Anthropocene as a geologic epoch that began in the mid-twentieth century. Micro-fibres, along with plastics, aluminium alloys and other human-made materials found in trace concentrations of sediment samples are forming 'technofossils' that will stain the geologic record.[13] This could in the future become what geologists refer to as an epoch-defining 'golden spike': a specific event marked in rock, sediment or glacier ice that denotes the onset of the Anthropocene.[14]

CONSUMING FAST FASHION

The clothing sector has unforeseen impacts on the global environment fuelled by the over consumption of fast fashion. What compels people to buy more and more clothes? The old twentieth-century fashion year of Spring–Summer and Autumn–Winter collections has broken down to be replaced by a continual process of re-invention. First mass-market retailers such as H&M and Zara promoted the rhythm of ever-changing trends by constantly refreshing their stock. Physical retailers have since been joined by efficient and assertive online stores like ASOS and Boohoo, the latter of which has the advertising tagline 'Twentyfour seven fashion' that encapsulates the relentless changes to their collections and the fast tempo of sales. Excessive consumption of clothing in the global North generates a surplus of unwanted clothes. T-shirts that are sold for £2 ($3) may be worn a few times and thrown away or donated for reuse. Oxfam estimate a quarter of Christmas party wear is only ever worn once.[15] Increasingly charity shops cannot sell donated clothes because they receive too many items and the garments are too low quality or already out of fashion. Boohoo sells some very cheap items, including dresses for as little as £5. The joint CEO Carol Kane has said that these dresses make up a small percentage of Boohoo's sales and are intentionally sold at a loss to drive web traffic. Kane argues fast fashion is fuelled by consumption: 'I believe this all comes back to consumer demand. I've been in the industry for 32 years, and within that time I've seen prices decline considerably.'[16] But does the fault really lay with customers when they are manipulated by a fashion industry that prices dresses artificially low to entice them to purchase more clothing?

Despite new patterns of retail and accelerated rhythms of change, fast-fashion brands still draw upon the material culture of seasonal fashion shows to inspire their ever-evolving offerings. Fashion weeks featuring tall, elegant models in couture designs in Beijing, London, Milan, New York, Paris, Tokyo and elsewhere are the apex of the broader fashion system of provision. Many clothes shown are outrageous and will inspire future fashions, rather than be worn in the real world. Other collections showcase new looks that will soon make it to retail. Between shows, bloggers, journalists, stylists, designers and retail buyers mix at exclusive receptions, enjoying cocktails and sharing trends on social media. In the days which follow, the designs showcased by runway models and the new trends worn by the fashion community are relayed online around the world. Outfits are rated and debated, fresh looks emerge and provide inspiration for new mass clothing products. Copying is rampant and budget versions of high fashions worn by celebrities are reproduced for the masses. Fashion Nova is one of the most popular brands on Instagram and infamously recreated Meghan Markle's Stella McCartney-designed evening wedding dress for what *Cosmopolitan* magazine praised as a 'dirt cheap' $44.99.[17]

Clothing culture is influenced by wider social processes, as Coco Chanel recognized: 'Fashion is not something that exists in dresses only. Fashion is in the sky, in the street, fashion has to do with ideas, the way we live, what is happening.'[18] The types of couture collections exhibited at fashion shows and shared by celebrities on social media help generate interest as consumer demand is shaped and manipulated by the fashion sector, as Alexandra Shulman, former editor-in-chief of British *Vogue* says: 'Fashion is smoke and mirrors. We create images, we create a world of stuff, yes, ultimately to make people want to have it.'[19] Fashion can literally produce smoke to ensure that brands maintain their exclusivity. In 2018 Burberry burned £30 million ($40 million) of unsold clothes, accessories and perfume rather than discounting these items and diluting the brand's appeal.[20] Image making led by the media, entertainment industry, fashion designers and retailers, creates new desires and simultaneously erodes the value of previous trends, placing consumers in a never-ending contest of purchases. Broader social norms and changing cultural values further influence how people think about colours and fabrics, the length of dresses or the design of logos.[21]

The majority of consumers in the global North are not 'slaves to fashion', and the symbolic value of clothing is just part of their decision-making process when they go shopping.[22] Many people claim to have little or no interest in fashion, but everyone adheres to some culturally constructed norms of dress; business suits for office work, jeans for the weekend, cocktail dresses for Christmas parties and so forth.[23] Trends are never static and are kept in motion by the material culture that surrounds fashion as the collective growth in demand for new products is essential for the clothing industry's business model.[24] The fact that clothing which can still be re-worn is regularly disposed of demonstrates that the market is very successful in stimulating new clothing purchases principally for their visual appeal. People continually buy clothes they do not really need because they like the look of them, although this is not everyone. Even in the affluent societies of the global North there are plenty of people whose choices are constrained by poverty. Thrift stores and charity shops still provide an important source of clothing for the poor. For the most disadvantaged access to clothing can be a fundamental issue of human welfare. Shockingly in Canada people have been so desperate for warm clothing that they have risked their lives climbing into clothing donation bins to tray to retrieve jackets. Sadly, two such deaths were reported in Vancouver in 2019.[25]

FAST-FASHION AND SECOND-HAND
CLOTHES IN THE GLOBAL SOUTH

In Africa and elsewhere in the global South clothing poverty is a reality of everyday life for the majority of people, yet this has not always been the case. Many countries had their own traditions and cultures of clothing production and consumption that have been decimated by globalization. For instance in Zambia, workers that laboured in the mines or industry, like the Mulungushi clothing factory, were part of an emerging modern society that could afford locally produced, and even international fashions in the 1970s and 1980s: 'Mineworkers in tattered clothes who were struggling to feed their families had to remind me that there was a time, not so long ago, when they could not only afford to eat meat regularly but could even buy tailored suits mail-ordered from London.'[26] Today, the urban poor in Zambia are unable to purchase locally made garments or attain international fashions. Second-hand garments provide the major source of clothing for most Zambians, other Africans and billions of people around the world.[27] The reasons are inter-linked with affluence in the global North and the structural inequalities and uneven development of the world economy.[28] From the colonial period onwards, the development of global trade and uneven exchange has enabled first cotton, and later completed clothing goods, to be traded from the global South to the North. Declining terms of trade and economic liberalization in developing countries have made clothing cheaper for consumers in Europe and North America, but have also weakened local markets and reduced the buying power of the poor. The excessive consumption of clothing in the global North leads to tens of billions of garments being exported back to the global South, sometimes to the very same locations which manufacture new clothes for export to Europe and North America, such as Kenya, Tanzania, the Philippines and Pakistan. Used-clothing imports erode opportunities for local manufacturers and lock poor societies into relationships of dependency.[29] New clothing sales are predicated on the exploitation of labour in places such as Zambian cotton farms and Pakistani clothing factories, yet the very people who grow the cotton or sew the clothes cannot afford to buy new fashions. Globalization means that some workers in Africa and Asia can make garments for export, but could only afford to buy them five years later on a second-hand market.

Policy-makers in the global South, including in major economies such as India and Nigeria, have tried to address the problems created through trade inequalities by imposing bans on used-clothing imports. India's efforts have been relatively successful, but Nigeria's have been undermined by cross-border imports from neighbouring African states. In 2015 Burundi, Kenya, Rwanda, Tanzania and Uganda, which together make up the East African Community (EAC), decided to phase out used-clothing imports. An estimated 67 per cent of East Africans purchase used clothing.[30] The EAC's aim is to encourage local garment production within member countries. In the 1970s, East Africa's clothing factories employed hundreds of thousands of people, but when the debt crisis hit Africa in the 1980s and 1990s, local manufacturing struggled to compete with international competition and factories were forced to close. In parallel, economic liberalization opened the EAC markets to cheap imports of used clothing as well as low-quality new garments from East and South Asia. Today, the small remaining clothing sector is geared towards production for exports.

Many economists disagree with banning imports because it goes against the principles of free trade. They argue it is bad for companies operating at a global scale and bad for the African poor. The EAC's move angered policy-makers in Washington because it would harm used-clothing exporters and lead to a loss of jobs and export revenue in the United States. Exporters might go out of business and rather than having the freedom to choose used clothing African consumers will have to buy higher-priced local garments or imported new clothes. Rising clothing prices will hit many low-income consumers in the short-term, but a revitalized local market could boost the EAC's economy by providing more jobs in manufacturing in the long run. Factory jobs could be better than work in second-hand markets and would employ many more people. There would also be jobs for people selling new clothing. Furthermore, retaining money in East African economies that currently goes to Europe and the US to pay for second-hand imports will improve their balance of trade and reduce economic dependency. Turning off the supply of used clothing will not enable the growth of local manufacturing on its own, especially if new-clothing imports from outside the EAC are cheaper than locally produced goods. Efforts to control used-clothing imports are therefore unlikely to be beneficial for the local economy unless there are similar controls on new-clothing imports. Clothing manufacturers in East Africa face other challenges. If countries such as Kenya are to revitalize their clothing factories, which once employed an estimated 500,000 people and now only has around 20,000 workers, then the EAC needs to promote industrial policies. These might include improving communication, transport infrastructure and power supplies to enhance distribution and avoid delays in production; providing tax relief for manufacturers; and offering export incentives. Links could also be established with East Africa's cotton-growing sector to improve its sustainability, to add value to this primary product, and help ensure a reliable local supply of raw materials.

Second-hand clothes are affordable for the poor, but trading in them reinforces an unequal relationship between haves and have-nots in the global economy. Successful nations that have developed in the last 50 years such as China and South Korea did not emerge from poverty by becoming dependent on exports from the West. Instead they protected domestic markets during the early stages of industrialization and enabled salaries to rise. If African leaders want to do more than maintain the status quo they need to take bold decisions, even if this means sometimes making choices that might be unpopular with international advocates of free trade. The intention of the EAC ban and the goal of promoting industrialization in the East African region is commendable, but for it to be successful more needs to be done to support industry and encourage the creation of good jobs to break the cycle of dependency and poverty.

Developing manufacturing capacity does not guarantee a route out of poverty for poor countries. Measures are required to protect workers' rights and enhance social welfare. Bangladesh has a massive clothing export sector that employees 40 million workers and contributes 83 per cent of Bangladesh's total exports.[31] The boom in fast fashion in the early twenty-first century fuelled the growth in Bangladeshi exports, but rather than there being an upswing in factory workers' livelihoods since the early 2000s, monthly wages actually marginally decreased from $93.67 in 2001 to $91.45 in 2011 (measured in 2001 US$ purchasing power parity (PPP)).[32] There have been some movements towards improving wages and health and safety since the devastating collapse of the Rana Plaza factory in 2013, which resulted in

1,134 deaths, focused attention on labour exploitation in South Asia. Minimum monthly wages were raised to $95 (or $242 in 2018 US$ PPP), yet this was only half the demands of local workers.[33] Labour exploitation is commonplace in the factories of Dhaka where many women from rural communities sew garments to supply global retailers including H&M and Zara.[34] Factory work is poorly paid, exploitative and driven by unrealistic targets. Less than 5 per cent of the Bangladeshi workforce are unionized and most workers do not get a living wage. They are overworked and tired, pushed hard to complete orders to meet the ever-changing trends in fast fashion. After long shifts, they struggle to feed their families on simple meals of rice and dried fish. Even so-called ethical products can be manufactured under appalling labour conditions. In 2019, female Bangladeshi workers who made Spice Girls T-shirts endorsed by the band to raise funds for the Comic Relief charity to help 'champion equality for women' were paid just 35p (0.50$) an hour, faced verbal abuse and harassment, and were forced to work 16-hour shifts to keep up with production targets.[35] In neighbouring India, other supplier factories for H&M as well as GAP have been accused of physical abuse and gender-based violence against female workers.[36] Women in South Asian factories are forced to work harder and harder by oppressive male managers to produce more and more fast fashion.

CLOSED-LOOP FAST FASHION

Throughout this book evidence has shown that the new and second-hand clothing sectors need to be considered in tandem by policy-makers, businesses and charities. The deep problems and international inequalities which provide the pre-conditions for the exploitative fast-fashion system are the same which have enabled the boom in the second-hand clothing trade. There is a social and environmental crisis in fashion. Too many cheap low-quality clothes are being produced under labour conditions that are exploitative. The unequal trade in these garments is constraining development in the global South and the pollution created by fashion is damaging environments everywhere. The scale of over-production is gross. In 2018 H&M — the world's second-largest apparel retailer — had a $4.3 billon pile of unsold deadstock, in the past some of this has been burned or used as fuel in electricity generation in an incredibly wasteful activity.[37] Elsewhere other unsold garments end up entering the international trade in used clothes.

In an attempt to resolve the problems of clothing and textile waste H&M alongside other influential voices in the fashion industry are championing new

closed-loop approaches to consumption and production. The Circular Fibres Initiative proposes
technological solutions to environmental problems
by reducing or even eliminating material waste.
Ellen MacArthur is a high-profile proponent of the
circular economy, as well as lending her celebrity
status to supporting campaigns on plastics pollution.
MacArthur enthusiastically discusses the initiative:
'The Circular Fibres Initiative aims to catalyse change
across the industry by creating an ambitious, fact-
based vision for a new global textiles system.'[38] This
is to be achieved by designing fashion garments that
can be remade into different clothing designs once the
owner has finished with them. As WRAP (the Waste
Resource and Action Programme), another advocate of
the circular economy, argues in their Clothing Action
Plan, closed-loop recycling will cut: 'the environmental impact of clothing across the supply chain' while
also 'generating value for business through collaboration, measuring and sharing best practice'.[39] What is
not on the agenda is challenging commercial interests,
or questioning high-tempo fast-fashion models of production and consumption. The technological solutions
for producing a circular system are uncertain. Various
fibres have been proposed as suitable for closed-loop
recycling, such as polyester, nylon, cotton and wool,

although so far no large-scale economically viable methods have emerged. Even when a target fibre is selected a further challenge is finding a cost-effective sorting process to accurately identify used garments. This is especially difficult when clothes tags are faded or missing, as the identification of any treatments or finishings on the garments, or blending of other fibres in trace volumes can make recycling unfeasible.[40]

Despite the technical barriers closed-loop recycling is a particularly appealing initiative for fast-fashion brands. Companies like H&M have a business model based on high-volume sales of low-price goods, and a circular consumption model can enhance the rapid cycle of purchase and disposal. Closed-loop models can forge a connection between throwing away unwanted items and buying new ones. Recycling points will be located in retail stores and every time consumers want to get rid of an item of clothing they have to first navigate the sales floor and its many incentives to buy a new outfit. Currently some retailers collect garments that enter the second-hand economy. However, the model is set to change in the near future as businesses are working towards prioritizing the recycling of material. H&M are working with I:CO to try to expand their recycling of waste garments. They imagine a future where:

re-loved clothing and shoes would circulate in closed product and material cycles and be used continuously in the manufacturing of new products. At I:CO, we are committed to this vision. Our innovative take back system is helping make it a reality and is used successfully by many companies around the world today.[41]

H&M and I:CO are companies driven by the underlying necessity to profit and expand their operations and they are leveraging global environmental crises to try to find a new money-making opportunity. Rather than reducing consumption, they will want to maximize the throughput of materials, as this is where revenue is generated. Shortening the phase of wearing clothes and making fashion consumption faster means that people keep clothes for a shorter time. In such a short-life scenario one can imagine that garments will be regularly returned and re-enter the circuit after being worn just once, like countless Christmas garments do already. Although it is not in their public business plans, it is conceivable that retailers such as H&M may become more of a subscription service akin to a Netflix or Uber for clothes. We can imagine a future where customers might not own their garments but, rather, subscribe to the opportunity to wear them, returning items for remanufacturing once they are finished with them. In between the garments would get remade in a new design, refashioned to match changing trends and climatic seasons. This could only be an ecologically sound system if the remanufacturing processes yielded little pollution — of micro-fibres and other emissions — and consumed limited energy. Given the huge environmental impacts of clothing production along with the complex physical and chemical processes and technical challenges associated with reusing textiles, this is an unrealistic proposal. Furthermore, the pressure to work hard and fast will remain on clothing factory workers in the global South. Closed-loop recycling is as likely to lead to further environmental degradation and social costs as it is to resolve the crises of overconsumption.

Within environmental management the maxim 'reduce, reuse, recycle' is a neat turn of phrase that encapsulates how the best way to alleviate the impact of consumption is, first, to reduce purchases; second, to reuse objects; and third, to make a new thing by recycling the material. The third option represents much greater use of energy and so is less favourable than reusing, which in turn is inferior to not producing and consuming the object in the first place. Reuse involves social change. In countries such as the United

Kingdom this means changing attitudes towards purchasing and wearing pre-owned clothing. But this type of social change represents a challenge to profitability, and therefore business has become attracted to a technical closed-loop solution that turns the developing global environmental crisis into a money-spinning opportunity.

WHAT SHOULD BE DONE WITH FAST FASHION?

There is already a circular economy operating at a global scale in the fast-fashion sector. Some clothes go from manufacturing in the global South to retail in the North and return back to the South where they are worn by the poor until they become rags and fall apart. This hidden under-belly of globalization has been exposed through this book. It is not a socially or environmentally sustainable system and needs to be challenged by legislation rather than enabled to continue as it reinforces rather than resolves global inequalities. What then should people do with their unwanted clothes? The simple answer is to start by modify their behaviour. Consumers in the global North urgently need to buy fewer clothes to reduce the environmental impacts of fashion. If someone can afford to buy lots of new clothes and discard their old clothes, then instead they could just buy fewer better clothes. Purchasing, higher-quality garments made using natural fibres, under good labour standards might be more expensive, but wearing them for longer to reduce the 'fastness' of fashion offers a simple solution for the individual. Fashion is inherently subjective, but well-made, crafted garments produced using natural fibres have intrinsic qualities that transcend short-term trends. Over time, as body shapes change and good clothes no longer fit, they can be sold online through auction sites or gifted or swapped with friends and family members. Another sustainable option is for consumers in the global North to shop locally for second-hand items. Stained or faded items can be dyed a darker colour. Ripped items repaired. When clothes are too worn-out to wear they can be reused around the home, for instance when doing domestic cleaning, or used as rags or dusters. Ultimately, though the answers lie at a global scale and not with individual action. Living more socially and economically sustainably can be an important personal political act, but is unlikely to resolve the major international problems.

Consumers cannot go into the market-place armed with their credit cards and swipe away the world's problems. Some people are interested in their personal social and environmental footprint.[42] They want to make sure *they* do the right thing, but individual adjustments to behaviour will not lead to widespread progressive change. More often when people go shopping they do not think about the broader impacts of their purchases or they are too busy to reuse their clothing sustainably.[43] The consumer cannot be either expected or trusted to consistently make the right decisions. That judgement may sound harsh, but is justifiable on three interconnected levels. First, it is unrealistic to expect consumers in the global North to be able to undertake an accurate ethical audit whenever they buy new clothes. Every time someone looks at a pair of jeans can they really be expected to 'get behind the veil, the fetishism of the market' and uncover the true story of the system of provision, given the incredible complexity of supply chains?[44] Secondly, shoppers cannot be trusted. Consumers are bombarded by social pressure, every time they venture into the market – including adverts, marketing and weblinks for tempting offers. The desire to consume makes even the most conscientious shopper corruptible to taking the 'wrong' choice.[45] Finally, although their individual buying power is weak, the vast majority of the world's consumers are poor people in the global South. Consumption decisions can be a matter of life and death for households with limited resources, like the millions surviving on a dollar or two dollars a day.[46] For example, a poor person in Mozambique cannot realistically be expected to ignore affordable imported second-hand clothing and choose more expensive sustainable locally manufactured garments.

To fix consumption, a more equitable distribution of the benefits of global clothing production should be fought for, which primarily means an increase in wage levels for the people who make clothing. To improve the conditions for labour in the global South, the price of clothes in the global North needs to increase. More expensive clothes should mean fewer purchases and a reduced environmental impact. Profits can also be reduced to increase the pay of garment workers as the American and European retailers that sell huge volumes of clothes in the global North like Walmart and Zara make a lot of money. Massive surplus is extracted from the labour of workers by the billionaire heads of clothing retail empires who are among an elite group of the wealthiest people on earth. The world's 26 richest people have as much wealth as the poorest half of the global population. Their assets are equal to those of 3.8 billion people. Among this group are the sixth richest person in the world, Amancio Ortega, former chairman of Inditex, which owns the Zara brand, who alone is worth $70 billion; and the 14th, 15th and 16th richest are three members of the Walton family, part owners of Walmart, with around $46 billion each. The number one spot is taken by Jeff Bezos with $112 billion. He is the owner of Amazon, which includes a growing portfolio of fast-fashion lines.[47] These individuals each have personal wealth that far exceeds the GDP of entire countries such as Mozambique ($12.33 billion) and Zambia ($25.81 billion).[48] Just 1 per cent of Bezos's wealth would be enough to fund the entire health budget of Ethiopia, a country of 105 million, for a whole year.[49]

How could redistribution be enacted? Rather than pitching different manufacturing countries like Bangladesh, India, Ethiopia or Zambia against one another in a race to the bottom for labour standards, one approach would be to regulate the market and raise minimum wages across the global South towards those of the global North. Comparing the different costs of garment manufacturing in the developed and developing world can demonstrate how this would affect retail prices. An estimate from the Institute for Global Labour and Human Rights calculates the costs of making a denim shirt in the US as $13.22 versus $3.72 in Bangladesh. This price disparity is mainly explained by differences in wages between the global

North and South. For instance, in Britain the hourly minimum wage is £8.21 ($10.60), yet labour activists argue that a living wage of £9 ($11.62) should be paid, which is not double or even ten times what a worker in the global South gets, but 23 times the $0.50 hourly wages in the Bangladeshi garment sector. Gradually increasing wages in countries like Bangladesh towards those in Britain would help human development by providing more income for workers to consume and improve their welfare. If this were to happen not just in clothing, but across the industrial base throughout the global South a self-sufficient working class could emerge, which would alleviate the relationships of dependency with the global North. The comparative costs difference for a denim shirt would be an increase of $7.25 (based on the difference in wage levels between the US and Bangladesh), which would be passed on to the consumer, but in a regulated market could also be offset by reduced profits for billionaire owners and shareholders. Ownership of the means of production could even be transferred to the workers following mutual and cooperative business models. The scenario set out here is utopian and such radical transformation in the value of labour in low-income countries is unlikely to occur, but the alternative is the persistence of clothing poverty.

NOTES

INTRODUCTION

1 See Chapter 3 n37 for a discussion of United Nations Comtrade data on the volume and value of second-hand clothes traded around the world.

CHAPTER 1

1 Ben Fine, *The World of Consumption: The Material and Cultural Revisited*, Routledge, London, 2002, p. 79.

2 Robert Ross, *Clothing: A Global History*, Polity Press, Cambridge, 2008.

3 James Sullivan, *Jeans: A Cultural History of an American Icon*, Gotham, New York, 2006.

4 David Harvey, *The Limits to Capital*, Verso, London, 2006, p. 7.

5 Daniel Miller, 'Anthropology in Blue Jeans', *American Ethnologist*, vol. 37, no. 3, 2010, pp. 415–28, p. 422.

6 Levi Strauss & Co., 'Our Team', 2013, www.levistrauss.com/careers/our-team.

7 Mylene Mizrahi, '"Brazilian Jeans": Material-
ity, Body and Seduction at a Rio de Janeiro Funk
Ball', in Daniel Miller and Sophie Woodward, eds,
Global Denim, Berg, Oxford, 2011, p. 103.

8 Daniel Miller and Sophie Woodward, 'Manifesto
for a Study of Denim', *Social Anthropology*, vol. 15,
no. 3, 2007, pp. 335–51, p. 339.

9 WWF, 'Cotton Farming', 2013, http://wwf.
panda.org/about_our_ earth/about_freshwater/
freshwater_problems/thirsty_crops/cotton.

10 Muhammed Khan and Christos A. Damalas. 'Occupational Exposure to Pesticides and Resultant
Health Problems among Cotton Farmers of Punjab, Pakistan', *International Journal of Environmental Health Research*, vol. 25, no. 5, 2015, pp. 508–21.
Francesca Mancini et al., 'Acute Pesticide Poisoning
among Female and Male Cotton Growers in India',
*International Journal of Occupational and Environmen-
tal Health*, vol. 11, no. 3, 2005, pp. 221–32.

11 Tony Allen, *Virtual Water: Tackling the Threat to
Our Planet's Most Precious Resource*, I.B. Tauris,
London, 2011, pp. 348–9.

12 A.K. Chapagain et al., 'The Water Footprint of Cotton Consumption: An Assessment of the Impact
of Worldwide Consumption of Cotton Products
on the Water Resources in the Cotton Producing

Countries', *Ecological Economics*, vol. 60, no. 1, 2006, pp. 186–203.

13 Cotton Campaign, 'Stop Forced and Child Labour in Cotton Industry of Uzbekistan', 2013, www.cottoncampaign.org.

14 Oxfam International, 'The Effect of the Free Trade Agreement with the US on Cotton Farmers in Peru: Cotton Is No Longer "White Gold"', 2007, www.oxfam.org/en/programs/development/samerica/peru_cotton.

15 All figures are in US dollars unless otherwise stated. Humphrey Hawksley, 'India's Exploited Child Cotton Workers', BBC News Asia, 19 January 2012, www.bbc.co.uk/news/world-asia-16639391.

16 Author's interview with cotton growers in Zambia.

17 Rachel Louise Snyder, *Fugitive Denim: A Moving Story of People and Pants in the Borderless World of Global Trade*, W.W. Norton, New York and London, 2008, pp. 46, 117.

18 Shelia MacVicar, 'Jean Factory Toxic Waste Plagues Lesotho', CBS Evening News, 8 January 2010, www.cbsnews.com/8301-18563_162-5205416.html.

19 Snyder, *Fugitive Denim*, p. 148.

20 Ibid., p. 95.

21 Kanchana N. Ruwanpura, 'Metal Free Factories: Straddling Worker Rights and Consumer Safety?', *Geoforum*, vol. 51, no. 1, 2014, pp. 224–32.

22 Jennifer Bair and Garry Gereffi, 'Local Clusters in Global Chains: The Causes and Consequences of Export Dynamism in Torreon's Blue Jeans Industry', *World Development*, vol. 29, no. 11, 2001, pp. 1885–903.

23 Julie McCarthy, 'Bangladesh Collapse: The Garment Workers Who Survived', National Public Radio, 10 July 2013, www.npr.org/blogs/parallels/2013/07/10/200644781/Bangladesh-Collapse-The-Garment-Workers-Who-Survived.

24 Cotton Incorporated, 'Historical Denim Ownership among U.S. Consumers', 2013, http://lifestylemonitor.cottoninc.com/historical-denim-ownership-among-u-s-consumers.

25 Miller and Woodward, 'Manifesto for a Study of Denim', p. 336.

26 Snyder, *Fugitive Denim*, p. 161.

27 Ellen R. Shell, *Cheap: The High Cost of Discount Culture*, Penguin, Harmondsworth, 2009.

28 Ben Fine, *Marx's Capital*, Macmillan, London, 1976.

29 David Harvey, *The Condition of Postmodernity: An Enquiry into the Origins of Cultural Change*, Blackwell, Oxford and Cambridge MA, 1990, p. 422.

CHAPTER 2

1 Ha-Joon Chang, *Bad Samaritans: The Myth of Free Trade and the Secret History of Capitalism*, Bloomsbury, London, 2007.

2 WTO, 'Chronological List of Dispute Cases', 2014, www.wto.org/english/tratop_e/dispu_e/dispu_status_e.htm.

3 'A Temporary Truce on Textiles', *The Economist*, 7 September 2005.

4 Michael White and David Gow, 'EU and China in "Bra Wars" Deal', *The Guardian*, 6 September 2005.

5 A trend documented by the classical economist David Ricardo as well as Karl Marx.

6 David Harvey, *The Urbanization of Capital*, Blackwell, Oxford, 1985, p. 128.

7 David Harvey, *The Enigma of Capital and the Crises of Capitalism*, Profile Books, London, 2010, p. 117.

8 David Harvey, *The Limits to Capital*, Verso, London, 2006, p. 440.

9 European Commission, 'Fashion Competiveness', 2014, http://ec.europa.eu/enterprise/sectors/fashion/competitiveness/index_en.htm.

10 Linda: The Bra Lady, 'How Long Do Bras Really Last?' 2012, http://blog.lindasonline.com/2012/01/09/how-long-do-bras-really-last.

11 Noel Castree, *Nature,* Taylor & Francis, London, 2005.

12 Neil Smith, *Uneven Development,* Blackwell, Oxford, 1985.

13 Jared Diamond, *Guns, Germs and Steel: A Short History of Everybody for the Last 13,000 Years,* Vintage, London, 1998.

14 James M. Blaut, 'Diffusionism: A Uniformitarian Critique', *Annals of the Association of American Geographers,* vol. 77, no. 1, 1987, pp. 30–47.

15 Eric R. Wolf, *Europe and the People without History,* University of California Press, Berkeley, 1982.

16 Lucinda Blackwell, Francesco d'Errico and Lyn Wadley, 'Middle Stone Age Bone Tools from the Howiesons Poort Layers, Sibudu Cave, South Africa', *Journal of Archaeological Science,* vol. 35, no. 6, 2008, pp. 1566–80.

17 Olga Soffer, 'Recovering Perishable Technologies through Use Wear on Tools: Preliminary Evidence for Upper Paleolithic Weaving and Net Making', *Current Anthropology,* vol. 45, no. 3, 2004, pp. 407–13.

18 Katka Krosnar, 'Now You Can Walk in Footsteps of 5,000-year-old Iceman – Wearing His Boots', *Daily Telegraph,* 17 July 2005.

19 Proverbs 31:10–24.

20 Marianne Vedeler and Lise Bender Jørgensen, 'Out of the Norwegian Glaciers: Lendbreen – a

Tunic from the Early First Millennium AD', *Antiquity*, vol. 87, no. 337, 2013, pp. 788–801.

21 Worshipful Company of Weavers, 'History', 2014, www.weavers.org. uk/history.

22 Robert Ross, *Clothing a Global History*, Polity Press, Cambridge, 2008.

23 Frederick Engels, *The Condition of the Working Class in England*, trans. Florence Kelly Wischnewetzky, George Allen & Unwin, London, 1942 (1844), p. 7.

24 Ben Fine, *Marx's Capital*, Macmillan, London, 1976.

25 See Chapter 5 for a detailed case study of labour exploitation in a contemporary factory.

26 J. Smith, *Memoirs of Wool*, vol. 2, 1747, p. 308; quoted by E.P. Thompson, *The Making of the English Working Class*, Vintage Books, London, 1966.

27 Eric Hobsbawm, *The Age of Revolution*, Abacus, London, 1962, p. 48.

28 Engels, *The Condition of The Working Class in England*, p. 7.

29 Karl Marx, *Capital: A New Abridgment*, Oxford University Press, Oxford, 1995, p. 274.

30 Ross, *Clothing*.

31 Jeremy Seabrook, 'Song of the Shirt', *Economic and Political Weekly*, vol. 49, no. 21, 24 May 2014.

32 Gregory Clark and Robert C. Feenstra, 'Technology in the Great Divergence', in Michael D. Bordo,

Alan M. Taylor and Jeffery G. Williamson, eds, *Globalization in Historical Perspective*, University of Chicago Press, Chicago, 2003.

33 Ross, *Clothing*.

34 Antonio Gramsci, *Selections from the Prison Notebooks*, Lawrence & Wishart, London, 1971.

35 Kate Fletcher, 'Other Fashion Systems', in Kate Fletcher and Mathilda Tham, eds, *The Routledge Handbook of Sustainability and Fashion*, Routledge, London, 2015, p. 18.

36 Peter Dicken, *Global Shift: Mapping the Changing Contours of the World Economy*, Sage, London, 2011, p. 305.

37 Ibid., p. 320.

CHAPTER 3

1 Based on the author's own observations when living and working in Papua New Guinea in 2006.

2 Beverley Lemire, 'Shifting Currency: The Culture and Economy of the Secondhand Trade in England, *c*. 1600–1850', in Alexandra Palmer and Hazel Clark, eds, *Old Clothes, New Looks: Second Hand Fashion*, Berg, Oxford, 2005.

3 Ann Matchette, 'Women, Objects and Exchange in Early Modern Florence', *Early Modern Women: An Interdisciplinary Journal*, vol. 3, 2008, pp. 245–51.

4 Terry Satuki Milhaupt, 'Second Hand Kimono Migrating across Borders', in Palmer and Clark, eds, *Old Clothes, New Looks*.

5 Adam Smith, *An Inquiry into the Nature and Causes of the Wealth of Nations*, vol. 1, Methuen, London, 1904, p. 27.

6 Kellow Chesney, *The Victorian Underworld*, Pelican, London, 1970, p. 230.

7 Charles Dickens, *Oliver Twist or The Parish Boy's Progress*, Baudry's European Library, Paris, 1839, p. 161.

8 Karl Marx, *Capital: A New Abridgment*, Oxford University Press, Oxford, 1995, pp. 279–80.

9 Susan Strasser, *Waste and Want: A Social History of Trash*, Metropolitan Books, New York, 1999, p. 49.

10 Aldous Huxley, *Brave New World*, Flamingo, London, 1994, p. 49.

11 Quoted in 'Fashion: Brave New Look', *Time*, 3 July 1950.

12 Strasser, *Waste and Want*.

13 WRAP, 'Valuing Our Clothes: The Cost of UK Fashion', July 2017 http://www.wrap.org.uk/sites/files/wrap/valuing-our-clothes-the-cost-of-uk-fashion_WRAP.pdf#page=4.

14 Kate Fletcher, 'Other Fashion Systems', in Kate Fletcher and Mathilda Tham, eds, *The Routledge*

Handbook of Sustainability and Fashion, Routledge, London, 2015, p. 18.

15 Interview with Paul Ozanne, National Recycling Coordinator, Salvation Army Trading Company Limited, 21 November 2008.

16 Research by Juliet B. Schor and Kristen Heim, cited by Juliet B. Schor, 'Prices and Quantities: Unsustainable Consumption and the Global Economy', *Ecological Economics*, vol. 55, no. 3, 2005, pp. 309–20, p. 314.

17 Oxfam, *Inside Oxfam*, Summer 2008, p. 17; Oxfam, 'How and What to Donate to Our Shops', 2011, www.oxfam.org.uk/donate/shops/index.html.

18 Andrew Brooks, 'Riches from Rags or Persistent Poverty? Inequality in the Transnational Second-hand Clothing Trade in Mozambique', Ph.D. thesis, Royal Holloway, University of London, 2012.

19 North West Leicestershire District Council, 'Door to Door Charity Bag Collectors Fined', 2011, www.nwleics.gov.uk/news/2011/01/31/door_to_door_charity_bag_collectors_fined.

20 Richmondshire District Council, 'Bogus Charity Collections on Rise', 2012, www.richmondshire.gov.uk/news-and-publications/press-releases/boguscharitycollections.aspx?theme=textonly.

21 Jennifer Shea and Patrick Brennan, *Addressing Commercial Threats to Charity Shop Collections*, nfpSynergy (unpublished report), London, 2008, p. 29.

22 'Clothing Donation Bins Spark Turf War in Ontario', CBC News, 30 January 2012, www.cbc.ca/news/canada/story/2012/01/26/charity-clothing-bins-millions.html.

23 Sharon Bernstein, 'Battle Erupts in California over Clothes Donation Bins', Reuters, 6 April 2013, www.reuters.com/article/2013/04/06/usa-charity-fight-idUSL2N0CR1OT20130406; Meghan Hoyer and Jayne O'Donnell, 'Clothing Bin Donations Don't Always Reach Needy', *USA Today*, 30 December 2012.

24 WRAP, 'Valuing Our Clothes'.

25 Interview with Brian Lincoln, Regional Team Leader, YMCA, 10 March 2009.

26 'Clothing Donation Bins Spark Turf War in Ontario', CBC News.

27 Interview with Paul Ozanne, 21 November 2008.

28 Interview with Steve Wooldridge, Head of Property and Stock Operations, Help the Aged, 3 December 2008.

29 Hoyer and O'Donnell, 'Clothing Bin Donations Don't Always Reach Needy'. Controversies

surrounding Planet Aid are discussed further in Chapter 7.

30 Interview with Steve Wooldridge, 3 December 2008.

31 British Heart Foundation, 'Charitable Public Misled by Commercial Collection Companies', 2011, www.bhf.org.uk/media/news-from-the-bhf/charitable-public-misled.aspx.

32 Interview with Brian Lincoln, 10 March 2009.

33 'Clothing Donation Bins Spark Turf War in Ontario', CBC News.

34 Strasser, *Waste and Want*, p. 225.

35 Shea and Brennan, 'Addressing Commercial Threats to Charity Shop Collections', p. 13.

36 Interview with Paul Ozanne, 21 November 2008.

37 United Nations Comtrade, *UN Comtrade Database*, 2019, http://comtrade.un.org/data. UN Comtrade statistics HS (as reported) commodity code 630900 'Clothing: worn, and other worn articles' in 2017, 117 nations reported exporting old clothing and the total value was $4.0 billion and weight was 4.1 billion kg. The equivalent weight calculations are based on an average weight for a pair of jeans of 523 grams and a T-shirt of 123 grams.

38 Pietra Rivoli, *The Travels of a T-shirt in the Global Economy: An Economist Examines the Markets,*

Power, and Politics of World Trade, Wiley, London, 2009, p. 219.

39 United Nations Comtrade, *UN Comtrade Database*, 2019, http://comtrade.un.org/.

40 Karen Tranberg Hansen, *Salaula: The World of Secondhand Clothing and Zambia*, University of Chicago Press, Chicago, 2000, p. 110.

41 Interview with Tony Clark, Oxfam Wastesaver, 13 March 2009.

42 'Wonder Where Your Donations Go? Oxfam Has Got It Sorted', *The Guardian*, 15 February 2014.

43 Interview with Tony Clark, 13 March 2009.

44 'Wonder Where Your Donations Go?', *The Guardian*.

45 Ben Fine, *The World of Consumption: The Material and Cultural Revisited*, Routledge, London, 2002, p. 26.

CHAPTER 4

1 Christopher Wrigley, 'Speculations on the Economic Prehistory of Africa', *Journal of African History*, vol. 1, no. 2, 1960, pp. 189–203.

2 Roland Oliver and John D. Fage, *A Short History of Africa*, Penguin, London, 1962.

3 Linda Newson, 'The Slave-trading Accounts of Manoel Batista Peres, 1613–1619: Double-entry

Bookkeeping in Cloth Money', *Accounting History*, vol. 18, no. 3, 2013, pp. 343–65, pp. 356–7.

4 Walter Rodney, 'African Slavery and Other Forms of Social Oppression on the Upper Guinea Coast in the Context of the Atlantic Slave Trade', *Journal of African History*, vol. 7, no. 3, 1966, pp. 431–43, p. 434.

5 Basil Davidson, *Africa in History*, Paladin, London, 1984.

6 Newson, 'The Slave-trading Accounts of Manoel Batista Peres, 1613–1619', p. 360.

7 Linda Newson, 'Africans and Luso-Africans in the Portuguese Slave Trade on the Upper Guinea Coast in the Early Seventeenth Century', *Journal of African History*, vol. 53, no. 1, 2012, pp. 1–24, pp. 22–3.

8 Karl Marx, *The Eighteenth Brumaire of Louis Bonaparte*, Wildside Press, Rockville, MD, 2008, p. 15.

9 Kathleen E. Sheldon, *Pounders of Grain: A History of Women, Work, and Politics in Mozambique*, Heinemann Educational Books, Portsmouth, NH, 2002.

10 Quoted in Eduardo Mondlane, *The Struggle for Mozambique*, Penguin, London, 1969, p. 79.

11 Sayaka Funada-Classen, *The Origins of War in Mozambique: A History of Unity and Division*, African Books Collective, Oxford, 2013.

12 Quoted in Mondlane, *The Struggle for Mozambique*, p. 87.

13 Ibid., p. 83.

14 Joseph Hanlon, *Mozambique: The Revolution under Fire*, Zed Books, London, 1984; Allen Isaacman, *Cotton Is the Mother of Poverty: Peasants, Work, and Rural Struggle in Colonial Mozambique, 1938–1961*, Heinemann, Portsmouth, NH, 1995.

15 Jean-Claude Berthelemy and François Bourguignon, *Growth and Crisis in Côte d'Ivoire*, World Bank, Washington DC, 1996.

16 John Rapley, *Ivoirian Capitalism: African Entrepreneurs in Côte d'Ivoire*, Lynne Rienner, Boulder, CO and London, 1993.

17 Kate Meagher, 'A Back Door to Globalisation? Structural Adjustment, Globalisation and Transborder Trade in West Africa', *Review of African Political Economy*, vol. 30, no. 95, 2003, pp. 57–75.

18 Kate Manzo, 'Modern Slavery, Global Capitalism and Deproletarianisation in West Africa', *Review of African Political Economy*, vol. 32, no. 106, 2005, pp. 521–34.

19 Rapley, *Ivoirian Capitalism*.

20 Manzo, 'Modern Slavery, Global Capitalism and Deproletarianisation in West Africa'.

21 Oxfam, *Pricing Farmers Out of Cotton*, Oxfam Briefing Paper, March 2007, www.oxfam.org.uk/ resources/policy/debt_aid/downloads/bp99_ cotton.pdf, p. 2.

22 Andrea R. Woodward, 'The Impact of U.S. Subsidies on West African Cotton Production', in Per Pinstrup-Andersen and Fuzhi Cheng, eds, *Food Policy for Developing Countries: Case Studies*, Cornell University Press, Ithaca NY, 2007, p. 12.

23 International Centre for Trade and Sustainable Development, *Cotton: Trends in Global Production, Trade and Policy*, 2013, www.ictsd.org/ downloads/2013/06/cotton-trends-in-global-production-trade-and-policy.pdf, p. 4.

CHAPTER 5

1 Franz Wild, 'China Swaps Gusto for Rigor as It Learns from Africa', Bloomberg, 3 June 2014, www.bloomberg.com/news/2014-06-02/china-swaps-gusto-for-rigor-in-africa-as-it-learns-from-mistakes.html.

2 Giovanni Arrighi, *Adam Smith in Beijing: Lineages of the Twenty-first Century*, Verso, London, 2007, p. 361.

3 Pun Ngai, 'Global Production, Company Codes of Conduct, and Labor Conditions in China: A Case

Study of Two Factories', *China Journal*, no. 54, 2005, pp. 101–13.

4 Xiaomin Yu, 'Impacts of Corporate Code of Conduct on Labor Standards: A Case Study of Reebok's Athletic Footwear Supplier Factory in China', *Journal of Business Ethics*, vol. 81, no. 3, 2008, pp. 513–29.

5 Robert B. Potter, Tony Binns, Jennifer A. Elliot and David Smith, *Geographies of Development: An Introduction to Development Studies*, Pearson, Harlow, 2008, p. 360.

6 Yongzheng Yang and Chuanshui Zhong, 'China's Textile and Clothing Exports in a Changing World Economy', *The Developing Economies*, vol. 36, no. 1, 1998, pp. 3–23, p. 4.

7 Pun Ngai, 'Global Production, Company Codes of Conduct, and Labor Conditions in China', p. 109.

8 Xiaomin Yu, 'Impacts of Corporate Code of Conduct on Labor Standards'.

9 Ha-Joon Chang, *Bad Samaritans: The Myth of Free Trade and the Secret History of Capitalism*, Bloomsbury, London, 2007, p. 9.

10 Rudolf Traub-Merz, 'The African Textile and Clothing Industry: From Import Substitution to Export Orientation', in Herbert Jauch and Rudolf Traub-Merz, eds, *The Future of the Textile and*

Clothing Industry in Sub-Saharan Africa, Friedrich-Ebert-Stiftung, Bonn, 2006.

11 TAZARA provided a route to the Indian Ocean that avoided apartheid South Africa. It is reflected upon fondly as a symbol of Sino-African solidarity by both parties.

12 Deborah Brautigam, *The Dragon's Gift: The Real Story of China in Africa*, Oxford University Press, Oxford, 2009, p. 216.

13 Alastair Fraser and John Lungu, 'For Whom the Wind Falls? Winners and Losers in the Privatisation of Zambia's Copper Mines', Mine Watch Zambia, 2007, p. 8.

14 James Ferguson, *Expectations of Modernity: Myths and Meanings of Urban Life on the Zambian Copperbelt*, University of California Press, Berkeley, 1999.

15 Antonio Gramsci, *Selections from the Prison Notebooks*, Lawrence & Wishart, London, 1971.

16 Miles Larmer, 'Reaction and Resistance to Neoliberalism in Zambia', *Review of African Political Economy*, vol. 32, no. 103, 2005, pp. 29–45.

17 Peter Gibbon and Stefano Ponte, *Africa, Value Chains and the Global Economy*, Temple University Press, Philadelphia, PA, 2005.

18 Dorothy McCormick, Mary Njeri Kinyanjui and Grace Ongile, 'Growth and Barriers to Growth

among Nairobi's Small and Medium-sized Garment Producers', *World Development*, vol. 25, no. 7, 1997, pp. 1095–110.

19 Traub-Merz, 'The African Textile and Clothing Industry', p. 17.

20 Raphael Kaplinsky, 'What Does the Rise of China Do for Industrialisation in Sub-Saharan Africa?', *Review of African Political Economy*, vol. 35, no. 115, 2008, pp. 7–22.

21 Ndubisi Obiorah, 'Who's Afraid of China in Africa? Towards an African Civil Society Perspective on China–Africa Relations', in Firoze Manji and Stephen Marks, eds, *African Perspectives on China in Africa*, Fahamu, Oxford, 2007, p. 39.

22 Stephen Breslin and Ian Taylor, 'Explaining the Rise of "Human Rights" in Analyses of Sino-African Relations', *Review of African Political Economy*, vol. 35, no. 115, 2008, pp. 59–71.

23 Fraser and Lungu, 'For Whom the Wind Falls?', p. 8.

24 Brautigam, *The Dragon's Gift*.

25 Henning Melber, 'The (Not So) New Kid on the Block: China and the Scramble for Africa's Resources – An Introductory Review', in Henning Melber, ed., *China in Africa*, Current African Issues No. 33, Nordiska Afrikainstitutet, Uppsala, 2007.

26 Brautigam, *The Dragon's Gift*, p. 218.

27 'New Form of Chinese Aid Revives Zambia's Largest Textile Company', *People's Daily*, 27 November 2003.

28 Quoted in Laurie Goering, 'China's Investment and Growing Clout in Africa Cause Concern', *Chicago Tribune*, 19 February 2006.

29 Interviews with ex-employees were carried out in Kabwe, 12–24 May 2008. All interviewees have been anonymized. Extended discussion is provided in an earlier article by Andrew Brooks: 'Spinning and Weaving Discontent: Labour Relations and the Production of Meaning at Zambia–China Mulungushi Textiles', *Journal of Southern African Studies*, vol. 36, no. 1, 2010, pp. 113–32. Unless otherwise stated, quotations from former workers throughout this chapter are taken from this article.

30 Duncan Gallie, *In Search of the New Working Class: Automation and Social Integration within the Capitalist Enterprise*, Cambridge University Press, Cambridge, 1978.

31 Ching Kwan Lee, 'Raw Encounters: Chinese Managers, African Workers and the Politics of Casualization in Africa's Chinese Enclaves', *The China Quarterly*, vol. 199, no. 1, 2009, pp. 647–66.

32 Melissa W. Wright, 'Factory Daughters and Chinese Modernity: A Case from Dongguan', *Geoforum*, vol. 34, no. 3, 2003, pp. 291–301.

33 Ministry of Defence, Zambia, *Report of Inter-Ministerial Technical Committee for Labour Reduction at Zambia–China Mulungushi Textiles (JV) Ltd (ZCMT)*, Lusaka, 2007, p. 1.

34 David Harvey, *The Limits to Capital*, Verso, London, 2006.

35 Gramsci, *Selections from the Prison Notebooks*.

36 Harvey, *The Limits to Capital*.

37 Yongzheng Yang and Chuanshui Zhong, 'China's Textile and Clothing Exports in a Changing World Economy'.

38 Ching Kwan Lee, 'Raw Encounters', p. 8.

39 Gallie, *In Search of the New Working Class*.

40 Gillian Hart, *Disabling Globalization: Places of Power in Post-apartheid South Africa*, University of California Press, Berkeley, 2002.

41 Ching Kwan Lee, 'Raw Encounters', p. 7.

42 Hart, *Disabling Globalization*.

43 Government of Zambia, *The Minimum Wages and Conditions of Employment Act*, Statutory Instrument No. 56 of 2006, Laws, vol. 15, cap. 276.

44 Kaplinsky, 'What Does the Rise of China Do for Industrialisation in Sub-Saharan Africa?'

45 'Chinese Textile Firm in Zambia Having Cash Flow Problems', *Africa Business*, 3 January 2007, http://africabusiness.wordpress.com/2007/01/03/chinese-textile-firm-in-zambia-having-cash-flow-problems.

46 Jacob Goldstein, 'Global Poverty and the Cost of a Pair of Jeans', NPR, 3 March 2010, www.npr.org/blogs/money/2010/03/how_much_does_a_pair_of_ jeans.html.

47 Peter Gibbon, 'AGOA, Lesotho's "Clothing Miracle" and the Politics of Sweatshops', *Review of African Political Economy*, vol. 30, no. 96, 2003, pp. 315–50, p. 320.

CHAPTER 6

1 NFL, 'Super Bowl XLVIII Most-watched TV Program in U.S. History', 3 February 2014, www.nfl.com/superbowl/story/0ap2000000323430/article/super-bowl-xlviii-mostwatched-tv-program-in-us-history.

2 World Vision, *World Vision News*, vol. 11, no. 1, 2007, http://media. worldvision.org/docs/Wv.Winternews07.pdf. The true worth of these goods is debatable given that gifts in kind are often valued at US retail prices, which are completely disproportionate to their true economic worth in developing countries.

3 Scott Bixby, 'The Super Bowl Loser 49ers Still Win in, Say, Chad', *Bloomberg Businessweek*, 4 February 2013, www.businessweek.com/articles/2013-02-04/the-super-bowl-loser-49ers-still-win-in-say-chad; Cathleen Falsani, 'The NFLs Donation to World Vision: Charity or Closet Cleaning?', *Huffington Post*, 20 February 2011, www.huffington-post.com/cathleen-falsani/nfl-steelers-world-vision_b_824864.html; Tim Rogers, 'Where New England Won the Super Bowl', *Time*, 15 February 2008, http://content.time.com/time/world/article/0,8599,1713846,00.html; Darren Rovell, 'Merchandise Donated to Charity', ESPN, 5 February 2013, http://espn.go.com/nfl/playoffs/2012/story/_/id/8918957/2013-super-bowl-san-francisco-49ers-championship-mer-chandise-donated-charity?src=mobile; CNN, 'Helping Clothe Countries in Need', 4 February 2011, http://edition.cnn.com/video/?/video/sports/2011/02/04/mckay.world.vision.cnn.

4 Uganda Manufacturers' Association, quoted by Carter Dougherty, 'Trade Theory vs. Used Clothes in Africa', *The New York Times*, 3 June 2004.

5 Author's own observations; Karen Tranberg Hansen, *Salaula: The World of Secondhand Clothing and Zambia*, University of Chicago Press, Chicago, 2000.

6   Myriam Velia, Imraan Valodia and Baruti Amisi, *Trade Dynamics in Used Clothing: The Case of Durban, South Africa*, SDS Research Report 71, School of Development Studies, University of Kwazulu-Natal, Durban, 2006.

7   Interview with Steve Wooldridge, Head of Property and Stock Operations, Help the Aged, 3 December 2008.

8   Hansen, *Salaula*, p. 116.

9   Quoted by Simone Field, 'The Internationalisation of the Second-hand Clothing Trade: The Zimbabwe Experience', Ph.D. thesis, Coventry University, 2000, p. 161.

10 Interviews, 27 May 2008. This confusion may be because used clothes have transited via Germany.

11 Hansen, *Salaula*, p. 182.

12 Maureen Chigbo, 'High Cost of an Imported Used Spiderman T-Shirt', *Electronic Journal of Governance and Innovation*, Southern African Institute of International Affairs, 25 April 2008, www.saiia. org.za/archive-eafrica/high-cost-of-an-imported-used-spiderman-t-shirt.html.

13 Hansen, *Salaula*, p. 118.

14 Field, 'The Internationalisation of the Second-hand Clothing Trade', p. 3.

15 Ragtex UK, 'About Ragtex UK', 2011, www. ragtexuk.com/about.htm; clothing is also exported by Ragtex to elsewhere in southern Africa and Pakistan.

16 See Chapter 3.

17 Michael Durham, 'The Clothes Line', *The Guardian*, 25 February 2004.

18 Interview with Tony Clark, General Manager, Oxfam Wastesaver, 13 March 2009.

19 Field, 'The Internationalisation of the Secondhand Clothing Trade', p. 159.

20 Ibid., p. 160.

21 Olumide Abimbola, 'The International Trade in Secondhand Clothing: Managing Information Asymmetry between West African and British Traders', *Textile: The Journal of Cloth and Culture*, vol. 10, no. 2, 2012, pp. 184–99, p. 192.

22 METL, 'Mohammed Enterprise Trading Limited: Company Profile', 2011, www.metl.net/about/ company-profile.

23 Pietra Rivoli, *The Travels of a T-shirt in the Global Economy: An Economist Examines the Markets, Power, and Politics of World Trade*, Wiley, London, 2009.

24 See Chapter 3.

25 Author's observations, August 2003.

26 Cyril Obi and Siri Aas Rustad, 'Introduction: Petro-violence in the Niger Delta: The Complex Politics of an Insurgency', in Cyril Obi and Siri Aas Rustad, eds, *Oil and Insurgency in the Niger Delta*, Zed Books, London, 2011.

27 Cyril Obi, 'Oil as a "Curse" of Conflict in Africa: Peering through the Smoke and Mirrors', *Review of African Political Economy*, vol. 37, no. 126, 2010, pp. 483–95.

28 Michael Watts, 'Petro-insurgency or Criminal Syndicate? Conflict and Violence in the Niger Delta', *Review of African Political Economy*, vol. 34, no. 114, 2007, pp. 637–60.

29 Ademola Oyejide, Olawale Ogunkola and Abiodun Bankole, 'Import Prohibition as a Trade Policy Instrument: The Nigerian Experience', in Peter Gallagher, Patrick Low and Andrew L. Stoler, eds, *Managing the Challenges of WTO Participation: 45 Case Studies*, Cambridge University Press, Cambridge, 2005, p. 440.

30 Reported used-clothing exports from global North calculated using OECD country data, 1981–2000, in United Nations Comtrade, *UN Comtrade Database*, 2014, http://comtrade.un.org/db/default.aspx.

31 Interview with Aloysius Ihezie, Director, Choice Textiles Division, 19 March 2009.

32 J. Joost Beuving, 'Nigerien Second-hand Car Traders in Cotonou: A Sociocultural Analysis of Economic Decision-making', *African Affairs*, vol. 105,
no. 420, 2006, pp. 353–73.

33 Gunilla Andræ and Björn Beckman, *Union Power
in the Nigerian Textile Industry*, Nordiska Afrikainstitutet, Uppsala, 1998; Economist Intelligence
Unit, *Country Reports: Nigeria*, London, November
2007.

34 *The Guardian*, January 2004, cited by Oyejide et al.,
'Import Prohibition as a Trade Policy Instrument',
p. 440.

35 Author's observations, May–July 2010.

36 'Smuggling, Used-Clothing Sales, Hurt Kenya
Textile Industry', *Voice of America*, 14 September
2010, www.voanews.com/english/news/africa/
Smuggling-Used-Clothing-Sales-Hurt-Kenya-
Textile-Industry-102953119.html.

37 Andrew Brooks, 'Networks of Power and Corruption: The Trade of Japanese Used Cars to Mozambique', *Geographical Journal*, vol. 178, no. 1, 2012,
pp. 80–92.

38 Tonia Kandiero, 'Malawi in the Multilateral
Trading System', in Gallagher, Low and Stoler,
eds, *Managing the Challenges of WTO Participation*,
p. 335.

39 See Andrew Brooks and David Simon, 'Unraveling the Relationships between Used-clothing Imports and the Decline of African Clothing Industries', *Development and Change*, vol. 43, no. 6, 2012, pp. 1265–90.

CHAPTER 7

1 'In Mozambique, Annan Sees Model of Progress for Africa and the World', UN News Centre, 2002, www.un.org/apps/news/story.asp?NewsiD=45 92&Cr=mozambique&Cr1.

2 'UN Chief Promotes Education, Gender Empowerment during Final Day of Mozambique Visit', UN News Centre, 21 May 2013, www. un.org/apps/news/story.asp?NewsID=44955#. U5gXlPldXms.

3 Andrew Brooks, 'Was Africa Rising? Narratives of Development Success and Failure among the Mozambican Middle Class', *Territory, Politics and Governance*, vol. 6, no. 4, 2018, pp. 447–67.

4 African Development Bank, *Mozambique Economic Outlook*, 2014, www.afdb.org/en/countries/southern-africa/mozambique/mozambique-economic-outlook.

5 World Bank, *Mozambique*, 2014, http://data.worldbank.org/country/mozambique?display=

default; UNDP, *Human Development Index*, 2014, https://data.undp.org/dataset/Table-1-Human-Development-Index-and-its-components/wxub-qc5k; USAID, *Mozambique*, 2014, www.usaid.gov/mozambique.

6 Anne Pitcher, *Transforming Mozambique: The Politics of Privatization, 1975–2000*, Cambridge University Press, Cambridge, 2002, p. 195.

7 Kathleen E. Sheldon, *Pounders of Grain: A History of Women, Work, and Politics in Mozambique*, Heinemann, Portsmouth, NH, 2002.

8 Peter Coughlin, Musa Rubin and L. Amedée Darga, 'The SADC Textile and Garment Industries: Towards a Global Vision?', in Dorothy McCormick and Christian Rogerson, eds, *Clothing and Footwear in African Industrialisation*, Africa Institute of South Africa, Pretoria, 2004, p. 20.

9 Peter Minor, *Strategies for Mozambique's Textile and Apparel Sector*, technical report by Nathan Associates for USAID, Washington, DC, 2005, p. 2.

10 World Bank, *Mozambique – CEM – Industry Section – Apparel Sector, Draft*, 7 May 2008, http://siteresources.worldbank.org/intdebtdept/resources/468980-1218567884549/5289593-1259608803444/Mo-zambiqueCeMapparel20090508.pdf, p. 1.

11 'Mozambique: Moztex Exporting Clothes to South Africa', *AllAfrica*, 16 December 2010, http://allafrica.com/stories/201012170661.html; 'Mozambique: Two Textiles Factories Expected to Re-launch Production This Year in Mozambique', *Maccauhub*, 5 September 2008, www.macauhub.com.mo/en/2008/09/05/5703.

12 Christopher M. Rogerson, 'Sunrise or Sunset Industries? South Africa's Clothing and Footwear Sectors', in Dorothy McCormick and Christian Rogerson, eds, *Clothing and Footwear in African Industrialisation*, Africa Institute of South Africa, Pretoria, 2004.

13 Caroline Skinner and Imraan Valodia, 'Labour Market Policy, Flexibility, and the Future of Labour Relations: The Case of KwaZulu-Natal Clothing Industry', *Transformation: Critical Perspectives on Southern Africa*, no. 50, 2002, pp. 56–76, p. 56.

14 Andrew Brooks, 'Networks of Power and Corruption: The Trade of Japanese Used Cars to Mozambique', *Geographical Journal*, vol. 178, no. 1, 2012, pp. 80–92; Jason Sumich, 'The Party and the State: Frelimo and Social Stratification in Post-socialist Mozambique', *Development and Change*, vol. 41, no. 4, 2010, pp. 679–98.

15 Pitcher, *Transforming Mozambique*, p. 173.

16 Research findings, including the various quotations and figures, are based on 13 months of ethnographic fieldwork in Maputo (July 2009–July 2010) carried out by the author.

17 Interview, 4 April 2010. He was asked to confirm if he was certain it was Nigeria; his answer remained unchanged.

18 Lucy Norris, personal communication, 5 February 2010.

19 Interview with Steve Wooldridge, Head of Property and Stock Operations, Help the Aged, 3 December 2008.

20 United Nations Comtrade, *UN Comtrade Database*, 2019, http://comtrade.un.org/data; for a full discussion, see Andrew Brooks and David Simon, 'Unraveling the Relationships between Used-Clothing Imports and the Decline of African Clothing Industries', *Development and Change*, vol. 43, no. 6, 2012, pp. 1265–90.

21 Andrew Brooks, 'Stretching Global Production Networks: The International Second-hand Clothing Trade', *Geoforum*, vol. 44, 2013, pp. 10–22.

22 These reflections were recorded in a diary in Portuguese kept by Maria between 1 March and 11 April 2010; they have been translated by

the author. Mary was one of nine traders who recorded all their daily business transactions in a research diary for a six-week period. For further discussion, see Andrew Brooks, 'Riches from Rags or Persistent Poverty? The Working Lives of Secondhand Clothing Vendors in Maputo, Mozambique', *Textile: The Journal of Cloth and Culture*, vol. 10, no. 2, 2012, pp. 222–37.

23 'Ghana Bans Second-hand Knickers', *BBC News Online*, 26 November 2010, www.bbc.co.uk/news/world-africa-11845851.

24 For sale in Vlinakulo Market, 25 March 2010.

25 The most extensive work has been done by Karen Tranberg Hansen, who undertook a detailed ethnographic investigation in Zambia: *Salaula: The World of Secondhand Clothing and Zambia*, University of Chicago Press, Chicago, 2000.

26 Textile Recycling Association, *'Textile Recycling Association Welcomes Research Papers about the Impact of Second Hand Clothing Industry on Sub-Saharan Africa*, 12 December 2005, www.textile-recycling.org.uk/press121205.htm.

27 Figures quoted by Francis N. Wegulo, 'Shoes for All: Second-hand Shoe Traders in Nakuru Town, Kenya', in Dorothy McCormick and Christian Rogerson, eds, *Clothing and Footwear in African*

Industrialisation, Africa Institute of South Africa, Pretoria, 2004, p. 580.

28 Salvation Army, 'Salvation Army Trading Company Limited', 2009, www.satradingco.org.

29 Total employment figures for the second-hand clothing trade in Mozambique are not available.

30 As there is great variance in second-hand clothing vendors' earnings, this figure in isolation is of limited utility, because it is based on a small sample size.

31 Andrew Brooks, 'Riches from Rags or Persistent Poverty? Inequality in the Transnational Second-hand Clothing Trade in Mozambique', Ph.D. thesis, Royal Holloway, University of London, 2012.

32 Wegulo, 'Shoes for All', pp. 578, 580.

33 ADPP, 'ADPP Mozambique', 2011, http://adpp-mozambique.org/index.php/about-us.html.

34 TRAID, 'TRAID History', 2011, www.traid.org.uk/history.html.

35 Michael Durham, 'Enigma of the Leader', *The Guardian*, 9 June 2003.

36 Monica Eng, 'Clothing Operations Linked to Controversial Danish Group Continue to Thrive', *Chicago Tribune*, 14 May 2011.

37 'DAPP in "Secret Money Swindling"', *Nyasa Times*, 1 March 2011.

38 See http://tvindalert.com.

39 'Mexican Police Tracking Down Cult School Leader', *Copenhagen Post*, 6 January 2014.

40 INE, *Inquérito sobre orçamento familiar 2008/09*, Instituto Nacional de Estatística, Maputo, 2010, cited in Margarida Paulo, Carmeliza Rosário and Inge Tvedten, '"Xiculungo" Revisited: Assessing the Implications of PARPA II in Maputo 2007–2010', Chr. Michelsen Institute, 2011, www.cmi.no/publications/publication/?4000=xiculungo-revisited-assessing-the-implications-of, p. 7.

41 Based on the author's observations in Kenya and Zambia. The upcycling of vintage clothes is discussed in the next chapter.

42 See Chapter 6.

43 Interview with Tony Clark, General Manager, Oxfam Wastesaver, 13 March 2009.

CHAPTER 8

1 Hazel Clark, 'Second Hand Fashion, Culture and Identity in Hong Kong', in Alexander Palmer and Hazel Clark, eds, *Old Clothes, New Looks: Second Hand Fashion*, Berg, Oxford, 2005.

2 Lucy Norris, 'Trade and Transformation of Secondhand Clothing: Introduction', *Textile*, vol. 10, no. 2, 2012, pp. 128–43.

3 Jacqueline P. Wiseman, 'Close Encounters of the Quasi-primary Kind: Sociability in Urban Secondhand Clothing Stores', *Journal of Contemporary Ethnography*, vol. 8, no. 1, 1979, pp. 23–51, pp. 30–31.

4 Janna Michael, 'It's Really Not Hip to Be a Hipster: Negotiating Trends and Authenticity in the Cultural Field', *Journal of Consumer Culture*, 2013, pp. 8–9.

5 Fabio Marzella, 'Second-hand Goods Use in the Italian Post-industrial Society: A First Theoretical view', n.d., http://univr.academia.edu/FabioMarzella, p. 1.

6 Tom Slater, 'The Eviction of Critical Perspectives from Gentrification Research', *International Journal of Urban and Regional Research*, vol. 30, no. 4, 2006, pp. 737–57, p. 738.

7 Karl Marx, *Grundrisse: Foundations of the Critique of Political Economy*, Vintage, London, 1973, p. 705.

8 'Wonder Where Your Donations Go? Oxfam Has Got It Sorted', *The Guardian*, 15 February 2014.

9 Steven Tyler was quoted as saying this in Season 10 of *American Idol*, 2011; Carlos Ramirez, 'Our 20 Favorite, Most Outrageous Steven Tyler One-Liners', *Noise Creep*, 25 May 2011, http://noisecreep.com/most-outrageous-steven-tyler-one-liners.

10 Michael, 'It's Really Not Hip to Be a Hipster'.

11 Elaine R. Hartwick, 'Geographies of Consumption: A Commodity-chain Approach', *Environment and Planning D*, vol. 16, no. 4, 1998, pp. 423–37.

12 Cold Summer, 'Why Are Japanese Jeans So Expensive?' RAWR Denim, 31 July 2013, www.rawrdenim.com/2013/07/why-are-japanese-jeans-so-expensive.

13 Shunya Yoshimi and David Buist, 'America as Desire and Violence: Americanization in Postwar Japan and Asia during the Cold War', *Inter-Asia Cultural Studies*, vol. 4, no. 3, 2003, pp. 433–50.

14 Rachel Louis Snyder, *Fugitive Denim: A Moving Story of People and Pants in The Borderless World of Global Trade*, W.W. Norton, New York, 2009, p. 142.

15 Kjeld Duits, 'The Quest for Perfect Jeans', Japanese Streets, 4 January 2012, www.japanesestreets.com/reports/1313/the-quest-for-perfect-jeans.

16 Jordan Caronm, 'Second Narrow: Perfect Jeans, Made in Japan, Water Resistant', Kickstarter, 2013, www.kickstarter.com/projects/864140473/second-narrow-perfect-jeans-made-in-japan-water-re5.

17 Cold Summer, 'Why Are Japanese Jeans So Expensive?'

18 Snyder, *Fugitive Denim*, p. 143.

19 Niko Besnier, 'Consumption and Cosmopolitanism: Practicing Modernity at the Second-hand Marketplace in Nuku'alofa, Tonga', *Anthropological Quarterly*, vol. 77, no. 1, 2004, pp. 7–45.

20 Examples in this section are based on the author's own fieldwork in Papua New Guinea in 2006.

21 Lamont Lindstrom, 'Cargo Cult', in Alan Barnard and Jonathan Spencer, eds, *Encyclopedia of Social and Cultural Anthropology*, Routledge, London and New York, 2002, p. 129.

22 Kate Maclean, 'Evo's Jumper: Identity and the Used Clothes Trade in "Post-neoliberal" and "Pluri-cultural" Bolivia', *Gender, Place and Culture*, vol. 21, no. 8, 2014, p. 964.

23 Ibid., p. 970.

24 Ibid., p. 968.

25 Lucy Norris, *Recycling Indian Clothing: Global Contexts of Reuse and Value*, Indiana University Press, Bloomington and Indianapolis, 2010, p. 181.

26 Lucy Norris, 'Recycling and Reincarnation: The Journeys of Indian Saris', *Mobilities*, vol. 3, no. 3, 2008, pp. 415–36, p. 415.

27 Authors own research in Kerala, South India, 2013.

28 Lucy Norris, 'Creative Entrepreneurs: The Recycling of Second Hand Indian Clothing', in Palmer and Clark, eds, *Old Clothes, New Looks*, p. 119.

29 B. Lynne Milgram, 'Reconfiguring Margins: Secondhand Clothing and Street Vending in the Philippines', *Textile*, vol. 10, no. 2, 2012, pp. 200–221, p. 206.

30 B. Lynne Milgram, '*Ukay-Ukay* Chic: Tales of Secondhand Clothing in the Philippine Cordillera', in Palmer and Clark, eds, *Old Clothes, New Looks*.

31 Amanda Ericsson and Andrew Brooks, 'African Second-hand Clothes: Mima-te and the Development of Sustainable Fashion', in Kate Fletcher and Mathilda Tham, eds, *The Routledge Handbook of Sustainability and Fashion*, Routledge, London, 2015.

32 Nelly and Nelsa Guambe, 'The Story behind Mima-te', 2013, www.mimate-maputo.com/?page_id=51.

CHAPTER 9

1 Toms, 'Our Movement', 2014, www.toms.com/our-movement/1#why-give-shoes.

2 Toms, 'Blake Mycoskie', 2014, www.toms.com/blakes-bio/1.

3 Christina Binkley, 'Charity Gives Shoe Brand Extra Shine', *Wall Street Journal*, 1 April 2011.

4 Toms, 'Our Movement'; Toms, 'Blake Mycoskie'.

5 From the author's own observation, lack of access to shoes is not a common development impasse in sub-Saharan Africa.

6 There have also been rumours that some distributions have been selective, with priority going to
   Christian groups when shoe drops are run with
   faith-based organizations.

7 Toms, 'Giving Report', 2013, www.toms.com/
   media/TOMS_Giving_Report_2013.pdf.

8 Andrew Brooks and David Simon, 'Unraveling the Relationships between Used-Clothing
   Imports and the Decline of African Clothing
   Industries', *Development and Change*, vol. 43, no. 6,
   2012, pp. 1265–90.

9 Bruce Wydick, Elizabeth Katz and Brendan Janet,
   'Do In-kind Transfers Damage Local Markets?
   The Case of TOMS Shoe Donations in EL Salvador', *Journal of Development Effectiveness*, vol. 6, no.
   3, 2014, pp. 249–67.

10 Henrik Serup Christensen, 'Political Activities on
   the Internet: Slacktivism or Political Participation
   by Other Means?' *First Monday*, vol. 16, no. 2, 2011.

11 Celia Lury, *Brands: The Logos of the Global Cultural
   Economy*, Routledge, London, 2004.

12 Blake Mycoskie quoted by Kevin Short, 'Toms
   CEO Blake Mycoskie Offers Surprising Answer
   to His Critics', *Huffington Post*, 14 November 2013,
   www.huffingtonpost.com/2013/11/14/toms-
   ceo-critics_n_4274637.html.

13 James Poulos, 'Toms Shoes: A Doomed Vanity Project?', *Forbes*, 11 April 2011, www.forbes.com/sites/jamespoulos/2012/04/11/toms-shoes-a-doomed-vanity-project.

14 Fredric Jameson, *Postmodernism, or, the Cultural Logic of Late Capitalism*, Duke University Press, Durham, NC, 1990.

15 Deirdre Shaw, Terry Newholm and Roger Dickinson, 'Consumption as Voting: An Exploration of Consumer Empowerment', *European Journal of Marketing*, vol. 40, no. 9/10, 2006, pp. 1049–67.

16 Patagonia, 'Don't Buy This Jacket, Black Friday and the New York Times', *The Cleanest Line*, 2011, www.thecleanestline.com/2011/11/dont-buy-this-jacket-black-friday-and-the-new-york-times.html.

17 Michal J. Carrington, Benjamin A. Neville and Gregory J. Whitwell, 'Why Ethical Consumers Don't Walk Their Talk: Towards a Framework for Understanding the Gap between the Ethical Purchase Intentions and Actual Buying Behaviour of Ethically Minded Consumers', *Journal of Business Ethics*, vol. 97, no. 1, 2010, pp. 139–58.

18 Michael Lee, Judith Moron and Denise Conroy, 'Anti-consumption and Brand Avoidance', *Journal of Business Research*, vol. 62, no. 2, 2008, pp. 169–80, p. 178.

19   Robert B. Potter, Tony Binns, Jennifer A. Elliot and David Smith, *Geographies of Development: An Introduction to Development Studies*, Pearson, Harlow, 2008, p. 360.

20   Matthias Zick Varul, 'Consuming the Campesino: Fair Trade Marketing between Recognition and Romantic Commodification', *Cultural Studies*, vol. 22, no. 5, 2008, pp. 654–79, p. 662.

21   Karl Marx, *Grundrisse: Foundations of the Critique of Political Economy*, Vintage, London, 1973, p. 92.

22   Antonio Gramsci, *Selections from the Prison Notebooks*, Lawrence & Wishart, London, 1971.

23   Caroline Wright, 'Consuming Lives, Consuming Landscapes: Interpreting Advertisements for Cafédirect Coffees', *Journal of International Development*, vol. 16, no. 5, 2004, pp. 665–80.

24   'Designer Vivienne Westwood Addresses at St Paul's Camp', *BBC News Online*, 19 November 2011, www.bbc.co.uk/news/uk-england-london-15806945.

25   Richard Tyler, 'Vivienne Westwood Undervalues Itself', *The Telegraph*, 28 August 2011.

26   ITC, 'Ethical Fashion: Not Charity, Just Work', International Trade Centre, 2012, www.intracen.org/trade-support/ethical-fashion.

27 Simome Cipriani, Jeremy Brown and Chloe Mukai, *The Ethical Fashion Programme. Not Charity, Just Work: 2011 Aid for Trade Global Review: Case Study*, International Trade Centre, Geneva, 2011.

28 ITC, 'Vivienne Westwood: Fashion Icon', International Trade Centre, 2012, www.intracen.org/trade-support/ethical-fashion/vivienne-westwood.

29 Cipriani, Brown and Mukai, *The Ethical Fashion Programme. Not Charity, Just Work*.

30 Clar Ni Chonghaile, 'From King's Road to Kenya: Westwood's New Fashion Journey', *The Guardian*, 24 November 2011.

31 Michael K. Goodman, 'Reading Fair Trade: Political Ecological Imaginary and the Moral Economy of Fair Trade Foods', *Political Geography*, vol. 23, no. 7, 2004, pp. 891–915.

32 Wright, 'Consuming Lives, Consuming Landscapes', p. 671.

33 These have been observed by the author in both Nairobi and rural Kenya.

34 Vivienne Westwood, 'Made with Love in Nairobi', 2011, www.viviennewestwood.co.uk/multimedia/made-with-love-in-nairobi.

35 Edward Said, *Orientalism*, Vintage Books, New York, 1979.

36 Author's interviews in Pokot, Kenya, 2010.

37 Stefano Ponte, Lisa Ann Richey and Mike Baab, 'Bono's Product (reD) Initiative: Corporate Social Responsibility that Solves the Problems of "Distant Others"', *Third World Quarterly*, vol. 30, no. 2, 2009, pp. 301–17; Jemima Repo and Riina Yrjölä, 'The Gender Politics of Celebrity Humanitarianism in Africa', *International Feminist Journal of Politics*, vol. 13, no. 1, 2011, pp. 42–62.

38 Quoted by Olivia Bergin, 'Vivienne Westwood's Mission to Save the World, One Handbag at a Time', *The Telegraph*, 9 August 2011.

39 Nicky Gregson and Louise Crewe, *Second-hand Cultures*, Berg, London, 2003.

40 H&M, 'Garment Collecting', 2014, http://about.hm.com/en/About/Sustainability/Commitments/Reduce-Reuse-Recycle/Garment-Collecting.html.

41 Olivier Balch, 'H&M: Can Fast Fashion and Sustainability Ever Really Mix?' *The Guardian*, 3 May 2013.

42 Kyle Stock, 'The Brilliant Business Model Behind H&M's Clothes Recycling Plan', *Bloomberg Businessweek*, 24 June 2013, www.businessweek.com/articles/2013-06-24/the-brilliant-business-model-behind-h-and-ms-clothes-recycling-plan#rshare=email_article.

43 Balch, 'H&M'.

44 H&M, 'Charity Star', 2014, www.hm.charitystar.
    com/en/home.

45 Whizz-Kidz, 'Matthew Pinsent Helps JJB
    Launch National Trainer Recycling Scheme for
    Whizz-Kidz', 2011, www.whizz-kidz.org.uk/
    news/2011/03/matthew-pinsent-helps-jjb-
    launch-national-trainer-re-cycling-scheme-for-
    whizz-kidz.

46 Oxfam, 'The M&S and Oxfam Clothes Exchange',
    2011, www.oxfam.org.uk/shop/content/second
    handstore/fashion/ms_clothes_exchange.
    html?ito=2841&itc=0.

47 I:CO, 'How Does I:CO Work?', 2014, www.ico-
    spirit.com/en/about-ico.

48 Kate Fletcher, *Sustainable Fashion and Textiles:
    Design Journeys*, 2nd edition, Routledge, London,
    2014.

49 Royal Society, *People and the Planet*, Royal Society
    Science and Policy Centre Report 01/12, Lon-
    don, 2012.

50 Kate Fletcher, 'Other Fashion Systems', in Kate
    Fletcher and Mathilda Tham, eds, *The Routledge
    Handbook of Sustainability and Fashion*, Routledge,
    London, 2015, p. 23.

51 Slavoj Žižek, *The Year of Dreaming Dangerously*,
    Verso, London, 2012, pp. 100–101.

52 Don Mitchell, 'The S.U.V. Model of Citizenship: Floating Bubbles, Buffer Zones, and the Rise of the "Purely Atomic" Individual', *Political Geography*, vol. 24, no. 1, 2005, pp. 77–100.

CHAPTER 10

1 Kelly-Leigh Cooper, 'Fast Fashion: Inside the Fight to End the Silence on Waste', 31 July 2018, https://www.bbc.co.uk/news/world-44968561.

2 'Great Pacific Garbage Patch', *National Geographic*, 2017, https://www.nationalgeographic.org/encyclopedia/great-pacific-garbage-patch/.

3 Edgar Hernandez, Bernd Nowack and Denise M. Mitrano, 'Polyester Textiles as a Source of Microplastics from Households: A Mechanistic Study to Understand Microfiber Release during Washing', *Environmental Science and Technology*, vol. 51, no. 12, 2017 pp. 7036–46.

4 Stephanie L. Wright, Richard C. Thompson and Tamara S. Galloway, 'The Physical Impacts of Microplastics on Marine Organisms: A Review', *Environmental Pollution*, vol. 178, 2013, pp. 483–92.

5 Brian Resnick, 'More Than Ever, Our Clothes Are Made of Plastic: Just Washing Them Can Pollute the Oceans. *VOX*, 11 January 2019, https://www.vox.com/the-goods/2018/9/19/17800654/

clothes-plastic-pollution-polyester-washing-mach ine?fbclid=IwAR0eysp78c1L0jQT3kvTlOwkSHEk 43NxMw7a3hALVbIf93hXRN1E0mjniGM.

6 Andrew Brooks, Kate Fletcher, Robert A. Francis, Emma Dulcie Rigby and Thomas Roberts, 'Fashion, Sustainability, and the Anthropocene', *Utopian Studies*, vol. 28, no. 3, 2017, pp. 482–504.

7 Paul J. Crutzen, 'The "Anthropocene"', in Eckart Ehlers and Thomas Krafft, eds, *Earth System Science in the Anthropocene*, Springer, Berlin, 2006, pp. 13–18.

8 Richard J. Hobbs, Salvatore Arico, James Aronson, Jill S. Baron, Peter Bridgewater, Viki A. Cramer, Paul R. Epstein, John J. Ewel, et al., 'Novel Ecosystems: Theoretical and Management Aspects of the New Ecological World Order', *Global Ecology and Biogeography*, vol. 15, no. 1, 2006, pp. 1–7.

9 Johan Rockström, Will Steffen, Kevin Noone, Åsa Persson, F. Stuart Chapin, Eric F. Lambin, Timothy M. Lenton, Marten Scheffer, et al., 'A Safe Operating Space for Humanity', *Nature*, vol. 461, no. 7263, 2009, pp. 472–5.

10 Stuart L. Pimm, Clinton N. Jenkins, Robin Abell, Thomas M. Brooks, John L. Gittleman, Lucas N. Joppa, Peter H. Raven, Callum M. Roberts and Joseph O. Sexton, 'The Biodiversity of Species and

Their Rates of Extinction, Distribution, and Protection', *Science*, vol. 344, no. 6187, 2014, 1246752.

11 *Ellen MacArthur Foundation*, 'A New Textiles Economy: Redesigning Fashion's Future', 2017, https://www.ellenmacarthurfoundation.org/assets/downloads/publications/A-New-Textiles-Economy_Full-Report_Updated_1-12-17.pdf.

12 Jason Clay, 'Cotton Carbon Emissions: How the Shirt on Your Back Affects Climate Change', *The Guardian*, 12 April 2012, https://www.theguardian.com/sustainable-business/cotton-reduce-environmental-impact-consumer-behaviour.

13 Camilla Royle, 'Marxism and the Anthropocene', *International Socialism*, vol. 151, 2014, pp. 63–84.

14 Jan Zalasiewi, Colin N. Waters, Juliana A. Ivar do Sul, Patricia L. Corcoran, Anthony D. Barnosky, Alejandro Cearreta, et al., 'The Geological Cycle of Plastics and Their Use as a Stratigraphic Indicator of the Anthropocene', *Anthropocene*, vol. 13, 2016, pp. 4–17.

15 Oxfam (@oxfamgb), 'Did You Know ¼ of Clothing Bought This Party Season Will Only Be Worn Just ONCE?' Tweet, 5 December 2018, https://twitter.com/oxfamgb/status/1070297763399823361.

16 BBC News, Fast Fashion: 'How Do You Justify Selling a £2 T-shirt?', 27 November 2018, accessed

2 May 2019, https://www.bbc.co.uk/news/business-46358969.

17 Shannon Barbour, 'Fashion Nova Answered Your Prayers and Is Selling a Meghan Markle Wedding Dress Replica for Dirt Cheap', *Cosmopolitan*, 5 November 2018, https://www.cosmopolitan.com/style-beauty/a24664988/fashion-nova-meghan-markle-wedding-dress-replica/.

18 Coco Chanel, quoted in Jessica Wolfendale and Jeanette Kennett, *Fashion – Philosophy for Everyone: Thinking with Style*, John Wiley & Sons, London, 2011, p. xiv.

19 Quoted by Deborah Orr in, 'Life in Vogue: The Fashionable World of Alexandra Shulman', *The Independent Magazine*, 31 January 2009.

20 Kelly-Leigh Cooper, 'Fast Fashion: Inside the Fight to End the Silence on Waste', 31 July 2018, https://www.bbc.co.uk/news/world-44968561.

21 Ben Fine, *The World of Consumption: The Material and Cultural Revisited*, Routledge, London, 2002.

22 Conrad Lodziak, 'On Explaining Consumption', *Capital and Class*, vol. 72, 2000, pp. 111–33.

23 Pierre Bourdieu, *Distinction: A Social Critique of the Judgement of Taste*, Routledge, London, 1984.

24 David Harvey, *The Enigma of Capital: And the Crisis of Capitalism*, Profile Books, London, 2010.

25 Wanyee Li, 'Poverty. Not Donation Bins, Cause Death, Say Advocates as Death Toll Mounts', *Star Vancouver*, 8 January 2019.

26 James Ferguson, *Expectations of Modernity: Myths and Meanings of Urban Life on the Zambian Copperbelt*, University of California Press, Berkeley, 1999.

27 Karen Transberg Hansen, *Salaula: The World of Secondhand Clothing and Zambia*, University of Chicago Press, Chicago, 2000.

28 Andrew Brooks, *The End of Development: A Global History of Poverty and Prosperity*, Zed Books, London.

29 Nicholas A. Phelps, John C.H. Stillwell, and Roseline Wanjiru, 'Broken Chain? AGOA and Foreign Direct Investment in the Kenyan Clothing Industry', *World Development*, vol. 37, no. 2, 2009, pp. 314–25.

30 USAID, 'Overview of the Used Clothing Market in East Africa: Analysis of Determinants and Implications', July 2017, https://d3n8a8pro7vhmx. cloudfront.net/eatradehub/pages/3552/ attachments/original/1503313183/East_Africa_ Trade_and_Investment_Hub_Clothing_Report-_ COMPRESSED.pdf?1503313183.

31 Ibrahim Hossain Ovi, 'RMG exports saw 8.76% growth last fiscal year', *Dhaka Tribune*, 5 July 2018,

https://www.dhakatribune.com/business/
2018/07/05/rmg-exports-saw-8-76-growth-last-
fiscal-year.

32 Howard Schenider, 'This Is Why the Textile
Industry Is Relocating to Places Like Bangladesh',
The Washington Post, 12 July 2015, https://www.
washingtonpost.com/news/wonk/wp/2013/
07/12/this-is-why-the-textile-industry-is-
relocating-to-places-like-bangladesh/?nore
direct=on&utm_term=.1e1e65d4e693.

33 Marjorie van Elven, 'Bangladesh Raises Minimum Wage for Garment Workers, *Fashion United*,
14 September 2018, https://fashionunited.uk/
news/business/bangladesh-raises-minimum-
wage-for-garment-workers/2018091438912.

34 Maria Zimmerman, 'Bangladesh: Sewing Full-
time for 61 Euros a Month', DW, 23 April
2017, https://www.dw.com/en/bangladesh-
sewing-full-time-for-61-euros-a-month/a-
38553216.

35 Simon Murphy, 'Revealed: Spice Girls T-shirts
Made in Factory Paying Staff 35p an Hour',
The Guardian, 20 January 2019, https://www.
theguardian.com/world/2019/jan/20/spice-
girls-comic-relief-tshirts-made-bangladesh-
factory-paying-staff-35p-an-hour.

36 Kate Hodal, 'Abuse Is Daily Reality for Female Garment Workers for Gap and H&M, Says Report', *The Guardian*, 5 June 2018, https://www.theguardian.com/global-development/2018/jun/05/female-garment-workers-gap-hm-south-asia.

37 Lucy Jones, 'H&M Is Sitting on $4.3 Billion Worth of Unsold Stock', *Well Made Clothes*, 2018, https://wellmadeclothes.com/articles/HM43BillionWorthOfUnsoldClothes/.

38 Ellen MacArthur, 'New Circular Fibres Initiative Brings Industry Together to Build a Circular Economy for Textiles', Ellen MacArthur Foundation, 11 May 2017, https://www.ellenmacarthurfoundation.org/news/new-circular-fibres-initiative-brings-industry-together-to-build-a-circular-economy-for-textiles.

39 European Clothing Action Plan, accessed 4 July 2017, http://www.ecap.eu.com/.

40 'Closing the Loop', Patagonia, 4 March 2009, http://www.patagonia.com/blog/2009/03/closing-the-loop-a-report-on-patagonias-common-threads-garment-recycling-program/.

41 'Join the I:Colution: Rethink, Reuse, Recycle, Renew', I:CO, accessed 4 July 2017, http://www.ico-spirit.com/en/.

42 Mathis Wackernagel and William E. Williams, *Our Ecological Footprint: Reducing Human Impact on the Earth*, New Society Publishers, Gabriola Island, Canada, 1998; Michael F. Maniates, 'Individualization: Plant a Tree, Buy a Bike, Save the World?', *Global Environmental Politics*, vol. 1, 2001, pp. 31–52.

43 Lodziak, 'On Explaining Consumption'.

44 David Harvey, 'Between Space and Time: Reflections on the Geographical Imagination', *Annals of the Association of American Geographers*, vol. 80, no. 3, 1990, pp. 418–34, p. 422.

45 Michal J. Carrington, Benjamin A. Neville and Gregory J. Whitwell, 'Why Ethical Consumers Don't Walk Their Talk: Towards a Framework for Understanding the Gap between the Ethical Purchase Intentions and Actual Buying Behaviour of Ethically Minded Consumers', *Journal of Business Ethics*, vol. 97, no. 1, 2010, pp. 139–58.

46 Daryl Collins, Jonathan Morduch, Stuart Rutherford and Orlanda Ruthven, *Portfolios of the Poor: How the World's Poor Live on $2 a Day*, Princeton University Press, Princeton, 2009.

47 Forbes, *The World's Billionaires*, 2018, http://www.forbes.com/billionaires/list/2018.

48 The World Bank, *Mozambique*, 2017, http://data.worldbank.org/country/mozambique; The World

Bank, *Zambia*, 2017, http://data.worldbank.org/country/zambia.

49 Larry Elliot, 'World's 26 Richest People Own as Much as Poorest 50%, Says Oxfam', *The Guardian*, 2 January 2019, https://www.theguardian.com/business/2019/jan/21/world-26-richest-people-own-as-much-as-poorest-50-per-cent-oxfam-report.

FURTHER READING

Brooks, Andrew, *The End of Development: A Global History of Poverty and Prosperity*, Zed Books, London, 2017.

Chang, Ha-Joon, *Bad Samaritans: The Myth of Free Trade and the Secret History of Capitalism*, Bloomsbury, London, 2007.

Cline, Elizabeth L., *Overdressed: The Shockingly High Cost of Cheap Fashion*, Portfolio, New York, 2019.

Engels, Frederick, *The Condition of the Working-Class in England*, trans. Florence Kelly Wischnewetzky, George Allen & Unwin, London, 1943 (1844).

Ferguson, James, *Expectations of Modernity: Myths and Meanings of Urban Life on the Zambian Copperbelt*, University of California Press, Berkeley, 1999.

Fine, Ben, *Marx's Capital*, Macmillan, London, 1976.

Fine, Ben, *The World of Consumption: The Material and Cultural Revisited*, Routledge, London, 2002.

Fletcher, Kate, *Sustainable Fashion and Textiles: Design Journeys*, 2nd edn, Routledge, London, 2014.

Fletcher, Kate, *Craft of Use: Post-Growth Fashion*, Routledge, London, 2016.

Fletcher, Kate, and Mathilda Tham, eds, *The Routledge Handbook of Sustainability and Fashion*, Routledge, London, 2015.

Gregson, Nicky, and Louise Crewe, *Second-hand Cultures*, Berg, London, 2003.

Hanlon, Joseph, and Teresa Smart, *Do Bicycles Equal Development in Mozambique?*, James Currey, Woodbridge, 2008.

Hansen, Karen Tranberg, *Salaula: The World of Second-hand Clothing and Zambia*, University of Chicago Press, Chicago, 2000.

Hart, Gillian, *Disabling Globalization: Places of Power in Post-apartheid South Africa*, University of California Press, Berkeley, 2002.

Harvey, David, *The Limits to Capital*, Verso, London, 2006.

Harvey, David, *The Enigma of Capital and the Crises of Capitalism*, Profile Books, London, 2010.

Marx, Karl, *Grundrisse: Foundations of the Critique of Political Economy*, Vintage, New York, 1973.

Marx, Karl, *Capital: A New Abridgment*, Oxford University Press, Oxford, 1995.

Norris, Lucy, *Recycling Indian Clothing: Global Contexts of Reuse and Value*, Indiana University Press, Bloomington and Indianapolis, 2010.

Palmer, Alexandra, and Hazel Clark, eds, *Old Clothes, New Looks: Second Hand Fashion*, Berg, Oxford, 2005.

Ross, Robert, *Clothing: A Global History*, Polity Press, Cambridge, 2008.

Smith, Neil, *Uneven Development*, Basil Blackwell, Oxford and New York, 1985.

Snyder, Rachel Louise, *Fugitive Denim: A Moving Story of People and Pants in the Borderless World of Global Trade*, W.W. Norton, New York and London, 2008.

St Clair, Kassia, *The Golden Thread: How Fabric Changed History*, John Murray, London, 2018.

Strasser, Susan, *Waste and Want: A Social History of Trash*, Metropolitan Books, New York, 1999.

Twigger Holroyd, Amy, *Folk Fashion: Understanding Homemade Clothes*, I.B. Tauris, London, 2016.

Wolf, Eric R., *Europe and the People without History*, University of California Press, Berkeley, 1982.

INDEX

ZED

Zed is a platform for marginalised voices across the globe.

It is the world's largest publishing collective and a world leading example of alternative, non-hierarchical business practice.

It has no CEO, no MD and no bosses and is owned and managed by its workers who are all on equal pay.

It makes its content available in as many languages as possible.

It publishes content critical of oppressive power structures and regimes.

It publishes content that changes its readers' thinking.

It publishes content that other publishers won't and that the establishment finds threatening.

It has been subject to repeated acts of censorship by states and corporations.

It fights all forms of censorship.

It is financially and ideologically independent of any party, corporation, state or individual.

Its books are shared all over the world.

www.zedbooks.net
@ZedBooks